Opening the Research Text

Mathematics Education Library
VOLUME 46

The titles published in this series are listed at the end of this volume.

Elizabeth de Freitas
Kathleen Nolan
(Editors)

Opening the Research Text

Critical Insights and In(ter)ventions into
Mathematics Education

 Springer

Elizabeth de Freitas
Adelphia University
Garden City, NY
USA
University of Prince Edward Island
Charlottetown, PEI
Canada
defreitas@adelphi.edu

Kathleen Nolan
University of Regina
Regina, Saskatewan
Canada
Kathy.Nolan@uregina.ca

Series Editor:
Alan Bishop
Monash University
Melboure 3800
Australia
Alan.Bishop@Education.monash.edu.au

Library of Congress Control Number: 2007936206

ISBN -13: 978-0-387-75463-5   e-ISBN-13: 978-0-387-75464-2

Printed on acid-free paper.

9 8 7 6 5 4 3 2 1

Contents

CHAPTER 4

CHAPTER 5

CHAPTER 6

Contributing Authors

Peter Appelbaum is Associate Professor and Coordinator of Mathematics Education and Curriculum Studies Programs at Arcadia University in Philadelphia, USA. At Arcadia he also directs the Strangely Familiar Music Group and is Director-at-Large of General Education. He is the author of *Embracing Mathematics: On Becoming a Teacher and Changing with Mathematics*; *Children's Books for Grown-Up Teachers: Reading and Writing Curriculum Theory*; and *Popular Culture, Educational Discourse and Mathematics*.

Marcelo Batarce is a lecturer at Universidade Estadual do Mato Grosso do Sul, Brazil. His first degree was in mathematics teacher education and, for the last two years, he has been studying Derrida as a fundamental aspect of his PhD at London South Bank University under Steve Lerman's supervision. Marcelo has always been interested in philosophical foundations of mathematics education and its relation to mathematics. His chapter in this book, co-authored with Steve Lerman, identifies the main directions of his current research.

Tony Brown (Bristol) is Director of ESCalate, the National Subject Centre for the Promotion of Teaching and Learning in Education, based at the University of Bristol. He has an MA in Psychoanalytic Studies from the University of Sheffield and a Ph.D. from the Open University. His doctoral thesis, entitled, *Transforming the Self* (2000), uses a psychodynamic approach to study student teachers' perceptions of identity. Prior to his position at the University of Bristol, Tony worked as a secondary school physics teacher, as a curriculum advisor and leader for mathematics, and as a programme leader for primary teacher education courses.

Tony Brown (MMU) is Professor of Mathematics Education and Head of the Research Student Programme at Manchester Metropolitan University, UK. His research work has focused primarily on issues relating to language in educational contexts. He has numerous international publications in the fields of mathematics education and teacher education. His books include: *New Teacher Identity and Regulative Government: the discursive formation of primary mathematics teacher education* (with McNamara), published by Springer; *Mathematics Education and Language: interpreting hermeneutics and post structuralism* in Kluwer's Mathematics Education Library Series; *Regulative Discourses in Education: A Lacanian perspective* (with Atkinson & England) and *Action Research and Postmodernism* (with Jones).

Ole Ravn Christensen has a Ph.D in science and mathematics education and is Assistant Professor in the Department of Education, Learning and Philosophy at Aalborg University, Denmark. His initial background is in mathematics and philosophy. Since 2000, he has been conducting research in the area of the philosophy of mathematics and science education, with particular emphasis on the social and historical dimensions of mathematics teaching and learning, and of science education. His research integrates studies on learning theories, philosophy of science and the practice of education and educational planning. He has published several papers in books and journals.

Brent Davis is Professor and David Robitaille Chair in Mathematics, Science, and Technology Education in the Faculty of Education at the University of British Columbia. His research is developed around the educational relevance of recent developments in the cognitive and complexity sciences. He is a founding co-editor of *Complicity: An International Journal of Complexity and Education* and current editor of *For the Learning of Mathematics*. He has published books and articles in the areas of mathematics learning and teaching, curriculum theory, teacher education, epistemology, and action research.

Elizabeth de Freitas is an Associate Professor at Adelphi University. Her research interests are mathematics education, cultural studies, teacher identity, and discourse analysis. She has published articles in *Educational Studies in Mathematics*, the *International Journal of Education and the Arts, Teaching Education, Language and Literacy, The Journal of the Canadian*

Association for Curriculum Studies, and *The Canadian Journal of Education.*

Brent Eidsness is a graduate student at the University of Regina, Sasakatchewan. He is a father of two boys, a husband, a secondary mathematics teacher, a school administrator, and a dabbler in all things mathematical. He is currently working on his Masters Degree in Educational Administration.

Paul Ernest is Emeritus Professor of the Philosophy of Mathematics Education at Exeter University, UK, where he directs the doctoral programme in mathematics education. He is also visiting professor in Oslo and Trondheim, Norway. He has published widely on the topics of the philosophy of mathematics, postmodernism and mathematics education, and more recently, on the semiotics of mathematics education. His books include *The Philosophy of Mathematics Education*, RoutledgeFalmer 1991, and *Social Constructivism as a Philosophy of Mathematics*, SUNY Press, 1998. Paul founded the Philosophy of Mathematics Education Journal, located at <http://www.ex.ac.uk/~PErnest/>. At the time of writing, the most recent issue is a two-part special issue on social justice.

Carol Fulton is an assistant professor in the Faculty of Education at the University of Regina, SK. She received a Ph.D. from the University of British Columbia, in the spring of 2006. Her dissertation is entitled: *Gazing in the Mirror: Reflections on Educating Pre-service Teachers for Collaborative Work with Indigenous Communities*. Carol teaches core study courses in a new middle years teacher education program oriented toward teaching for social justice. Her research interests include narrative inquiry, complexity science and teaching for social and ecological justice.

Shana Graham is a M.Ed. student at the University of Regina, Saskatchewan. After nine years of teaching mathematics, science, and chemistry at the secondary level, she chose to pursue a graduate degree in mathematics curriculum and instruction. In her thesis, Shana embraces situated learning and complexity theories in (re)considering learning and teaching in mathematics education.

Eric (Rico) Gutstein teaches mathematics education at the University of Illinois—Chicago. His interests include teaching mathematics for social justice, Freirean approaches to teaching and learning, and urban education. He has taught middle and high school mathematics. Rico is a founding member of *Teachers for Social Justice* (Chicago) and is active in social movements. He is the author of *Reading and Writing the World with Mathematics:*

Toward a Pedagogy for Social Justice (Routledge, 2006) and the co-editor of *Rethinking Mathematics: Teaching Social Justice by the Numbers* (Rethinking Schools, 2005). He currently works as a mathematics support staff member at the Greater Lawndale/Little Village High School for Social Justice in Chicago.

Una Hanley is a Senior Lecturer in Mathematics Education at the Manchester Metropolitan University. She teaches primarily in masters and doctoral programmes where she works with practising teachers researching their everyday practices. Her own research interests span teacher identity and teacher development. She has recently completed a project funded by the UK Economic and Social Research Council evaluating a teacher development initiative. She has published widely in journals including papers in the *British Education Research Journal* and the *Journal for Mathematics Teacher Education*.

Kathy Lawless is a physics teacher and vice principal at a high school in Moosomin, Saskatchewan. She completed a Masters Degree in Curriculum and Instruction at the University of Regina in December of 2006.

Carl Leggo is a poet and professor in the Department of Language and Literacy Education at the University of British Columbia where he teaches courses in English language arts education, creative writing, narrative research, and postmodern critical theory. In addition to degrees in English literature, education, and theology, he has a master's degree in Creative Writing. He is the author of three collections of poems: *Growing Up Perpendicular on the Side of a Hill*, *View from My Mother's House* (Killick Press, St. John's), and *Come-By-Chance* (Breakwater Books, St. John's), as well as a book about reading and teaching poetry: *Teaching to Wonder: Responding to Poetry in the Secondary Classroom* (Pacific Educational Press, Vancouver).

Stephen Lerman is Professor of Mathematics Education at London South Bank University and Head of Educational Research. He was a secondary teacher of mathematics for 15 years before beginning research towards a PhD. He is a former President of the International Group for the Psychology of Mathematics Education (PME). Steve's research interests are in sociocultural and sociological studies of mathematics education.

Paul Muir is a professor in the Department of Mathematics and Computing Science, Saint Mary's University, Halifax, Nova Scotia, where he has just completed his 23rd year of service. Dr. Muir is a long time member of the

Saint Mary's University's Senate Quality of Teaching Committee and, in 1997, won the universities' highest award for teaching, the Father William Stewart S.J. Medal for Excellence in Teaching. His research is in numerical computing and involves the development and analysis of mathematical theory, algorithms and software for the treatment of mathematical models of complex phenomenon.

Kathleen Nolan is Associate Professor in the Faculty of Education, University of Regina, where she teaches undergraduate and graduate courses in mathematics and science curriculum. Her research interests include mathematics and science teacher education, poststructural and sociocultural studies of teacher identity, critical and narrative research methodologies, and performative scholarly research-writing. Kathleen has published several articles and book chapters with Peter Lang, Open University Press, and University of Toronto Press. She is author of a new book entitled *How Should I Know? Preservice Teachers' Images of Knowing (by Heart) in Mathematics and Science* (SensePublishers).

Devona Putland is principal and grade five teacher at an elementary school in Moosomin, Saskatchewan. She completed a Masters Degree in Educational Administration at the University of Regina in December of 2006.

Nathalie Sinclair works in the Faculty of Education at Simon Fraser University in British Columbia, Canada. She teachers undergraduate mathematics courses as well as pre-service and graduate courses in mathematics education. Nathalie's research focuses on the aesthetic dimension of mathematics thinking and learning, and also on the use of dynamic geometry software across the mathematics curriculum.

Ole Skovsmose has a special interest in critical mathematics education. Recently, he published *Travelling Through Education*, which investigates the notions of mathematics in action, students' foreground, globalisation, and ghettoising with a particular reference to mathematics education. He is professor at Aalborg University, Department of Education, Learning and Philosophy. Ole has participated in conferences and given lectures on mathematics education in many different countries, including Australia, Austria, Brazil, Canada, Colombia, Germany, Norway, Sweden, USA, England, Hungary, Iceland, South Africa, Greece, Portugal, Spain, and (naturally) Denmark.

Diana Stentoft is a doctoral candidate in the Department of Education, Learning and Philosophy, Aalborg University, Denmark. Her background is in language and international relations. Diana's thesis research is focused on student and teacher identities as they are brought into the mathematics classroom context and their influence on the teaching and learning of mathematics. She works from a multi-disciplinary perspective integrating social and post-structural analysis.

Tara Stuckless is a doctoral candidate in the Faculty of Education at the University of Regina, Saskatchewan. She has a B.Sc. in mathematics from Memorial University of Newfoundland, and M.Sc. in mathematics from Simon Fraser University. Her research interests include discourse analytic, sociolinguistic, and semiotic approaches to understanding mathematics education.

Dalene M. Swanson is a SSHRC postdoctoral scholar at the University of Alberta. Her research interests span mathematics education, curriculum studies; arts-based research and education; critical theory; cultural studies; and global and social justice. Dalene was born and educated in South Africa, and holds degrees in mathematics and education from the University of Cape Town, and a Ph.D. in Curriculum Studies and Mathematics Education from The University of British Columbia. She has published locally and internationally. Dalene received four prestigious Canadian and international awards in Qualitative Research and Curriculum Studies for her doctoral research in South African schools with socio-economic and cultural differences in a post-apartheid context.

Paola Valero has a Ph.D in mathematics education and is Associate Professor in the Department of Education, Learning and Philosophy at Aalborg University, Denmark. Her initial background is in Linguistics and Political Science. Since 1990, Paola has been doing research in the area of mathematics education, with particular emphasis on the political dimension of mathematics teaching and learning, and of mathematics teacher education. Her research integrates sociological and political analyses of mathematics in different institutional settings, and in different aspects of mathematical learning and teaching. She has published several papers in books, journals and conferences proceedings.

Margaret Walshaw is a senior lecturer at Massey University, New Zealand. Her main research interest is in making connections between education and social theories of the postmodern. She has recently completed a project funded by the Royal Society of New Zealand, exploring young women's place in mathematics and society. Currently, she is engaged as co-principal investigator in a Ministry of Education project on teaching and learning in junior secondary school mathematics classrooms. She is editor of the book *Mathematics Education within the Postmodern*, published by Information Age, and is author of the book *Working with Foucault in Education*, recently published by Sense Publishers.

Chapter 1

FOREWORD TO THE RESEARCH TEXT

Mathematics education under cross-examination

Kathleen Nolan and Elizabeth de Freitas
University of Regina; Adelphi University & University of Prince Edward Island

Each of the chapters in this collection embraces a socio-political perspective on mathematics education. Taking such a perspective cannot be translated into a single methodological principle, but it does indicate a shared commitment to cultural and critical analyses of school mathematics. This book uses multiple lenses to explore the political context of school mathematics, focusing less on the "situated" nature of learning, and more on the power relations that structure learning experiences within dominant educational discourses. Emphasis on the discursive mapping of power relations and subject positions within mathematics education is crucial in further developing the "social turn" (Lerman, 2000) in mathematics education research. This book represents an important contribution to the expansion of the research field because of its unremitting interrogation of "common sense" practices. Contributors were asked to take risks in their writing, to critique and disrupt cherished notions embedded in the field, and to "speak truth to power" by whatever means they deemed necessary. The result is a collection that is sometimes uncomfortable to read; a collection that troubles many taken-for-granted assumptions about mathematics education and research.

The recent burgeoning interest in socio-cultural readings of mathematics education has produced a number of excellent edited books (Allen & Johnston-Wilder, 2004; Boaler, 2000; Gates, 2001; Jacobs, Becker & Glimer, 2001; Secada, 2000; Valero & Zevenbergen, 2004; Walshaw, 2004a) to which this book pays tribute. The emphasis on equity, social justice and new research methodologies in many North American and European publications offers further evidence of this shifting focus in the Western mathematics education research community. The new focus comes as a result of an increased awareness that previous models for research, which have been tied perhaps too closely to cognitive theory and large-scale quantitative methods, are enhanced by new methodologies and theoretical frameworks that explore the underbelly of mathematics education.

Although research paradigms are constantly in flux, we have chosen the umbrella term of "poststructural" to describe these new directions in mathematics education research. Poststructuralism inherits from structuralism a focus on signifying systems and discursive patterns (as opposed to earlier Humanist notions of the subject as the source of all signification), but it is a far more political project that aims to destabilize or disrupt established knowledge claims. Indeed, it attends to the contingency and political provisional status of knowledge claims. Poststructuralism aims to interrupt the master narratives of social science and reject claims to complete or coherent explanations that essentialize the human subject. It also demonstrates the inadequacies and ideological inscriptions that underscore foundationalist theories of identity and culture.

In *Poststructuralism and Educational Research*, Peters & Burbules (2004) describe the theory as follows:

> Poststructuralist thought has developed a range of different methods or approaches (e.g., archaeology, genealogy, deconstruction) that operate according to their own logics but tend to emphasize notions of difference, local indeterminacy, historical breaks or discontinuities, serialization, repetition, and a mode of critique as 'dismantling' or 'disassembling' (read, deconstruction). (p. 22)

In focusing on difference, ambiguity, and indeterminacy, poststructuralism seeks out the aporias, the silenced voices, the inconsistencies in texts, the moments of surplus meaning, the asymmetries within power relations, the inherent alterity of the speaking subject—all of which establish the very conditions of discourse. The agenda of poststructuralism is not to resolve the contradictions but rather to reveal the continuous deferral of meaning and signification that constitutes subject positions within discourse. Theorists such as Michel Foucault, Jacques Derrida, Judith Butler, John Caputo, to name only a few who are now commonly cited by educational researchers, aim to problematize our epistemic assumptions and reveal the political, contingent nature of all knowledge claims.

The poststructuralist philosophy that informs this collection demands a vigilant critique of the cultural habits associated with mathematics education - a critique sustained indefinitely because the job of interrogating the status quo is never complete, and readers are not allowed, or at least not encouraged, to settle for easy answers and comforting narratives. The writing in this collection is therefore "sous rature" (under erasure) (Derrida, 1976, p. 3) in the sense that the authors' claims to research truth or insight are subject to the same inquisitive probing that each has tactically deployed as a means of examining school mathematics. This kind of deconstruction is the hallmark of poststructuralism– building on the strengths of structuralist programs (in this case, traditional semiotics, psychology and Marxist-inspired sociology), but employing these theoretical frameworks reflexively and without reliance on positivist epistemologies. In practice, a poststructuralist approach to research in mathematics education means accessing these powerful theoretical frameworks with humility; that is to say, employing these tools while simultaneously denouncing them as enlightenment ideals. The contradiction in this endeavor is deliberate. The difficulty lies in finding ways of enacting this philosophy in our scholarship so that readers gain meaning and insight into the lived experience of school mathematics. This collection does so by juxtaposing core chapters with arts-based response chapters.

Each set of core and response chapters is meant to be read together. The core chapters in this collection, described in more detail below, pose difficult questions about school mathematics, educational research, and power. These core chapters tackle the political facets of mathematics education using different theoretical lenses to examine the ways that power relations constitute, and are constituted by, the cultural practices of mathematics education. The response chapters in this collection open up the research texts and offer diverse reading practices that are both inventions and interpretations of the core chapters. These "insights and in(ter)ventions" function as linking responses and "what if not" exercises, building on and extending the discussions found in each core chapter. Our hope is that such responses will assist readers in engaging the research text and actively pursuing its implications. Each response is meant to complement the research paper by triggering critical reflection, dialogue and action. In creating a dialogic text in which a variety of voices and positions are enacted, and in relying on arts-based forms of representation that fly in the face of more traditional forms of research text, we hope to have created a research-based text that breaks the norm in mathematics education. The arts-based responses underscore the fabrication of research texts. Maggie Maclure argues that all educational research texts are fabrications, and that neutrality and realism are "the most spectacular" signs of rhetorical artfulness (Maclure, 2003, p. 80). Research texts are granted authority, claims Maclure, when they erase their own artfulness and appear to be transparent in their persuasiveness, as though unproblematic in their relation to the 'external' or 'internal' situation that they describe. As a means of confronting this artfulness, and in some sense celebrating the fabrication of research, the response chapters in this collection focus on the "writtenness" (Maclure, 2003, p. 105) of research texts, and invite the reader to do the same.

This book creates more openings than closures, and does so by actively and critically engaging the reader in multiple ways, thereby reaching different readers differently. The response chapters – the "insights and in(ter)ventions" - are not intended as authoritative applications of the more theoretical research text, but rather as suggestive multi-directional supplements that challenge reader ambivalence and engender dialogue. They open up the research text and invite the reader to speculate on the implications of the research for their own practice and the community at large. By sustaining a dialogue on the research issues and offering different ways of conceiving the research, we hope to address the fragmented reading experience that often besets the reader of an isolated article.

Response formats in this collection include narrative, fiction, teacher self-study, collage, concept maps, graphic novels, conversations, and poetic renderings. Many of these responses use some form of narrative. Narrative research in general - in which experience and identity are seen as narratively constructed - has become a mainstream staple of qualitative research (Denzin & Lincoln, 2000). As a sub-genre of narrative research, fictional narratives draw more explicitly on literary forms. Peter Clough uses the term "research fictions" to describe the short stories he composes based on his research (Clough, 2002). Clough's narratives are character-based explorations of the politics of educational research. Other scholars use fiction to explore the lived experiences of students and teachers and mathematical learning (Doxiadis, 2003). Because fiction has the power to subjunctify truth by generating "what if" scenarios, it is an excellent vehicle for exploring social justice issues. Fiction draws on the reader's capacity to empathize and imagine the world differently (de Freitas, 2003, 2004). As a response to a work of theory or expository text, fictional narratives can playfully take-up and interrogate the research paper from divergent positions which may have been only partially addressed in the original text.

Self-study and life history narratives have been used to supplement and envision some of the core chapters. A "first-hand" autobiographical narrative pertaining to experiences in the mathematics classroom engenders an empathic response on the part of the reader and possibly triggers other kinds of intervention and action. Teacher self-study has become an incredibly successful form of professional development that can lead to transformative change (Miller, 1992; Ellis & Bochner, 2002). Povey et al (2004) have argued that student life history narratives can reveal to researchers the reasons why certain students continue to be disenfranchised from school mathematics. Autobiographical narratives, or acts of self-study, respond explicitly to the issues raised in a core chapter by re-contextualizing them in particular lived experiences. Such responses trouble all truth claims by generating a more nuanced and empathetic understanding of the issues.

Poetic transcription and poetic representation have been employed by qualitative researchers as a means of representing research in emotionally provocative ways (Cole & Knowles, 2003). Anderson Norton (2000a, 2000b) has used poetic transcription to convey the correlations between the belief structure of mathematicians and their conception of mathematics. Poetic transcription is a way for researchers to dwell on the phrasing and speaking rhythms found in their interview data. It can be used to supplement a more traditional assessment of research findings precisely because poetry evokes without prescribing meaning. A poetic rendering dwells on the ambiguity, tentativeness, and multiplicity of meaning making and can help readers explore the contradictory associations affiliated with an experience or belief (Richardson, 2001).

The graphic novel or graphic story employs comic visuals to integrate dialogue and narrative with image. Art Spiegelman's *Maus* and Chris Ware's *Jimmy Corrigan* have shown readers that the traditional comic-book art form can be used to treat serious and complex issues. These "drawn books" are increasingly popular with adults everywhere (Arnold, 2005). Because a graphic story uses image as a narrative tool while also incorporating written dialogue or text, it is a form that highlights multi-literacy (Eisner, 1996; Weber & Mitchell, 2004). As a response or complement to a core chapter, the graphic story offers a revisioning of the research context in which students, teachers and researchers are portrayed. Similarly, collage as a response format uses non-verbal stimuli to evoke the complexity of a situation in ways that words cannot do. This form of multi-sensory response draws on both emotional and intellectual modes, triggering a long-lasting memory that can be accessed in the future.

Several of the response chapters play with visual and unusual forms of representing text. A concept map by a graduate student reveals new and different relationships between ideas. The linking between concepts is represented by the particular diagram structure which has been constructed. The concept map is a visual reading of the core chapter and an attempt to make the ideas more messy and life-like. The responses function as examples of interpretive devices, as well as sources for future discussion amongst students in mathematics education courses. Some of the responses highlight the messiness and ambiguity of the research/writing process—a process that is often only acknowledged by its absence in a "finished" text. Some authors have deliberately included the details of their deliberations as they construct their response. According to Blumenfeld-Jones & Barone (1997), masking process and doubt in our research texts as we "work with" the text, erases the crucial facets of negotiation and recursion which are inherent in knowledge production (p. 83). A seemingly simple response, like a conversation between a mathematics researcher and a mathematics education researcher, disrupts images of the unilateral academic voice of the research text, and begins to indicate how a dialogical mode of knowing is always and only in process. The give-and-take of a conversation, even in an asynchronous environment like an e-mail exchange, highlights the moments when language constitutes and divides different domains of inquiry.

The diverse response formats in this collection return again and again to the struggles and challenges of theory-practice transitions in mathematics education research. What research calls for in theory, on the one hand, often seems elusive in practice. What is needed is a "lived theory" where the ideas being advocated in the author's research text are lived out through diverse and multiple forms. The arts-based response chapters, together with the core chapters, draw attention to the methods by which we might interweave theory and practice in new styles of research-writing. Roth & McRobbie (1999) argue for w/ri(gh)ting research that "allows us to resist epistemic violence of traditional master narratives by encompassing heterogeneity" (p. 518). Similarly, Nolan (2005) strives to not only write a research text *about* different ways of knowing mathematics and science but to write the text *through* different ways of knowing, highlighting textual performance and non-linearity in an attempt to interrupt the reader along the journey of coming to know.

Our hope is that this book will inspire scholars in mathematics education to play with form in/as content. New scholars in the field are searching for fresh theoretical perspectives that point to different ways of communicating and interpreting their research, and this book offers tangible alternative strategies for writing research texts. We caution the reader, as we also caution our selves, to be mindful of the socio-political perspectives that must always be at the heart of the enterprise. The freedom to play with alternative methodology comes with the responsibility to address the needs of others who may not be privileged with such freedom. As Smith (1997) reminds us, deconstruction is used "to reveal possibilities of freedom from the systems in which we are entrapped while avoiding any presumption of a meta-discourse" (p. 108). In education, the first step of poststructuralism is to acknowledge the prevalent hierarchy of discourses as social constructions full of "cracks"—contradictions, inconsistencies, ambiguities, and arbitrary rules that privilege some while placing others and their ideas on the margins (Bloland, 1995, p. 7). Poststructuralism is both a theoretical tool and a political device. At the heart of these strategies lies a dismantling of the discourses of power, and herein lie their usefulness as research and classroom tools.

The collection opens with a chapter by Margaret Walshaw that speaks directly to our desire to "open the research text" and consider alternative research paradigms in mathematics education research. By focusing on debates surrounding the evidence based movement (in New Zealand, but with far reaching implications), Walshaw offers a postmodern approach to exploring mathematics pedagogical practices that take seriously the issues of teaching and learning as complex processes. In response to Walshaw's text, Tony Brown provides a perspective that corroborates Walshaw's New Zealand story through his discussion of UK policies and decisions that have served to "ignore the inherent messiness of classrooms". Nathalie Sinclair offers a different take on Walshaw's critique of 'best practices' by considering comparisons between evidence based movements in mathematics education and in the field of obstetrics. Sinclair draws on the dialogue between Socrates and Theatetus as a means to round out her midwifery analogy.

   Building on the discussion begun by Walshaw regarding the political status of research in mathematics education, Marcelo Batarce & Stephen Lerman engage with the theme of 'math wars' as they explore the conflict (in general, and in the particular instance of the Brazilian context) between mathematics and mathematics education. Theirs is a chapter that attempts to bring a closer reading of Derrida to mathematics education by noting that "[m]athematics education as a condition of reading mathematics… is, first of all, already in its trace, a debate about mathematics". Una Hanley refers to her response as a 'supplement' to Batarce & Lerman's chapter, as she offers a deconstruction of the insider/outsider binary and draws attention to how the authors' discussion is "a relationship of fluidity and movement… where nothing can be pinned down". Elizabeth de Freitas, drawing on a Socratic dialogue for her response, further questions the act(s) of writing mathematics and asks if the writing of mathematics "might be the very condition of mathematical knowledge".

   Paul Ernest picks up the 'writing' thread introduced by Batarce & Lerman and extends the discussion to consider the content and function of mathematical text, where 'text' refers to the many semiotic systems of inscription embedded in all forms of mathematical communication. In his chapter, Ernest states that "to open the mathematical text is to explore its social uses and functions, as well as its inner meanings and textures." Perhaps Brent Davis' response to Ernest best expresses a dilemma inherent in our desire to uncover these inner meanings and textures when he states that "[in] the desire to pull learners along a smooth path of concept development, we've planed off the bumpy parts that were once the precise locations of meaning and elaboration". Tara Stuckless, presented by the editors with the challenge of constructing a response that attempts to speak to both Ernest's and Davis' texts, presents her inter(ven)tion in the form of a messy text— one that is rich with in-between spaces and 'isolated' signs of her learning process. Elizabeth de Freitas presents an apt closure to these texts (and an opening to the subsequent Brown chapter and responses) through her imaginative fiction about Agnes—a character who seeks to trouble the epistemic authority of mathematics as she takes pleasure in her identity as a (female) mathematician.

Grappling with issues of identity is the main focus of Tony Brown's psychoanalytic enquiry into trainee primary teachers' accounts of themselves as they story themselves and their (past, failed) relationships with mathematics, while en route to becoming mathematics teachers. Brown shows how these trainee teachers internalize comforting narratives about their practice as a means of erasing the difficulties they experienced. It seems most apropos then, that the response texts to Brown's chapter about trainee and new teachers of mathematics would come from several current mathematics teachers. The visual and poetic sojourns of five mathematics teachers/graduate students (Brent Eidsness, Shana Graham, Kathy Lawless, Devona Putland, and Tara Stuckless)—as they ventured away from a comfortable, linear form of academic text—bring to light some of the promises of alternative arts-based representation formats. Kathleen Nolan enters the scene, as the graduate course instructor, to present an autobiographical account of the possible ensuing compromises when taking up such alternative formats in graduate curriculum courses, Nolan introduces questions regarding who has the power when it comes to deciding *how* and *what* one should know in/through arts-based formats in education.

The trio of Ole Ravn Christensen, Diana Stentoft, and Paola Valero deliberate on the presence and meaning of power in mathematics education. These authors trace three different perspectives on power—intrinsic, technical, and structural inequality—supporting their discussions with brief illustrative fictions. As the sole example (in this collection) of authors intervening in their own research text, Christensen, Stentoft, and Valero construct a response which interrogates their three perspectives on power, inviting readers to participate in the same kind of conversation in order to imagine new possibilities, or frameworks, for viewing power. Kathleen Nolan then picks up on the three perspectives of power, presenting a playful, autobiographical 'thrice-told story' of her experience living through/within the three perspectives.

Ole Skovsmose explores power enacted in particular mathematical practices in and out of schools, focusing on the role that mathematics in action plays in a knowledge society. His examination of the mathematical competencies required in the knowledge market takes him on a journey of questioning his own critical-versus-functional binary, leading him ultimately to a critical state of doubt. Authors Kathleen Nolan & Paul Muir share their own doubts—about the mark(et) driven system, about skill-based mathematics, and, ultimately, about Skovsmose's run away concepts—as they discuss their own run away ideas for cha(lle)nging mathematics education. An auto-biographical, poetic rendering, presented by Carl Leggo, follows with an evocative reflection on the emotional imprint of school mathematics, and the need to recognize the poetic role of language. He states: "like Ole Skovs-mose's concepts, poetry pushes at edges into spaces where language refuses clarity, coherence, composition, even comprehensibility…".

Eric (Rico) Gutstein's chapter brings the issue of "mathematics in action" to the forefront by considering the many challenges of teaching mathematics for social justice. He asserts that "[d]iscussions that name racism, examine historical lessons of struggle, and politicize the overall context of mathemat-ics can be important to developing political relationships with students, even/especially in mathematics classes". The three responses to Gutstein's chapter dwell on the nature of those political relationships by drawing on life experiences in teacher education. Both Elizabeth de Freitas and Carol Fulton recount recent experiences with pre-service mathematics teachers' direct and deliberate resistance to the kinds of discussions that Gutstein proposes. Da-lene Swanson, taking up Gutstein's challenge, demands that the political impetus behind mathematics social justice pedagogy be grounded in the par-ticular needs of particular contexts.

The book closes with Peter Appelbaum's afterword in which he insight-fully weaves together the various contributor's ideas, while tracing the many divergent paths of inquiry and diverse forms of representation that comprise the collection. Appelbaum playfully encourages the reader to view this col-lection through metaphorical lenses such as "static electricity", "waking up", and "stop making sense", asking, for example: What if we, as educators, stopped trying to make sense for our students, "and instead worked together with students to study the ways in which mathematics does and does not make sense?" He reads the collection through the philosophy of Kierkegaard who, like the authors in this book, attempted to problematize that which was taken for granted by others. Appelbaum suggests that what defines this col-lection is the commitment to understanding mathematics education as a *critical* cultural practice, and the passion and persistence to leverage re-search texts as vehicles for "imagining new worlds".

REFERENCES

Allen, B. & Johnston-Wilder, S. (Eds.) (2004), *Mathematics Education: Exploring the Cul-ture of Learning*. New York, NY: Routledge-Falmer.
Arnold, A. D. (2005). The all-time graphic novels. *Time Magazine*, Oct. 19, Wednesday.
Boaler, J. (Ed.) (2000). *Multiple perspectives on mathematics teaching and learning*. London, UK: Ablex Publishing.

Bloland, H.G. (1995). Postmodernism and higher education. *The Journal of Higher Education, 66*(5), 521-559.

Blumenfeld-Jones, D.S. & Barone, T.E. (1997). Interrupting the sign: The aesthetics of research texts. In J.A. Jipson & N. Paley (Eds.), *Daredevil research: Re-creating analytic practice* (pp. 83-107). New York, NY: Peter Lang.

Clough, P. (2002). *Narratives and fictions in educational research.* Philadelphia, PA: Open University Press.

Cole, A.L. & Knowles, J.G. (2003). *Provoked by art: Theorizing arts-informed inquiry.* Lanham, MD: Rowman & Littlefield.

de Freitas, E. (2003). Contested positions: How fiction informs empathic research. *International Journal of Education & the Arts: A journal of scholarship, 4(7).*

de Freitas, E. (2004). Plotting intersections along the political axis: The interior voice of dissenting mathematics teachers. *Educational Studies in Mathematics, 55.* 259-274.

Denzin, N.K. & Lincoln, Y. (Eds.). (2000). The seventh moment: Out of the past. In N.K. Denzin & Y. Lincoln (Eds.), *The Sage Handbook of Qualitative Research*, 2nd Edition. Thousand Oaks, CA: Sage Publications.

Derrida, J. (1976). *Of grammatology.* [Translation by Gayatri Chakravorty Spivak.] Baltimore: John Hopkins University press.

Doxiadis, A. (2003). *Embedding mathematics in the soul: Narrative as a force in mathematics education.* Opening Address to the 3rd Mediterranean Conference of Mathematics Education. Available: [http://www.apostolosdoxiadis.com/files/essays/embeddingmath.pdf].

Ellis, C & Bochner, A.P. (2002). *Ethnographically Speaking.* Lanham, MD: Altamira Press.

Eisner, W. (1996). *Graphic storytelling and visual narrative.* Tandrac, Florida: Poorhouse Press.

Gates, P. (Ed.) (2001). *Issues in mathematics teaching.* New York, NY: RoutledgeFalmer.

Jacobs, J.E., Becker, J.R. & Glimer, G.F. (Eds.) (2001). *Changing the faces of mathematics: Perspectives on gender.* Reston, VA: NCTM Publishing.

Lerman, S. (2000). The social turn in mathematics education research. In J. Boaler (Ed.), *Multiple perspectives on mathematics teaching and learning* (pp 19-44). London, UK: Ablex Publishing.

Maclure, M. (2003). *Discourse in educational and social research.* Philadelphia, PA: Open University Press.

Miller, J. (1992). Teachers, autobiography, and curriculum: Critical and feminist perspectives. In B. B. Swadner & S. Kessler (Eds.), *Reconceptualizing the early childhood curriculum* (pp.103-122). New York: Teachers College Press.

Nolan, K.T. (2005). Publish or cherish? Performing a dissertation in/between research spaces. In R. Barnett (Ed.), *Reshaping the university: New relationships between research, scholarship and teaching* (p. 119-135). Berkshire, England: Open University Press.

Norton, A. (2000a). Mathematicians' religious affiliations and professional practices: The case of Joseph. *The Mathematics Educator, 12*(1), 17-23.

Norton, A. (2000b). Mathematicians' religious affiliations and professional practices: The case of Charles. *The Mathematics Educator, 12*(2), 28-33.

Peters, M. & Burbules, N.C. (2004). *Poststructuralism and educational research.* Rowman & Littlefield Pub., Inc.

Povey, H., Burton, L., Angier, C. & Boylan, M. (2004). Learners as Authors in the Mathematics Classroom. In B. Allen & S. Johnston-Wilder (Eds.), *Mathematics education: Exploring the culture of learning.* New York, NY: Routledge-Falmer.

Richardson, L. (2001). Alternative ethnographies, alternative criteria. In L. Neilsen, A.L. Cole & J.G. Knowles (Eds.), *The art of writing inquiry* (pp. 250-252). Halifax, NS: Back-along-books.

Roth, W-M & McRobbie, C. (1999). Lifeworlds and the 'w/ri(gh)ting' of classroom research. *Journal of Curriculum Studies, 31*(5), 501-522.

Secada, W.G. (Ed.) (2000). *Changing the faces of mathematics: Perspectives on multiculturalism and gender equity.* Reston, VA: NCTM Publishing.

Smith, D. (1997). *Procedures of power and curriculum change: Foucault and the quest for possibilities in science education.* New York, NY: Peter Lang Publishing, Inc.

Valero, P. & Zevenbergen, R. (Eds.) (2004). *Researching the socio-political dimensions of mathematics education: Issues of power in theory and methodology.* Dordrecht: Kluwer Academic Publishers.

Walshaw, M. (Ed.) (2004a). *Mathematics education within the postmodern.* Greenwich, Connecticut: Information Age Publishing Inc.

Weber, S & Mitchell, C. (2004).Visual Artistic Modes of Representation for Self-Study, Chapter 10. In J. Loughran, M. Hamilton, V. LaBoskey, & T. Russell (Eds.), *International Handbook of Self-Study of Teaching and Teacher Education Practices.* Spring 2004, Kluwer Press.

Chapter 2

BEST EVIDENCE RESEARCH REDEFINED IN MATHEMATICS EDUCATION

Margaret Walshaw
Massey University

Abstract: This chapter focuses on the evidence based movement and draws attention to the debates surrounding its application to education. An alternative meaning for evidence based research in mathematics education is proposed in response to issues raised in those debates. The particularly postmodern approach offered in this chapter explores mathematics pedagogical practices while taking into account the complexity of teaching as well as the limits of knowing.

Key words: evidence based movement; research; policy development; complexity; redefined outcomes.

1. INTRODUCTION

In their closing chapter in the *Handbook of International Research in Mathematics Education*, English et al. (2002) write that "the field of mathematics education research appears to be at a critical stage in its development" (p. 802). New ways of thinking enable "closer and more meaningful working partnerships between many levels and types of both researchers and practitioners" (p. 803). The authors also make the point, however, that these new ways of thinking bring to the fore a whole set of issues for assessing and improving the quality of research. The issues form part of the debate, conducted largely in negative terms, about research as a governed site, about researcher accountability, and about transparency and standards. In this chapter, putting critical approaches to use, I join the debate and recount my efforts to tell the story, through a literature synthesis, of what quality pedagogical practice looks like. I describe a version of policy-informing evidence-based research that takes issue with current narrowly defined understandings of pedagogical practice.

Not so long ago, the crossover between best evidence forms and traditional research in any discipline had many common denominators. Orthodox notions of observation, authority, representation and the transparency of language all sat comfortably with the base assumptions underlying the best evidence movement. Much of the strategic thinking about the purpose of research and how it informs policy has revolved around a widely held belief in its capacity to make classrooms and schools effective, efficient and better places.

A number of researchers within mathematics education (see Walshaw, 2004b), taking the lead from other disciplines, have recently broadened the repertoire of research. In particular, they ask important questions about the measurement of social phenomena and about the validation of causal relationships. These questions came to the fore recently for me when I, together with a colleague, entered into a contractual arrangement with the Ministry of Education in New Zealand to write a best evidence synthesis of mathematics pedagogical practices. The task was to produce a systematic review of best evidence in relation to mathematics pedagogical practices that facilitate positive outcomes for students from early years to senior secondary school. The synthesis was subsequently published (Anthony & Walshaw, 2006) and made available in the public domain. Its stated use was to inform policy and practice.

Researching and writing the literature synthesis drew us into contemporary methodological and philosophical debates within education on the trend towards evidence based practice. In the first section of this chapter I draw attention to issues in the debates, outlining the genesis and the fundamental assumptions that ground the belief that the movement can contribute significantly to the improvement of practice. I document critical insights from others who have questioned the orthodox notions of truth and causality that inhere, and map out how those notions tend to overlook uncertainty, contingency, and complicity.

In the second section I make a case for an alternative meaning for evidence based research as it is operationalised in current educational policy. As a consequence of carrying out the synthesis, I propose an intervention in the form of a research paradigm that is not simply a surface treatment to the current push for mastery of cause/effect relations, but one that acknowledges the "messy real-life classroom" (Sfard, 2005, p. 398) processes that characterise mathematics teaching. In advocating for a new approach to research, the purpose is to encourage a move away from the desire to establish true and accurate accounts of quality teaching and suggest how we might rethink best evidence research to lay bare the complexity of teaching through a critical awareness of the limits of knowing.

2.   BEST EVIDENCE RESEARCH

Evidence based research syntheses are the current preoccupation of many English speaking policy makers and funding agents, searching for answers to pressing pedagogical problems. Driven to a large extent by the example of improved practice synthesis in health care (Lather, 2004; NCTM Research Advisory Committee Report, 2003; Oakley, 2002), such syntheses signal a major shift in thinking within academic and policy circles in relation to the gap between academic research and real world policy and practice. The movement calls for greater accessibility of sound educational research evidence, and a greater respect for the perspectives and investments of diverse stakeholders in the educational research process. As a lever for policy, the movement carries "enormous potential to influence school audiences, consumers and funders of research" (Chatterji, 2004, p. 3).

Luke and Hogan (2006) have historicised the evidence based movement and shown how the seeds were sown in the U.S., the U.K., Canada, Australia, and New Zealand in the "discourses of markets and corporatism, economic rationalism and accountability" (p. 171) that have dominated many nations. Trinder (2000a) adds a further layer to our understanding by arguing that this is a context in which "there is a heightened sense of risk, and increasing reliance upon as well as increased distrust of expertise" (p. 3). The research-informing-policy-informing-practice grand narrative, as a significant characteristic of our 'contemporaneity' (Foucault, 1998), is presented as a radical approach that invites collaboration between practitioners and consumers in knowledge building. Needless to say, it has attracted both critics and champions alike (see Eisenhart & Towne, 2003; Hammersley, 2004; Thomas & Pring, 2004; Trinder, 2000b) who remain divided on its merits. For some commentators, the evidence based movement represents a way of systematising and disseminating what is known to make sense (Hargreaves, 1996). For others, it both follows and supports an increasingly centralised control over policy and practice (Atkinson, 2000). It presents as part of a "new panopticon" (Davies, 2003, p. 91) within the managerialist strategies of education and "must be revised" (Chatterji, 2004, p. 3).

In her Foucauldian analysis, Lather (2004) describes the policy movement as a state intervention that represents "one of the three technologies of governmentality," whose primary objective is to "regulate behaviour and render populations productive" (p. 765). Governmentality, in its application to the best evidence movement, targets individuals as the means with which to maintain control over research practice by "naming, classifying and analysing" (Lather, 2004, p. 765). Systems and practices are reformed through mandating, standardisation, and implementation of that which comes to be perceived as normal. Lather writes: "In terms of the recent governing mentality of educational research, the 'privilege accorded to ... 'the sciences of man' is based on the political arithmetic' (Foucault, 1998, p. 323) that makes particular kinds of discourse both possible and necessary" (p. 765).

At issue for many scholars in debates over evidence based work is the autonomy of educational research. In particular, changes to the government funding of and support for educational research have been questioned in relation to academic freedom, for their attempt to draw an analogy between education and the positivism of the natural and medical sciences (Lather, 2004; NCTM Research Advisory Committee Report, 2003). Lather reminds us that an analogy such as this "ignores the last 40 years of contestation regarding the definition of science, particularly in the social sciences" (p. 762). In its application to mathematics education, it has the effect of marginalising the huge inroads made over recent decades by postmodern and critical scholars who needed a counterpoint to the behaviourist tradition for understanding the practices they were studying in mathematics classrooms and schools. It ignores scholarly interventions within the discipline that confronted the difficulty of measuring educational outcomes and the limitations of causal models.

Measurement of educational phenomena and assessments of causality within the evidence based movement derive from the Hegelian concept of complete and 'absolute knowledge.' Complicit within this regime of truth is a core assumption that reality and truth have "generalisable and universal efficacy across and in spite of contexts" (Luke & Hogan, 2006, p. 174). In this regime "paradigmatic instances of the best knowledge possible, for everyone in all circumstances" (Code, 1995, p. xi) hold true.

In a postmodern assessment, the myth of universality, in its application to pedagogy, taken together with an "embarrassingly naïve trust in the objectivity of...research" (Lather, 2004, p. 762) does "not remove the subjectivity of researchers" (Davies, 2003, p. 99). Rather, the drive to find security and certainty works merely to keep researcher subjectivity out of view. What emerges is a staging of truth, in which the concepts of objectivity and universalism play a central role.

Advocates of best evidence discourses define their key priority as the immediate and obvious application of evidence based research to the classroom (NCTM Research Committee Report, 2003). 'What works' in terms of teacher effectiveness, irrespective of setting or circumstance, is under investigation and subject to the whims and wishes of consulted users and interested parties. The particular version of this instrumental model in the political toolkit, as exemplified in research on teacher effectiveness, views the production of conclusive and long-term knowledge about causes of teacher effectiveness as unproblematic. It then attempts to rationalise policy in relation to knowledge developed through these empirically derived indicators.

Prototypically, evidence based research determines the sort of design model to be employed and the sort of data that will count as evidence. Key elements endorsed include classical experimentation and randomised trials as the principal research design, and standardised achievement test scores and national data weigh in as the chief means to establish system and teacher effectiveness. Among others, Berliner (2002) opposes the promotion of a single method for educational research. In making a case for context sensitive approaches to the generation and explanation of knowledge, Kilpatrick (2001) supports the stand of the NCTM Research Advisory Committee (2003), maintaining that: "[f]or many reasons, it is a mistake to take the controlled experiment as the archetype for research that can improve school mathematics. Educational research is not simply a matter of comparing methods in the way one might compare medical treatments." (p. 424)

If experimentation has been subject to a contested discourse, so too has the issue of causal explanation. Under interrogation in evidence based research is the validation of positivist causal relationships amongst the mechanisms and techniques of pedagogical phenomena, based on 'if x then y' claims. A tightly-knit epistemological infrastructure that includes prediction, explanation and verification bypasses the complexity within educational settings. By ensuring that only proof-based empirical studies ground evidence, the movement excludes non-cognitive and social student outcomes and tends to prevent important local studies of diverse communities to surface. What are concealed are the critical realities of different contexts, policies, systems, resources, approaches, and practices as well as the different ways in which they impact on students.

3.   ALTERNATIVE APPROACHES

A Foucauldian response to the current evidence based movement highlights the historically specific nature of knowledge production. Such knowledge is circumscribed by particular forms of governance, yet precisely because the knowledge is discursively and politically constituted, it is also open to change. In the section that follows I describe an alternative epistemological and methodological toolkit for undertaking best evidence work. In the description, governmentality assumes an analytic function through which to explore 'other' forms of "strategic possibilities" (Foucault, 1998,

p. 320) for undertaking evidence based research. The alternative approach proposed offers one possible solution to problems associated with the recent traditions of the movement.

This is not by any means the first challenge to be mounted "to the clarity of vision, degree of organisation and tightly focused approach of evidence based practice" (Trinder, 2000b, p. 218). Oakley (2002), for example, reporting on major literature reviews undertaken within the Evidence for Policy and Practice Information and Coordinating (EPPI) Centre at the Social Science Research Unit, University of London Institute of Education, offers a different take on the episteme of evidence based synthesis. Oakley has shown "that it is possible to develop collaborative, democratic and systematic structures for reviewing research evidence, which will help to open up the traditionally rather esoteric world of educational research to public scrutiny" (p. 284).

Similarly, Luke and Hogan (2006) report on the Centre for Research in Pedagogy and Practice (CRPP) that responds to "the key policy issue" concerning "what will count as performance, efficacy, outcome, consequence and indeed learning, knowledge and capital" (p. 172). In redefining the construction of educational policy, they offer a "version of evidence-based educational policy formation [that is] not narrowly determined by standardised achievement test scores but rather one that is based on triangulated quantitative and qualitative research" (p. 170). Addressing the core questions of schooling in Singapore, the CRPP research programme focuses on the pedagogical, "social, demographic and cultural factors that impact upon school performance and outcomes" (p. 176).

4.   THE NEW ZEALAND RESPONSE TO EVIDENCE BASED POLICY DEVELOPMENT

The Best Evidence Synthesis of Pedagogical Approaches that Facilitate learning for Diverse Students in Pāngarau/Mathematics in Centres and Schools (Anthony & Walshaw, 2006) was produced as part of the Iterative Best Evidence Synthesis (BES) Programme established within the Medium Term Strategy Policy Division of the New Zealand Ministry of Education (see Alton-Lee, 2005, 2006). It represents a synthesis of the literature on quality mathematics teaching across settings and learners. Like other syntheses undertaken in the *Iterative Best Evidence Syntheses Programme*), it attempts to systematically identify, evaluate, analyse, synthesise and report on the evidence of quality teaching, taking into account the histories, cultures, language, and practices within New Zealand and comparable international contexts.

The primary objective of this particular best evidence synthesis was to identify and explain the characteristics of pedagogical approaches that enhance proficiency and equity in Pāngarau/Mathematics. In the "almost overwhelming task" (Cobb, 2006) of meeting those objectives, the Best Evidence Synthesis (BES) was shaped by the *Guidelines for Generating a Best Evidence Synthesis Iteration* (Ministry of Education, 2004) and informed by dialogue with policy makers, educators, practitioners and researchers. Interactions with these diverse communities revealed the central role that infrastructure, context, settings, and accountabilities play within the educational system.

4.1 Conceptual Framework

The particularly postmodern mode of dealing with meaning construction in the mathematics BES owes a large debt to Deleuze's (2001) ideas on process, emerging relationships and interconnections that parallel, in some important respects, current applications of complexity science in mathematics classrooms. It has, in particular, many synergies with the work of Davis and Simmt (2003) in which classrooms are read as adaptive as well as self-organising complex systems. The idea of teaching as a complex context-dependent process also draws inspiration from the work of post-Vygotskian activity theorists such as Davydov and Radzikhovskii (1985) and Lave and Wenger's (1991) well-known social practice theory. Both propose a close relationship between conceptual development and social processes.

Building on those ideas, the BES conceptualises teaching as nested within an evolving network of systems. The system itself functions like an ecology in which the activities of the students and the teacher, as well as the school community, the home, the processes involving the mandated curriculum and education-at-large, are constituted mutually through their interactions with each other. It is within the nested system that "individual and collective knowledge emerge and evolve within the dynamics of the spaces people share and within which they participate" (Walshaw, 2004a, p. 5).

Within the nested system, teaching is influenced by adaptive and interactive variables, rather than additive and isolated variables. Teachers adapt their day to day pedagogical practice in relation to their subject and pedagogical subject knowledge, to their personal understandings and inclinations, to the system-level processes at the school, to the 'apparatus' of education itself, and to the understandings and the level of support from the family and wider school community. Student outcomes, in turn, are shaped, in no small measure, by teachers' active engagement with processes and people within the classroom and beyond.

Complexity has emerged in this BES as the capstone of pedagogical practice and making that complexity transparent has been a central methodological concern. It required attending to the constituent parts of a large matrix of practice—those located at both the macro-level of the system (e.g., policy, institutional governance, families and communities) and those at the micro-level of the classroom—as well as the complex relationships between those parts. Within that constituency, specific components of the matrix of practice were identified. These have been characterised as a) the organisation of activities and the associated norms of participation in each phase, b) discourses, particularly norms of mathematical argumentation, c) the instructional tasks, and d) the tools and resources that learners use. It is these multiple aspects of pedagogical practice that lend coherence to the identification of a range of student outcomes.

4.2   Redefining Outcomes

Given the complexity of pedagogical practice, the interpretation of quality pedagogical practice in the BES magnifies more than pedagogical descriptions and explanations that implicate high stakes assessment. Core academic student outcomes were expanded from mastery of skills and concepts to exemplify mathematical proficiency that traced out the dispositions and habits of mind underlying what mathematicians do in their work. These aspects tap into and incorporate curriculum content, classroom organisational structures, instructional and assessment strategies, as well as classroom discourse regarding what mathematics is, how and why it is to be learned and who can learn it. Proficiency outcomes include the ability to think creatively, critically and logically; to structure and organise; and to process information. Outcomes also encompass an enjoyment of intellectual challenge and extend to the development of skills to interpret and critically evaluate mathematical information in a variety of contexts, and to solve problems that contribute to an understanding of the world.

In addition to these academic outcomes, a range of social outcomes was identified in relation to affect, behaviour, communication, and participation. These social outcomes include: a sense of cultural identity and citizenship, a sense of belonging, contribution, well-being, communication, exploration, community spirit, values (e.g., respect for others, tolerance, fairness, caring, diligence, generosity), and preparation for democratic and global citizenship. The wide range of student outcomes took into account "human volition, programme variability, and collateral effects such as cultural diversity, and multiple perspectives" (Lather, 2004, p. 762), and implicated *interactions* between people. We found that productive interactions enhance not only skill and knowledge, but also contribute to the construction of mathematical identity and disposition.

Luke and Hogan (2006) have noted that what is distinctive about the approach taken in the New Zealand Best Evidence programmes "is its willingness to consider all forms of research evidence regardless of methodological paradigms and ideological rectitude, and its concern in finding contextually effective appropriate and locally powerful examples of 'what works'…with particular populations, in particular settings, to particular educational ends" (p. 174). The BES in mathematics is at odds with that body of research that documents "the learning of the individual student while concentrating on the result rather than on the process of teaching and learning" (Sfard, 2005, p. 398). Its emphasis, rather, is on "the broadly understood social context of learning" (p. 398).

Using a "jigsaw methodology" (Alton-Lee, 2006, p. 1) different kinds of evidence were documented, drawn from data collection methods of diverse research designs. The pluralism of methods included large-scale studies, as well as local classroom based action research and design studies. Each form of evidence, characterised by its own way of looking at the world, led to different kinds of truth claims, and different ways of investigating the meaning of quality teaching.

4.3   Influences Rather than Causes

The multilayered data base provided by the BES did not offer linear causal explanations simply because the sheer complexity of the teaching-learning relation "precludes the possibility of identifying clear-cut cause-effect relationships" (Sfard, 2005, p. 407). Instead, the intent was to seek out those pedagogical practices that produced particular student outcomes in particular settings and to particular educational ends, rather than to make generalised pronouncements of 'effective' or 'quality' practice.

The critical realist sensibility implied in the conceptual framework brings to the fore the contingency of student outcomes on a network of interrelated factors and environment. Student outcomes are not so much *caused* by teaching practice, as they are *occasioned* by a complex web of relationships around which knowledge production and exchange revolve (Tower & Davis, 2002; Walshaw, 2004a). Thus, the focus shifted from familiar 'evidence base' struggles of establishing causality towards an emphasis on context dependence. In doing so, this alternative approach did not overlook cultural specificity, and because it stayed "close to the complexities and contradictions" of teaching and learning it did not "divest experience of its rich ambiguity" (Lather, 2004, p. 767). Instead of making assessments about the causes of student outcomes from the vantage point of scientificity, the mathematics BES explored, bottom-up, how teaching might be character-ized, case by case, in specific contexts for specific students.

We were searching for those studies that were able "to offer a developing picture of what it looks like for a teacher's practice to cultivate student [out-comes]" (Blanton & Kaput, 2005, p. 440). The commitment was towards studies that offered a "detailed look at how [teachers'] actions played out in the classroom and how students were involved in this" (Blanton & Kaput, p. 435), and the sorts of mathematical proficiency and non-cognitive out-comes that resulted. Specifically we sought those studies that not only of-fered robust descriptions of pedagogy and outcomes but were also able to provide rigorous explanations for a close association between the two.

Research rigor, however, is a highly contestable term. A central chal-lenge in the production of the BES revolved around what (and whose voice) would count in relation to rigorous evidence. From the early days of work on the BES, a vision of shared understanding and shared ownership guided the development. To this end, a brokerage role was adopted between not only the mathematics education research and practice communities, but also at the policy level. Specifically, in order to attain a high level of agreement be-tween stakeholders, the process was one of coordinated broad outreach. We actively sought input from a wide range of stakeholders and negotiated consensus with them on the basis of feedback received from national, inter-national and practitioner advisors, teacher union representatives, and presen-tations of work-in-progress at national conferences.

The issue concerning the communication of the research findings to wider communities was addressed by including vignettes of narrative data drawn directly from the studies, thus making the literature synthesis more accessible. The vignettes expand upon broad findings and bring the reality of classroom life to the fore. In particular, they exemplify "theoretical tools that are localised, adapted and used by actual teachers" (Alton-Lee, 2006, p. 18) within the complexity and contradictions of mathematics teaching in the classroom.

From that eclectic body of evidence, certain patterns about teaching emerged that enabled us to foreground ways of doing and being that charac-terise effective pedagogical practice. Each aspect, of course, constitutes but one piece of evidence and must be read as accounting for only one variable, amongst many, within the teaching nested system. When all these aspects are taken together, however, what one obtains is a fairly cohesive view of what quality teaching looks like.

5. CONCLUSION

Mathematics educational policy need not be informed by research that admits only the criteria of classical experimental design and performance indicators for establishing evidence. The 'proof' of quality pedagogical practice, as many commentators have argued, demands a form of science that does not establish closed standards in the name of 'scientific rigor.' State educational policy formation requires an approach that is open to "all forms of research evidence regardless of methodological paradigms and ideological rectitude" (Luke & Hogan, 2006, p. 174). Above all, it requires a science "that can cope with the multiplicity of the social world…, attentive to the demands of different contexts, and different communities" (Lather, 2004, p. 768).

In this chapter, I have described an alternative and critical approach to research synthesis that challenges (even shifts) current meanings of evidence based research in many countries. The New Zealand model does not seek to synthesise and explain scientific evidence about what works for learners. Rather, capturing the Derridean (1976) realisation about the end to 'pure presence', it trades certainty's promise for the contradiction of classroom life. It offers instead a critical interpretive counter-science that foregrounds the fundamental role of context in explanations of mathematics educational phenomena.

The mathematics BES has been designed to help strengthen policy development in ways that effectively address both the needs of diverse learners and the patterns of systematic underachievement in New Zealand education. Having sparked discussion and debate, it is anticipated that the mathematics BES will stimulate activity across policy makers, practitioners, and researchers with a view towards capacity building of systems that are responsive to outcomes for all students. "Research," as Krainer (2005) has argued, "is a powerful means of keeping the negotiation and decision processes vivid" (p. 77). It is hoped that reflection on the findings of this synthesis, by a wide range of stakeholders, will create an understanding about the different inflections pedagogical practice takes within diverse classrooms and schools, and how different practices contribute to varying social and academic outcomes for students. It should be acknowledged, however, that even if these findings hold for this particular time and place, we can never be certain they will do so in the future. All research is of-the-moment, and in due ciurse, consensus about pedagogical practice will be renegotiated as new research comes to hand. Those new findings will initiate new discussions, prompt new questions and renew productive engagement with mathematics education.

REFERENCES

Alton-Lee, A. (2005). *Collaborating across policy, research and practice: Knowledge building for sustainable educational development.* Paper prepared for the OECD, Linking evidence to practice: Evidence based policy research workshop, the Netherlands, 14-15 September 2005.

Alton-Lee, A. (2006). *Iterative best evidence synthesis: Strengthening research, policy and practice links to improve .* Paper presented at the 4th annual policy conference: Policy Evolution, 29 March 2006.

Anthony, G., & Walshaw, M. (2006). *The Best Evidence Synthesis of Pedagogical Approaches that Facilitate learning for Diverse Students in Pāngarau/Mathematics in Centres and Schools.* Wellington: Learning Media.

Atkinson, E. (2000). In defence of ideas, or why 'what works' is not enough. *British Journal of Sociology of Education, 21*(3), 317-330.

Berliner, D. C. (2002). Educational research: The hardest science of all, *Educational Researcher, 31*(8), 18-20.

Blanton, M., & Kaput, J. (2005). Characterizing a classroom practice that promotes algebraic reasoning. *Journal for Research in Mathematics Education, 36*(5), 412-446.

Chatterji, M. (2004). Evidence on 'what works': An argument for extended-term mixed-method (ETMM) evaluation designs. *Educational Researcher, 33*(9), 3-13.

Cobb, P. (2006). Report to the New Zealand Ministry of Education on the Best Evidence Synthesis: *Characteristics of pedagogical approaches that facilitate learning for diverse students in early childhood and schooling in Pāngarau/mathematics.* Paper presented at the Quality Assurance day, 13 February, 2006.

Code, L. (1995). *Rhetorical spaces: Essays on gendered locations.* New York: Routledge.

Davies, B. (2003). Death to critique and dissent? The politics and practice of new managerialism and of 'evidence-based practice'. *Gender and Education, 15*(1), 91-103.

Davis, B., & Simmt, E. (2003). Understanding learning systems: Mathematics education and complexity science. *Journal for Research in Mathematics Education, 34*(2), 137-167.

Davydov, V. V. & Radzikhovskii, L. A. (1985). Vygotsky's theory and the activity-oriented approach in psychology. In J. V. Wertsch (Ed.), *Culture, communication, and cognition: Vygotskian perspectives* (pp. 35-65). New York: Cambridge University Press.

Deleuze, G. (2001). *Logic of sense* (Trans: M. Lester with C. Stivale; Ed: C. V. Boundas). London: Athlone.

Derrida, J. (1976). *Of grammatology.* Baltimore: The John Hopkins University Press.

Eisenhart, M., & Towne, L. (2003). Contestation and change in national policy on 'scientifically based' education research. *Educational Researcher, 32*(7), 31-38.

English, L., Jones, G., Lesh, R., Tirosh, D., Bartolini Bussi, M. (2002). Future issues and directions in international mathematics education research. In L. English (Ed.), *Handbook of international research in mathematics education* (pp. 787-812). Mahwah, NJ: Lawrence Erlbaum.

Foucault, M. (1998). On the archaeology of sciences: Response to the epistemology circle. In J. Faubion (Ed.), *Michel Foucault: Aesthetics, method, and epistemology* (Vol. 2, p. 297-333). New York: The Free Press.

Hammersley, M. (2004). Some questions about evidence-based practice in education. In G. Thomas, & R. Pring (Eds.), *Evidence-based practice in education* (pp. 133-149). Berkshire: Open University Press.

Hargreaves, D. (1996). *Teaching as a research-based profession: Possibilities and prospects.* Teacher Training Agency Annual Lecture. London: TTA.

Kilpatrick, J. (2001). Where's the evidence? *Journal for Research in Mathematics Education, 32*, 421-427.

Krainer, K. (2005). What is 'good' mathematics teaching, and how can research inform practice and policy? *Journal of Mathematics Teacher Education, 8*, 75-81.

Lather, P. (2004). Scientific research in education: A critical perspective. *British Educational Research Journal, 30*(6), 759-772.

Lave, J. & Wenger, E. (1991). *Situated learning: Legitimate peripheral participation.* Cambridge: Cambridge University Press.

Luke, A., & Hogan, D. (2006). Redesigning what counts as evidence in educational policy: The Singapore model. In J. Ozga, T. Popkewitz, & T. Seddon (Eds.), *Education research and policy: Steering the knowledge-based economy. World handbook of education* (pp. 170-184). London: Routledge.

Ministry of Education. (2004). *Guidelines for generating a Best Evidence Synthesis Iteration 2004.* Wellington: Ministry of Education.

NCTM Research Advisory Committee Report (2003). Educational research in the No Child Left Behind environment. *Journal for Research in Mathematics Education, 34*(3), 185-190.

Oakley, A. (2002). Social science and evidence-based everything: The case of education. *Educational Review, 54*(3), 277-286.

Sfard, A. (2005). What could be more practical than good research? On mutual relations between research and practice of mathematics education. *Educational Studies in Mathematics, 58*, 393-413.

Thomas, G., & Pring, R. (2004). *Evidence-based practice in education.* Berkshire: Open University Press.

Tower, J., & Davis, B. (2002). Structuring occasions. *Educational Studies in Mathematics, 49*(3), 313-340.

Trinder, L. (2000a). Introduction: The context of evidence-based practice. In L. Trinder (Ed.), *Evidence-based practice: A critical appraisal* (pp.1-16). Oxford: Blackwell Science.

Trinder, L. (2000b). A critical appraisal of evidence-based practice. In L. Trinder (Ed.), *Evidence-based practice: A critical appraisal* (pp. 212-241). Oxford: Blackwell Science.

Walshaw, M. (2004a). A powerful theory of active engagement. *For the Learning of Mathematics, 24*(3), 4-10.

Walshaw, M. (Ed.) (2004b). *Mathematics education within the postmodern.* Greenwich, CT: Information Age.

PSYCHOSOCIAL PROCESSES IN MATHEMATICS AND MATHEMATICS EDUCATION
A Response to Margaret Walshaw

Tony Brown
Bristol University

TB[1]: I remember you recalling a quote of Winnicott's. He draws a parallel between the inner world of the child and the external world of learning in the mathematics classroom.

DT: I invited Winnicott to speak at the Association of Teachers of Mathematics Conference in 1967. I don't think many people saw the point of it all, but I enjoyed his contribution. What he said appeared later in one of his essays.

> What I think you must not expect is that a child who has not reached unit status can enjoy bits and pieces. These are frightening to such a child and represent chaos.
> (Winnicott, 1966, p. 61)

Winnicott was hinting at another representational feature of mathematics and making the point that for many students not only does mathematics fail to add up, it can also come to *represent* the failure of things to add up. Winnicott was a UK government adviser during World War 2, helping to organise the evacuation of thousands of children from cities into relatively safer rural areas. He was influential in shaping a national response to a general unconscious anxiety that the devastation of war could become manifest in disturbing ways in the next generation. Medical and psychological models of learning were very influential immediately after the war and teachers naturally turned (or were turned) to psychological theories of individual development in order to understand their role in the education process. Caleb

Gattegno's founding of the group that later became the Association of
Teachers of Mathematics (ATM) and his translation of Piaget's writing into
English can be seen as practical ways that made contemporary models of
learning available to mathematics teachers, helping them adopt scientifically
informed approaches to teaching.

TB: Following Winnicott, if we take the view that the power of mathematics lies in its gener-
alisability, then perhaps we should not be surprised that the school student might make an
unconscious connection between their inner world of relations and the inner processes of
cognition. For me the limitation of hard-core constructivist psychology is its lack of engagement with the affective constructions that are being made alongside the logico-mathematical.
To imagine that these can coexist in the mind during the same period of human development
but never be mutually influential seems naïve beyond belief. Gattegno's (1987) later - almost
mystic – references in his *Science of Education* publications seem to me to be an attempt to
bridge the gap between the inner world of mathematical processing and the relational world. I
imagine that John Mason's (2001) *noticing paradigm* has similar roots.

The internalising of experience associated with learning mathematics can
become bound up with other internal dynamics. Part of the power of mathematical laws, processes and symbols is their applicability to the particular –
an infinity of particulars. The dominant pedagogy of school mathematics
tacitly assumes that the learner's mathematical associations will be made
with the cognitive; that is, with learners creating internal mathematical models to represent the physical world and the structures and patterns within
mathematics itself. However, learners are likely to be more promiscuous
with the mathematics they internalise than the prevailing pedagogy can risk
acknowledging—with students making unconscious associations between
mathematical elements and the relational dynamics that they are exploring in
the transitional adolescent space between child and adult.

In recent times, few writers have worked on psychodynamic interpretations of education. One example, however, is Deborah Britzman (2000;
2003) who has reworked Anna Freud's lectures given to teachers in 1930.
Fewer writers still have developed alternative views of mathematics pedagogy: Claudine Blanchard-Laville, a professor of mathematics in Paris,
writes about the vulnerability of the psychic space of teaching (vulnérabilité
de l'espace psychique d'enseignement) (2001) and the sado-masochistic potential of the teacher's role created by classroom dynamics (2006). Jacques
Nimier[2] provides many examples of the power of mathematics to influence
the inner life of teachers, school pupils and student teachers, as well as its
potential to disrupt and shape their engagement with, and response to,
mathematics.

TB: It seems possible to mount an argument that it is a weakness of pedagogy to assume that
the learner automatically restricts the internalisation of mathematical experience to the cognitive domain. I wonder what Winnicott would make of the prevalent notions of evidenced-

based practice that teachers are being encouraged to draw upon. Margaret Walshaw's chapter reminds us that these notions "tend to overlook uncertainty, contingency and complicity" (p. 14). Never mind mathematics, these words have a strong resonance vis-à-vis adolescence! But how can we respond to the new 'big idea' of evidence-based practice?

DT: It reminds me of an earlier conversation we had, when I said that I was appalled that the teaching establishment was going through one of its BIG IDEAS – following Piaget, sets, numeracy, logic – and then discovering problem-solving. I cannot see that we have much to teach children about problem solving. People seem to forget that the most important issue is that one person's problem easily becomes another's exercise.

TB: How do we engage with evidence-based practice when the sources of evidence that are tolerated by the dominant forces in education policy are so skewed? One person's evidence is another person's distraction. Teachers face regular onslaughts about what they 'ought to be doing' and what constitutes a 'professional' response to the latest big idea.

From a Foucauldian perspective, one can see that it is inevitable that teachers' claims to knowledge of classroom practices will be systematically under-valued and undermined. This is a necessity for those who wish to impose the power of the state. These days, there is a huge political desire to dominate the process of state education and what passes for an appropriate education of the masses. Walshaw gives a useful reminder that the "messy real-life classroom processes that characterise maths teaching" (p. 14) pose a threat to centralised ambitions to regulate discussion of teaching quality and the achievements of learners. First Thatcher and then Blair chose education as an arm of what Foucault (1991) calls "the technology of government". This makes the selection and approval of particular fields of education research a crucial area for centralised control. In order to serve the dominant political will, approaches to understanding teaching and learning must ignore the inherent messiness of classrooms and instead support the normalising process that follows from the government's preferred discourse on what is possible and necessary for education; that is, for it to become an education that is desirable.

Orchestrating the research base and driving the debate towards mechanistic curriculum delivery, target setting and so on, requires the production of knowledge in these areas to follow particular forms of teachers' and pupils' experiences of educational exchanges and, in so doing, privileges the rationalising of policy over local needs of teachers and learners. Complexity is the victim of the political desire for simple solutions to problems in education— simple solutions that education is expected to offer learners. The challenge for mathematics education in these times, when there is a huge resistance to the study of mathematics by students in countries like the UK, is to find ways to re-engage the learner without trivialising the learning process and without adopting policies that marginalise those directly involved. To this end, it is appropriate that Walshaw draws on Luke and Hogan's (2006) observation that we need to be open to "all forms of research evidence regardless of methodological paradigms and ideological rectitude" (p. 21).

The complexity of the mathematics classroom extends well beyond the conscious processes of teaching and learning, of curriculum delivery and assessment practices. It includes the unconscious desires of those within the psychic space of the classroom. It includes the natural applicability of mathematics to representations of phantasy[3] and of the desired worlds of the protagonists who teach and learn in classrooms.

DT: I am amazed at the loyal response teachers continue to make as the educational scene staggers from one temporary position to the next. Is it a question of being governed? Like the feeling I get visiting the stately homes of England and discovering in them that the governed have always colluded with the governing in a curious way that is at once the strength and the weakness of the system.

Classroom spaces are becoming more difficult places for teaching and learning. There is a sense of global disturbance 'in the air,' emanating in part from anxieties about climate change and the consequences that will follow the ending of the 'century of oil.' Adolescents in western cultures are both projecting and introjecting[4] these anxieties in addition to the troubling personal work they necessarily have to engage with when revisiting Oedipal relations for a second time. Teachers have to contain the anxieties felt in our society about the need to control adolescents. They are often blamed when teenagers behave badly. They also have to contain the anger of adolescents who can feel scapegoated by politicians and others. Many adults harbour ambivalent attitudes towards adolescents, often projecting onto teachers their fears that the next generation of adolescents might not be able or willing to engage with the big problems in society. At the same time we also harbour unconscious fears that adolescents will renege on us and refuse to buy into adulthood and its concomitant responsibilities. As complex dynamics are played out in classrooms, the relational laws and structures of mathematics become available for unconscious representations in the psyche of learners and teachers. They are used to represent both success and failure—in mathematics, in personal development and in personal relations. How to develop and use this perspective as an evidence base remains a considerable challenge for mathematics educators.

REFERENCES

Blanchard-Laville, C. (2001) Les Enseignants entre Plaisir et Souffrance. Paris: Presses Universitaires de France – PUF

Blanchard-Laville C. (2006) *Potentialités sadomasochistes chez l'enseignant dans sa pratique, Connexions, 86*(2), 103-119.

Britzman, D. (2000) Teacher Education in the Confusion of our Time. *Journal of Teacher Education, 51*(3), 200-205.

Britzman, D. (2003). *After-Education: Anna Freud, Melanie Klein, and Psychoanalytic Histories of Learning.* NY: State University of New York Press

Foucault, M (1991) Governmentality, in G Burchell, C Gordon & P Miller (Eds.), The Foucault Effect: Studies in Governmentality, pp 87-104 (London: Harvester Wheatsheaf)

Gattegno, C. (1987). *The science of education: Part I. Theoretical considerations.* New York: Educational Solutions.

Luke, A. and Hogan, D. (2006) Redesigning what counts as evidence in educational policy: The Singapore model. In J. Ozga, T. Popkewitz, and T. Seddon (Eds.) *Education research and policy: steering the knowledge-based economy. World handbook of education* (pp. 170-184). London: Routledge.

Mason, J. (2001) *Researching Your Own Practice: The Discipline of Noticing.* London: Routledge Falmer Press.

Nimier, J. Les Facteurs Humains dan l'enseignement et la formation d'adultes http://perso.orange.fr/jacques.nimier/fantasmes.htm. Retrieved 10 March 2007

Winnicott, D. W. (1966) The Child in the Family Group. In D. W. Winnicott, (1986) *Home is where we start from: Essays by a psychoanalyst.* Harmondsworth: Penguin

---

[1] I was hit hard by the loss I felt following Dick Tahta's death in December 2006. This piece was among several 'works in progress.' By retaining the references to our conversations and correspondence I am acknowledging, in a simple way, Dick's generous gift of wisdom and encouragement and the pleasure I gained from our long friendship.

[2] http://perso.orange.fr/jacques.nimier/nos_eleves.htm; retrieved 10 March 2007

[3] *Phantasy*, - unconscious desires, anxieties and fears.

[4] *Projection* and *introjection* are terms used in psychoanalytic theory to describe defence mechanisms whereby a subject expels or takes in unconscious material. A child anxious over the absence of her parents may introject comforting experiences of being mothered. A subject who is overwhelmed by feelings of anger may project these feelings into another person who is then perceived as having those qualities rather than the subject who now feels rid of them.

THE TEACHER AS MIDWIFE: WHAT CAN MATHEMATICS EDUCATION RESEARCH LEARN FROM OBSTETRICS?
A Response to Margaret Walshaw

Nathalie Sinclair
Simon Fraser University

As Margaret Walshaw points out in her chapter, research in the medical sciences is often favourably compared to research in mathematics education. The former has perfected the "gold standard" of research; that is, the double-blind, large-scale randomized, controlled trials. We are told that these trials—unlike our own, "softer" efforts in educational research—produce both true and accurate knowledge.

Interestingly, one medical field in which this particular gold standard is almost never used, has, strikingly, contributed more to saving human lives than perhaps any other: obstetrics. In a recent *New Yorker* article, physician Atul Gawande (2006) provides an illuminating history of the field. This author's analyses and reflections are provocative, and if one takes the (admittedly fairly big) analogical jump of comparing research in obstetrics to research in mathematics education (and, so, doctors to teachers, and giving birth to teaching mathematics to students), then I think these provocations might offer new ways of thinking about the kind of research and evidence we might seek in our work as mathematics education researchers. For this chapter, I chose to mine this analogy, in part because of the way comparisons to medicine have been used rhetorically in the past (mostly against our field), and in part because of the way in which some of the developments in obstetrics speak so well to Walshaw's criticisms of traditional evidence based research. And, as the title of this chapter suggests, Plato's *Theaetetus* played a part in my choice as well; in it, Socrates is questioning the young man Theaetetus about the constitution of knowledge, and he introduces the metaphor of teaching as midwifery.

Before continuing, it seems judicious to point to some of the more egregious problems with my proposed analogy, if only as a way to lend some playfulness to the exercise. First, childbirth usually goes well, but when it goes wrong, the consequences are often life-threatening and always heart-wrenching. Whether teaching mathematics usually goes well may depend on your point of view and individual experience, but we can agree that when it goes badly, the consequences are usually less extreme. Second, far more mothers have babies than teachers teach mathematics—and arguments about social populations are often scale-dependent. Third, teaching takes place in schools; birthing most often in hospitals (though this is a new phenomenon). Gawande helps us agree on one clear point of similarity, though: in North America, obstetrics, like teaching, is not a highly-valued profession.

Major changes began to occur in both fields in the 19th century, largely because of developments in hospitals and schools. More children were being educated in schools and more women were having their babies in hospitals. In obstetrics, the shift from midwives, who worked on a small scale, to doctors, who had many births to oversee, paralleled an increase in the spread of bacteria and infection, including the deathly Puerpail fever. A different tension occurred in schools, where teachers began having to deal simultaneously with a wide diversity of students. In both cases, the institution brought different goals, including in particular a new need for accountability—producing, among other things, a desire for a flatter, more uniform range of practices, expectations, and standards.

In his article, Gawande describes the most basic problem of obstetrics as the "obstruction of labor—not being able to get the baby out."[1] The history of obstetrics is the history of myriad tactics and tools that have been devised to overcome this problem. We might see the history of teaching, and research on teaching (which is much younger as a field), in a similar way— as the history of finding better ways of overcoming "the obstruction of mathematical learning." In Plato's dialogue, Socrates comments not so much on the basic problem of obstetrics, but on the tremendous power of the midwife: "Moreover, with the drugs and incantations they administer, midwifes can either bring on the pains of travail or allay them at their will, make a difficult labor easy and at an early stage cause miscarriage if they so decide." His perspective improves upon my proposed analogy if we consider, in a similar way, the power of the teacher.

Early on in the field of obstetrics, doctors invented devices like the crochet, which was used to save the life of the mother by extracting the fetus from the womb. They also invented "maneuvers" to help get babies out of complicated positions. These maneuvers range from careful sequencing of tugs and pulls at limbs to fracturing the collar bones in order to pull the baby out. In looking back over the history of teaching, we could also identify a number of tools and maneuvers; they might include abaci, manipulatives, films, calculators and computers, as well as problem solving, applications, group work, or even yelling at, encouraging, ignoring, and so on. As with the crochet and the maneuvers of obstetrics, such teaching tools work well in particular cases, but also have a high failure rate (whether we take failure rates in mathematics education to be in terms of the people's general fear and loathing of it, or in terms of students' often disappointing results on international comparison tests).

Within the past century, two major developments in obstetrics have produced important improvements in delivering babies alive, and in saving mothers' lives. I briefly consider each here, pointing to some interesting parallels to research in mathematics education in terms of the kind of research that led to them and the assumptions they make about the nature of the problem that research is meant to solve. These parallels support Walshaw's arguments about how educational research can look for and communicate best practices in mathematics teaching. Her proposals include using a wider variety of research methodologies to gather evidence about effective teaching, acknowledging the complexity of teaching situations and the impossibility of obtaining both true and accurate knowledge about it, and using nonparadigmatic means of communicating best practices to teachers.

The first major development in obstetrics, according to Gawande, was the introduction of the Apgar score. In the 1930s in the United States, two national reports showed that childbearing still resulted in a surprising number of deaths despite advances made in anesthesia and infection control. In response, the field "turned to a strategy of instituting strict regulations on individual practices. Training requirements were established for physicians delivering babies." Twenty years later, a woman named Virginia Apgar (who had never given birth herself, or delivered a baby) proposed a simple idea that transformed obstetrics.[2] Apgar worked mostly on providing anesthesia for child deliveries and thus witnessed first hand the number of babies that were born malformed or weak, deemed unlikely to survive, and thus left to die. She developed a score, which could be used by nurses to rate the condition of a baby at birth: "An infant got two points if it was pink all over, two for crying, two for taking good, vigorous breaths, two for moving all four limbs, and two if its heart rate was over a hundred. Ten points meant a child born in perfect condition." Almost immediately, "the Apgar score changed everything. It was practical and easy to calculate, and it gave clinicians at the bedside immediate information on how they were doing."

The score had comparative and competitive influence. In terms of the former, it became quickly obvious that even infants with very low scores could survive, which meant fewer malformed or weak babies were left to die. In terms of the latter, hospitals now had a quantitative way of rating their achievement, and this compelled lower-achieving hospitals to try to improve their methods and practices. The score also helped guide practice: certain forms of anesthesia were shown to produce higher-scoring babies than others, and so were favoured over others. Thus, Apgar tests were assessments of tremendously high-stakes, not just for the infants, but for their mothers, doctors, and the institutions surrounding their birth.

Despite its immediate impact, the Apgar test could by no means be said to have emerged as a result of "gold standard" research. It was developed by someone who was knowledgeable about her work, passionate about saving children's lives, very perceptive, and in a position to observe a considerable number of cases. While mathematics educators may shudder at the thought of capturing the quality of a teacher or the success of a student with a single number between one and ten, it is worth noting that the Apgar score is not a pedagogical content knowledge score, an IQ score or a standardized test score; in its sum, it is a measure of the human "as a whole." By contrast, Walshaw's critique of our own field's 'best practices' forces us to ask if such practices allow us to see only particular symptoms rather than the student as a whole.

The case of the Apgar score challenges the usual medical research belief that nothing should be introduced into practice unless it is based on "gold standard" research. Strangely enough, the "gold" metaphor, which refers to currencies that are tied to the value of gold, carries within it its own warnings about institutionalized standards of best or most certain knowledge. In the past, gold (or silver, or any other commodity chosen by the institution) has been an arbitrary substantive basis for currency definition. But historians and economists have shown over and over again that using such an arbitrary commodity leads to market instabilities. Most countries now use flat currency, which is not linked to the value of any external commodity. While not an elegant metaphor, "flat" research might better suit the mathematics education enterprise. A flat standard floats with changing problems and changing contexts; it neither abides by a singular, static conception of how best to teach nor how best to evaluate that teaching.

The Apgar score illustrates this floating mechanism in that it gave rise to a new practice in obstetrics that offered a different teleological possibility in research. Instead of aiming to solve a given, fixed problem (preventing deaths in childbirth), it created a new problem (assigning a number reflecting the health of newborns) whose solution acted as a stepping stone to solving the original problem. The new problem offered formative assessment strategies that complicated the binary judgment of life or death.

If the first major development in obstetrics was about qualitative ways of assessing the newborn child, the second focused on surgical ways of getting that newborn child out of the womb. Rather than providing a whole new technique that had little historical precedent, it offered a significant improvement on an existing technique—that of using forceps. "The story of the forceps is both extraordinary and disturbing, because it is the story of a life-saving idea that was kept secret for more than a century." The secrecy allowed the 16th century French doctor, Peter Chamberlain, to retain a coveted position among aristocrats needing the services of a doctor at childbirth. In the 1960's, almost four hundred years after the introduction of the forceps, some forty percent of all North American childbirths involved their use. At that time, only five percent were performed by Caesarean-section, which (as its name suggests) is a medical practice with a much older history. Surprisingly, just four decades later, the number of C-sections in the United States now exceeds thirty percent (much higher than most other countries), and forceps are rarely ever used. Behind such a rapid upheaval, one might infer the presence of some startling, gold-standard finding that forceps do not work as well as C-sections. But, that's not quite right. Instead, studies show that forceps are extremely effective. But here's the rub: unlike the C-section, forceps require practical expertise.

Now I consider two aspects of the C-section take-over, while keeping in mind possible parallels to issues in mathematics education research. First, I'll look at the training of doctors (interns in obstetrics), and imply parallels to the training of teachers. Second, I'll consider the ways in which "effectiveness" is defined in the context of childbearing, and relate it to struggles to define "effectiveness" in the context of mathematics teaching.

In the 1960s, Dr. Watson Bowes, a professor of obstetrics and acknowledged masterly user of the forceps, wrote the definitive textbook chapter on their use. In Gawande's article, Bowes describes the difference between teaching interns how to use forceps and teaching them how to do C-sections: "With a C-section, you stand across from the learner. You can see exactly what the person is doing. You can say, 'Not there. *There.*' With the forceps, though, there is a feel that is very hard to teach. 'Just putting the forceps on a baby's head is tricky. You have to choose the right one for the shape of the mother's pelvis and the size of the child's head—and there are at least half a dozen types of forceps. You have to slide the blades symmetrically along the sides, travelling exactly in the space between the ears and the eyes and over the cheekbones. For most residents, it took two or three years of training to get this consistently right,' [Bowes] said. Then a doctor must apply forces of both traction and compression—pulling, his chapter explained, with an average of forty to seventy pounds of axial force and five pounds of fetal skull compression. 'When you put tension on the forceps, you should have some sense that there is movement.'"

Using forceps is thus a matter of craft. Doing a C-section is like following a recipe: it may require some skill, but that skill can be translated into the kind of propositional, paradigmatic presentation that is so well-suited to the textbook. Gawande writes, "The question facing obstetrics was this: Is medicine a craft or an industry? If medicine is a craft, then you focus on teaching obstetricians to acquire a set of artisanal skills—the Woods corkscrew maneuver for the baby with a shoulder stuck, the Lovset maneuver for the breech baby, the feel of a forceps for a baby whose head is too big. You do research to find new techniques. You accept that things will not always work out in everyone's hands." Having a "feel" for the shape of the womb and the baby has a very local and immediate sensation which sounds so much like that of teaching—knowing when to push the student a little harder and knowing when to back off; knowing when to ask a question and knowing when to give an answer; knowing when to pull out the manipulatives and knowing when to take them away. These are all decisions that are made in the moment, often defying the categorization of simple lists and escaping the prescriptive mechanics of methods texts.

The "strategic possibilities" promoted by Margaret Walshaw seem to be more about craft than industry. For example, she describes offering some narrative descriptions of practice in her 'best evidence' framework—these provide alternative forms of communicating with teachers that do not rely on paradigmatic knowledge, and that can only be captured by non-quantitative research methods. In a similar vein, we might imagine future medical interns being able to engage in simulations of childbirth with forceps, so that they have more visceral opportunities to learn what forty to seventy pounds of axial force might mean as well as what the simulated effects of 'getting it wrong' might look and feel like.

Walshaw argues that a general assumption behind the evidence based movement is that it can provide the best knowledge possible for everyone everywhere, and that it is the *same* knowledge. Another way of saying this, drawing on the C-section analogy, is that this movement is choosing industry over craft. What might the consequences of such a choice involve? For obstetrics, there are many, and they range from losing a practice or technique that might be useful in different or extenuating circumstances (some that we can imagine, and some that we have yet to encounter), to insulting the knowledge, experience and expertise of individual doctors or midwives. Similarly, in prescribing 'best practices' in mathematics education, we run the risk of losing practices that are hard to learn—or that simply fail to be captured by our limited paradigms of evidence—and of treating our teachers as exchangeable followers of rote procedures.

C-sections have definitely saved the lives of many women and children: they are a wonderful part of the obstetric repertoire. They have also become extremely practical in the sense that they can be scheduled in advance, and they involve very little risk—many C-sections are now even done in cases where no obstruction of labour is involved. However, in its narrow focus on getting the baby out of the womb safely, C-sections have engendered widespread complaints in their apparent disregard for the well-being of the mother, and the different conditions in which women want to experience childbirth. Obstetrics has risked losing sight of the complex, contextual set of relations involved in every birth. A C-section exerts both physical and psychological damage on the mother by increasing the amount of time it takes to recover from childbirth and by decreasing the quality of some mothers' experience of childbirth. Having a baby, in the Caesarean regime, is having surgery, and the role of "the mother" has been displaced by the role of "the patient."

Walshaw warns of the danger of ignoring the contextual factors in teaching and learning; she speaks of the "ecology" in which the many different participants involved in mathematics education live, including the children, the teachers, the school and the home. Part of taking the complexity of this ecology seriously requires acknowledging the ways in which efforts to solve certain problems will ripple across much larger domains. Certainly we want to improve the effectiveness of mathematics education. But even if we could do this reliably and effectively through true and accurate accounts of high-quality teaching, should we not also consider the well-being of our teachers, and, for that matter, of our schools and families? It seems worthwhile to explicitly draw out the parallels of this analogy now. The criterion by which an obstetric procedure (such as a C-section) is deemed 'effective' seems to go beyond saving the life of the child to the easy teachability, ready practitioner-replicability, and convenient advance-schedulability of the procedure. And somewhere in this "beyond" is a sense of loss—loss of specialization for special circumstances, loss of regard for the mother, and loss of context and context sensitivity. Likewise, for mathematics education to be deemed 'effective,' the goal seems to be to promote procedural 'best practices' and "gold standard" research. In so doing, however, there is a risk of ignoring key contextual factors such as the well-being of the teacher, the particularity of each student, and the specificity of every unique teaching moment.

The two cases of the Apgar score and the C-section takeover are interesting to compare. Gawande suggests that the simple and predictable Apgar score is in part responsible for the takeover of the equally simple and predictable C-section. The two cases are, however, very different from each other. The Apgar score guides choice and action, and was developed using knowledge that no "gold standard" research could produce. The C-section has been improved over the years thanks to medical research in other fields, and has grown into a seductive solution to more than the given problem. Can we learn from obstetrics—a field that seems to resemble our own in more ways than other medical fields with which we are always being compared?

At the very least, perhaps we can refine our critical perspectives on research in mathematics education by asking new questions: Can we ensure that our 'best practices' are not creating problems that did not exist before? Can we think more creatively—like Virginia Apgar—about the relationship between problems and solutions in the process of improving our field? Can we help Theaetetus explain to Socrates what it is about teaching and learning that resists a formulaic "gold standard" approach to research?

REFERENCES

Gawande, A. (2006). The Score. *The New Yorker*, October 9, 2006, 59-67.

Plato. *Theatetus*. Retrieved April 22, 2007 from http://plato.stanford.edu/entries/plato-theaetetus/.

---

[1] Unless otherwise indicated, all the quotations I use are taken from Gawande's article.

[2] Oddly enough, returning to the Plato parallel, Artemis, who was seen as the patroness of childbirth, and who insisted that midwives be not only experienced at childbirth themselves, but past the age of giving birth again, never had children of her own.

Chapter 3

MATHEMATICS AND MATHEMATICS EDUCATION—DECONSTRUCTING THE MATH WARS

Marcelo Batarce & Stephen Lerman
London South Bank University, London, UK

Abstract: In this chapter, we draw on Derrida's concept of writing in order to bring a closer reading of his work to mathematics education. We engage with the theme of the 'math wars' by looking at the transcriptions of a panel debate held in Brazil between two mathematicians and two mathematics educators. We explore the conflict of mathematics versus mathematics education by noticing that it already exists as a grammatological conflict — mathematics education imposes a condition over mathematics, that is, the condition of reading it together with education. We consider the proposal in 1998 to hold the International Congress on Mathematics Education (ICME) in Brazil along with the polemics that led to Brazilian mathematicians impeding Brazilian mathematics educators from holding such a conference in Brazil, despite having support for the proposal across the entire ICMI Committee.

Key words: Derrida; grammatology; mathematics education; math wars; ICME.

Now we tend to say "writing" for all that and more: to designate not only the physical gestures of literal pictographic or ideographic inscription, but also the totality of what makes it possible; and also beyond the signifying face, the signified face itself. And thus we say "writing" for all that gives rise to an inscription in general, whether it is literal or not and even if what it distributes in space is alien to the order of the voice: cinematography, choreography, of course, but also pictorial, musical, sculptural "writing". (Derrida, 1976, p. 9)

1.   INTRODUCTION

In this chapter we interrogate the debate between mathematicians and mathematics educators. This debate is widely recognized in the United States, for instance, where the term 'math wars' is often used in reference to the heated disagreements between mathematicians and mathematics educators. Such recognition might suggest that this topic itself has relevance both for the academy and for educational policy pertaining to mathematics education. We propose to locate this debate, unavoidably, whenever and wherever *mathematics education* is written. Our aim is to show how the debate itself gives rise to the inscription *mathematics education*. Indeed, we contend that 'mathematics education' cannot be defined outside of, or prior to, the debate, for it is precisely through the debate that it is constituted as a domain for deliberation. The debate is more primordial than any *epistémè[1]* or domain implied by it. In other words, we argue that mathematics and mathematics education do not exist epistemically prior to the debate.

In order to engage this issue we consider a transcription of a panel debate between mathematicians and mathematics educators held in Brazil in 1998[2]. There is at least a double meaning for the word 'debate': it may mean a meeting having a beginning and an end, well-localized in space and time and with a specific proposal or focus, as in the following sentence 'I am going to see on TV the debate between Bush and Blair tomorrow at 5 pm'. But also, 'a debate' may mean a discussion of a particular subject that often continues for a long time and in which different people over time express different opinions. In this case it refers to something more abstract and not well-localized in a specific time and space.

Whenever we refer to the debate we are referring to both meanings at the same time. That is, to the panel debate in 1998 (its transcription) and to any abstract or general concept of a debate between mathematicians and mathematics educators. In unifying the panel debate with the more general meaning of that debate, including its concrete historical instantiation, we are drawing on Derrida's concept of writing. We understand the transcription as a *writing of a debate* in Derrida's sense of "writing". Paraphrasing Derrida, the writing of the debate designates not only the typed transcription of that panel but also some totality of what makes the typed transcription of a debate between mathematicians and mathematics educators *possible*.

2.   THE ORIGINS OF THE DEBATE

> ... a meditation upon the trace should undoubtedly teach us that there is
> no origin, that is to say simple origin; that the questions of origin carry
> with them a metaphysics of presence. (Derrida, 1976, p. 74)

There would be no sense in denying the concrete historical instantiation
of the panel debate in Brazil. However, the panel debate between mathematicians and mathematics educators does not have an origin prior to the origin
of the general idea or concept of the debate. And the concept of the debate—the concept that is known as the signified— is always already in the
position of the signifier. If there is a general concept of the debate supervis-
ing the meaning of the concrete panel debate, it is written into the transcripts
of the debate somehow. Our reading of the typed transcripts of the debate is
driven by our awareness of this double meaning.

The panel discussion apparently began with the ill-formed question, articulated by the chairperson, "Why does SBM [The Brazilian Mathematics
Society] and SBEM [The Brazilian Mathematics Education Society] fight so
much, in those terms?"[3]

Since the question posed is somehow disturbing, it seems that a satisfying answer is not an easy task. The question looks like an incomplete sen-
tence-question, a question poorly constructed. One could ask that the word
"terms" be defined. The problem, however, is that "those terms" cannot be
uttered explicitly, objectively, or clearly. What should the terms of a fight
be? Presumably the reason, or lack of reason, for the fight should be in the
'terms'. What are the reasons for a fight? Both a debate and a fight have no
reasonable terms. How could one know the meaning of such indeterminate
terms? We must follow the chairperson, from the very beginning, and com-
mence with that question. We try to identify the unsaid in the given *terms*;
we try to hear the babble of the unsaid. We note that the Chairperson starts
promisingly:

> The idea of the debate emerged in conversations, during and after a visit,
> to a very remote territory, which 30 years ago was Xavante[4] territory, and
> where nowadays there is a mathematics teacher training course. The idea
> of the debate actually appeared in a dinner with a teacher from there, who
> asked that question: "why do SBM and SBEM fight so much, in those
> terms?" (Chairperson)[5]

Could a real debate be planned? If it could, who should plan it? Should it
be planned by both opponents of the supposed debate? What should a
planned debate be like? Should it be a debate where each party is aware of
the opponent's move? Should it be a kind of combined debate? The Chair-

person attempts to convince the audience that the debate was indeed planned, giving us details of the occasion when the idea of the debate appeared. It sounds a little like a confession voiced in a court and used as an alibi or indeed a condemnation. Although he has given us details of the place and moment where and when the idea of the debate appeared, he did not make it clear what the debate was about. He did not show us the *terms* of the debate. It seems that he and the teacher with whom he was talking at the dinner knew very well the reasons for the debate which they were about to plan. It was simply not said. It was unsaid. He chose to leave those reasons unsaid and retained within that geographic place, captured in that conversation at that dinner table.

If we paint this picture with some ambiguity, it is not to confuse the reader. Instead, it is because we suspect that the debate overflows itself. This kind of chance environment (a dinner in a remote territory), which can always be described in detail but always also almost lost and far away, locates the origin of the debate, but not its indefinite history prior to that conversation. This issue of origins is important because we suspect that the debate involves an eternal agreement of differences. After all, what could mathematics education be without mathematics? This dependency or need seems so apparent that one suspects that the disagreements are, also, a form of agreement, an original agreement, perhaps the original condition of mathematics education. This strong dependency of the one on the other causes us to suspect that the limits which would separate the opponents, and would define the debate itself, have never been well demarcated. We do not deny that there are two sides. Rather, we claim that the two sides can replace each other indeterminately.

Anyone who is interested in the debate has already taken part in it. Any claim that one makes about the debate is part of the debate. Whenever one points to the origin of the debate this pointing is part of the debate. That is the uncomfortable position which everyone becomes subject to:

Well, it is true, let us say frankly ... neutral in this fight ... I am the general secretary of SBEM [...] Well, this is not an official debate between the two societies, the people who are present here represent informally both societies, but it is not an official thing. (Chairperson)[6]

3.   THE TRACE OF MATHEMATICS IN MATHEMATICS EDUCATION

From the *old linguistics*, the linguistics of the word (Derrida, 1976, p. 20-21), we probably should never consider the signified *mathematics education* prior to the transcendental signified *mathematics* and *education*. *Mathemat-*

ics education could never be a transcendental signified, a unity, prior to *mathematics* and prior to *education*. There are two words *mathematics* and *education* and bringing them together as one transcendental signified would obliterate the unity of the original transcendental signified. In this way many people understand, for instance, *mathematics* in the term *mathematics education*, as an adjective of *education*. *Mathematics education* would be a special kind of education. In most cases then, the term *mathematics education* attempts to preserve the full meaning of an original transcendental signified *mathematics*. In the community of mathematics education, one finds this position implicitly taken up, but perhaps never defended and assumed as clearly and precisely as in Bicudo (2003) when he talks about the etymology of the word *mathematics*.

> This name [mathematics], within the very small space taken up by it, includes so many perfections, not just accidental but natural ones, and causes noble effects in human hearts and actions; and, in the same way that smoke brings the idea of fire, this name includes the essential part of the idea from which it proceeds, and in virtue of which it moves and persuades. (Bicudo, 2003, Original in Portuguese)

Bicudo's words convey both what appears to be an intended message and also its opposite. He appears to claim that *mathematics* is a transcendental signified – a foundational fire from which the smoke emerges. And yet smoke is always the originating signifier for fire. In a sense, it is the smoke that designates the fire. However, there is no precedence: the transcendental *mathematics* is subjected to "the play of signifying references that constitutes the language" (Derrida, 1976, p. 1). The very need to venture forth with the metaphor of an ultimate source for meaning – the fire - is a measure of the desire for some unadulterated origin of meaning. By disrupting the hierarchy and giving precedence to, for instance, *mathematics education*, the transcendental signified of mathematics is threatened. We are suggesting that *mathematics education* can be read at one go. We are suggesting that the term *mathematics education* is a condition of reading the word *mathematics*, that is to say, a "grammatological appropriation" (Derrida, 1976) of the two previously distinct notions.

4.   ~~MATHEMATICS~~[7] EDUCATION

Following the chairperson, a mathematics educator who researches in the field of mathematics teacher education started his speech by telling the history of his career in mathematics teacher education. In order to identify differences between SBM and SBEM, he discusses how mathematics educators emerge in Brazil:

> I was working on mathematics analysis and also I watched the same students through the teaching practice at primary and secondary schools. Then I realized some contradictions, [he reinforces] contradictions on both sides. On one hand I was, in the course on Analysis, trying to offer a solid qualification in mathematics, one which I supposed to be solid … however, observing the student teachers' deficiencies in trying to explore mathematical ideas, to produce meaningful mathematics teaching, I realized they had a need for a deeper mathematics knowledge and the content which I was working with in Analysis courses did not take account of this necessary qualification … What did I find in the teaching practice? Too much emphasis on technique teaching, generalist, especially by the teacher of didactics who did not know mathematics content, and therefore, a way of teaching, dissociated from the nature of that knowledge … It lead me to new readings and studies … Then, I searched for a way to discuss mathematical ideas, to talk more about meaning historically produced, to explore the multiple forms of representation and signification of mathematics, that is, a different view. (Debater A)[8]

This mathematics educator describes his own development in understanding different possible significations of the word *mathematics*. This development was initiated when the word *mathematics* was added to the word *education* in order to signify something together as a unity. In fact, it is not hard to recognize this same trend in most references to mathematics education. One sees a similar conjunction in conceptions such as ethno-mathematics, socio-cultural studies of mathematics education, critical mathematics education and also specific notions such as mathematics for teaching, or everyday mathematics. Such occurrences carry on a movement of, and support a need for, saying something about mathematics which would be beyond mathematics itself. The result of this trend is to promote a meaning for *mathematics* that is not exactly the meaning of mathematics, to promote a *mathematics* for those who fail in mathematics, to promote a *mathematics* which does not come from the *ethnos* of mathematics, and so on.

Despite the fact that we can localize the debate between mathematicians and mathematics educators, and thereby speak about the particularities of the Brazilian context, we cannot remove the ever-haunting trace of the classical centrality of an original mathematics epistémè. On the one hand, mathematics education, at some point, must mistrust the nature of mathematical knowledge (for instance, for not being adequate for mathematics teacher education); on the other hand, mathematics education, when it attempts to delimit itself and institute its epistémè (for instance, by its notion of methods or research), must ask for help from the nature of mathematical knowledge. Is mathematics education any education at all?

Susan Pirie (1998) has also pointed out the contradiction which we have just raised, but in the reverse way, which in the end points to the same contradiction. She questions whether scientific proof is appropriate for mathematics education research methods:

> It is certainly inappropriate for our research to be evaluated solely from the standpoint of scientific proof. The appeal of the scientific paradigm lies both in its appearance of certainty and in its common acceptability, which stem from a long tradition of established practice. The methods devised within the paradigm have evolved over time and have been shaped and mathematically developed so that generally acceptable criteria for evaluation of the results exist. We must not be seduced by this history... (p. 19)

If the notion of research has always been bound to the notion of scientificity, and if both are bound to mathematics (the science of the sciences, the science of the scientific method, method of all sciences, science of scientific proof, science of evaluation) then we must trouble these implicit associations. Although Pirie (1998) asserts, "[o]ur interests lie in the realm of *mathematics* [sic] education..." (p. 19), she does not avoid admitting that mathematics is an influence on the subjects of mathematics education research, stating "...and we cannot disregard the influence and peculiar nature of the subject matter, namely, the mathematics, on the teaching and learning that concerns us" (Pirie, 1998, p. 19). Italicising the word 'mathematics' (in the original text), is a trick of writing, an unphatic thought, but it shows us the place from where mathematics education effects a deconstruction; that is, it shows us how mathematics education is served by the same structure which it questions. The italics do not put the current legitimacy of the term into doubt, but they do put the 'currentness' and the legitimacy themselves into doubt.

Mathematics education thereby overwhelms the original epistémè and cannot be closed - it is *in debate*. It is a debate against itself, a struggle of its own, a debate of mathematics education with the name 'mathematics' which is marked within its own name. It is a move which effaces the 'mathematics' word written within the term 'mathematics education'. The addition of the word 'education' after 'mathematics' pronounces the effacement of mathematics. Mathematics education should be read as ~~mathematics~~ education. The effacement of the mathematics sign is written in the trace of mathematics education.

One could suggest that the psychology of mathematics education might question this trend toward the effacement of *mathematics*. It is true that the psychology of mathematics education, generally, has attempted to keep itself peacefully away from any challenge to the subject mathematics. It has developed methodologies to study the social effects of dealing with mathematics, but has kept itself away from challenging the very nature of it. It has locked mathematics inside a black box. The resulting limitations have been recently felt in the community, as Lerman (2006) suggests:

> I am suggesting that 'psychology' is much broader than many perceive and hence the concerns of many of those who want to present their work at PME meetings but worry that 'psychology' is too narrow and thus excludes them are working under an illusion. It must be said that those who wish to tighten the brief to restrict the definition of 'psychology' are perhaps working under a similar illusion (p. 349)

5.   WHO DOES THE TEACHING OF MATHEMATICS BELONG TO?

The debater continues, posing the political question of ownership. His phrasing is enigmatic. He proposes that mathematics education is, "a field that, I will posit firstly, in principle, well, a field of nobody, or of everybody, it is the field of teaching of mathematics" (Debater A)[9]. The indeterminacy of "the field of teaching of mathematics" makes one ponder the grammatical possibilities for the preposition "of". Was the debater treating "of teaching" as belonging to, or being associated with, mathematics? Or, is he speaking of teaching as containing, comprising or being made from mathematics? Or, is *mathematics*, in the term "teaching of mathematics", an object of the noun 'teaching' derived from the verb 'to teach'?

The next debater, a mathematician, touches on this point in a mathematical way; that is, firstly proposing to make the debate more objective, and then claiming to be the owner of the teaching of mathematics:

> I would like to make some points… my talk will be very quick, and actually my talk is focused on the debate, well… what are we facing? We have two societies: the Brazilian mathematics society and the Brazilian mathematics education society and each one has its own specific research field, as was well remarked by [the first debater, a mathematics educator]. The Brazilian mathematics society has its field of research which is mathematics research and Brazilian mathematics education society has

also its research field which is the research in mathematics education. (Debater C) [10]

This debater seems to get to the heart of the debate, and he seems to have provided us with mathematical certitude. He takes for granted the distinction between the two domains. He also points out the struggle of the debate: "What we have to discuss here is how these two societies could work together in a common program." (Debater C) [11]

Let us examine the complexity of the meaning of "work together"— the complexity of joining and understanding the other. Is accepting the other a matter of making him/her understandable to us? Or, is it accepting the *lack* of understanding in us? Is it making the other like us, performing and including it in us? Or, is it the stranger (our shadow, our complement) in us? That which is other to us is also the absence within us, the counterpart that undermines the totality. It is the invisible. It is what haunts us. The debater uses the authority of being the Brazilian mathematics society president, and the rhetoric of emphasis and accountability, to claim the space of ownership:

> There is a last question which I would wish to put as another point of this debate that, I think, is fundamental. We must exert a strong vigilance and work on the assessment of mathematics teacher education courses [four year courses in mathematics and mathematics education for future high school teachers] as much as on mathematics bachelor degree courses. The government, through the education ministry, is influencing assessment of these courses. There is a discussion about what should be in the Masters courses for mathematics teachers. I mean, what should mathematics teacher education at the higher education level look like? ... The SBM has struggled and fought for adequate expectations in mathematics education. The MPhil degree for teachers should be in mathematics and **NOT IN MATHEMATICS EDUCATION**. (Debater C) [12]

6. MATHEMATICS (AND) MATHEMATICS EDUCATION: THE MEETING THAT HAS NOT HAPPENED

Debater D, the other mathematics teacher educator, complains that mathematics education is paying an unfair debt to mathematics. He presents a brief account of the history of mathematics education, and considers the charges that have been brought against it. He explicitly points out how the debate is political. He brought nothing new to the debate, but raised the po-

lemic issue of the International Congress of Mathematics Education (ICME).
This is a tense moment:

> When SBEM was founded ... the first reaction of SBM was to immedi-
> ately try to create something called the Brazilian Committee of Mathe-
> matics Instruction. A short time ago there was again an attempt to do so
> by the Latin-American Committee of Mathematics Instruction, because
> Mathematics Education is becoming stronger in Latin America as a
> whole. One of the e-mail messages was saying something like, in Brazil
> the problem is UB. [silence] Do you know what 'the UB' is? [silence]
> Ubiratan D'ambrósio! 'The problem is the UB', that was in a message of
> the official group which was trying to organize the thing. So, this conflict
> exists. If we do not accept it we are not going to advance, because trying
> to pretend we are both working towards a 'better teaching of mathemat-
> ics' - by the way this is an expression which I do not use ... at the same
> time thinking there is an action by the other, ... and in some way a sabo-
> tage or stealing of legitimate space or something ... it certainly does not
> work. (Debater D)[13]

What is often missed, especially by the new generations of mathematics
educators, is the important fact that within Brazil mathematics education
was, and is, attempting to move away from mathematics. The move which
led to the foundation of SBEM, came from the 'inner group' of SBM, or at
least from the mathematicians, including Ubiratan D'ambrosio and many
other important players. What does such a move represent? Do we see a
"new area", "a new field of research", "a new community of practice", "a
new mathematics to be thought", "new methodologies", "new aims", a new
epistémè? Or do we see an ongoing and indeterminate debate?

> I went to Servilha and presented the pre-proposal of Brazil to hold the
> 2004 ICME. The reaction was the following: There were 2 other candi-
> dates, United States and Argentina, they withdrew their candidacies and
> said that they supported us. We had, therefore, support across the whole
> Committee. I was surprised when I received a letter from the General
> Secretary (of IMU), [...] signed by SBM through its president Paulo
> Cordano who was the representative in ICMI, saying: they did not sup-
> port the proposal that ICME should be held in Brazil for two reasons:
> first the financial crisis [...] Second, that the Brazilian community was
> not..., was too weak, and would not have any relevant contribution to
> make. Now I am going to mention four or five of the principal journals in
> the field: Educational Studies in Mathematics, (...), Journal for Mathe-
> matics Teacher Education, Recherche en Didatique de Mathematique,

Union Quadrante and For the Learning of Mathematics. In all of them there are Brazilians on the editorial committees. (Debater D)

7.   THE FINAL ANSWER

Since the beginning of this chapter, our attempt has been to consider the issues through the lens of Derrida's Grammatology. We have meditated upon writing, upon mathematics education as writing. We have tried to implement a meditation on writing, as Derrida suggests: "It is thus the idea of the sign that must be deconstructed through a meditation upon writing" (Derrida, 1976, p. 73). Mathematics education as a condition of reading mathematics (that is to say, as a condition of reading mathematics together with education) is, first of all, already in its trace, a debate about mathematics. Mathematics is threatened in the trace of mathematics education. That is why the debate is more primordial than any *epistémè* or domain implied by this name. And no one can avoid the weight of this debate when writing this name, when writing under the umbrella of this name, when writing about this name, when writing against this name. But, at this point, mathematics education is just an artificial notion which we have called 'mathematics-education-read-at-one-go'. We argue that 'mathematics-education-read-at-one-go' does not only obliterate mathematics' name, but also the name of *mathematics education.*

While Derrida is concerned with deconstructing the western tradition of philosophy, it is worth noting that the kernel of this tradition is an 'epoch of mathematics'. We argue that mathematics education, although not under the closure of its own name, nor yet under the name mathematics, is nonetheless that which deconstructs this structural kernel. The voice of mathematics education, ingenuously or not, shakes the foundations of the very structure of mathematics. The signifier 'mathematics' is subjected to/by the signifier 'mathematics education' through "the play of signifying references that constitute the language" (Derrida, 1976, p. 7). Mathematics education is the effacement of the sign mathematics, which, ironically, is what makes mathematics education legible.

When the mathematics educator quoted above spoke about the proposal of the ICME to be held in Brazil, he directed his speech to the only man who could answer his question: the mathematician who sat at his side debating with him; that is, the mathematician who had signed the letter sent to the International Mathematical Union (IMU) against the ICME being held in Brazil.

We have proposed to interrogate the debate between mathematicians and mathematics educators. We have questioned the terms of the debate. We leave the whole weight of our questions at this moment when the mathematics educator speaks (or asks) this final question:

> This is a problem that must be posed clearly and must be sorted out. I could not understand [at this point he looks to the mathematician and calls his name] […] what I came to say here today is that we have tried to work together, we did everything clearly, what happened? I am finished [speaking]. (Debater D)

To answer the questions that we have raised, in the full meaning of the word 'answer' within the Western philosophical tradition, would be to return to the 'epoch of mathematics' and impose an answer on an intruder question. That is why the last words must be from a mathematician who is in the International Mathematical Union:

> Just remember one thing - from inside the organization of the International Mathematics Union, the ICMI is the organisation for the instruction of mathematics, but it is the SBM which is associated with the Union. So, it is SBM who proposes, or not, to hold the congress. This means that we did not come as an intruder. I mean, we were asked to give an opinion […]. We did. (Debater C)

ACKNOWLEDGEMENTS

We would like to thank Roberto Baldino for his comments on previous versions of this chapter.

REFERENCES

Bicudo, I, (2003). Todos os nomes: o Nome Matemática. In Anais do V Seminário Nacional de História da Matemática, Marcos V. Teixeira e Sergio Nobre-editores, (pp. 115-123). Rio Claro.

Derrida, J (1976). *Of Grammatology*. London: The Johns Hopkins University Press

Lerman, S. (2006). Socio-cultural research in PME. In A. Guitérrez, P. Boero (Eds), *Handbook of research on the psychology of mathematics education: Past, Present and Future*, (pp 347-366). Rotterdam: Sense.

Pirie, S.E.B. (1998). Towards a definition of research. In A. Teppo (Ed.), *Qualitative Research Methods in Mathematics Education* (pp. 17-22). Journal of Research in Mathematics Education Monograph Series. Reston, VA: National Council of Teachers of Mathematics.

[1] The English translation of *Of Grammatology* that we have been reading has kept the word epistémè in French, we are following this rule.

[2] The debate was held at Instituto de Matemática e Estatística – Universidade De São Paulo Brazil. The transcription is an unpublished document made by Mirian Marquez, at the time a post graduate student. The tape is available at Programa de Pos Graduação em Educação Matemática - Departamento de Matemática, Unesp – RC – Brazil.

[3] "Por que a Sbm e a SBEM brigam tanto, nesses termos?" We have carried out a free translation of the transcriptions. All passages will be footnoted with the original in Portuguese. We are going to introduce the debaters to the reader as they have been introduced by the chairperson on the beginning of the panel, then we are going to use a notation to quote them through this chapter as it follows: Chairperson. '[Debater A] - Dario Fiorentini who has a mixed qualification, he has both his first degree (undergraduate) and his master in Mathematics, he has a doctorate in Education, he is current Lecturer at Unicamp, (state university of Campinas) he teaches post graduate and mathematics teacher education as well. [Debater B] – Eduardo Wagner, who is a mathematics lecturer and editor of Eureka a journal of SBM and also is member of editorial committee to Revista do Professor de matemática and an executive member of committee of Brazilian Mathematics Olympics games. [Debater C] – Paulo Cordano, most of the audience knows, he has the whole of his mathematics qualification here at IME (institute of mathematics and statistic) and after that he went to USA and he is the current president of SBM. [Debater D] - Rômulo Lins, who also got a mixed qualification, he did his first degree in mathematics here at IME, and is doctored in mathematics education at United Kingdom, he was president of SBEM and he is Lecturer at UNESP at Rio Claro he is working through undergraduate and post graduate courses in mathematics education.' (Chairperson, the original of this quotation follows below in Portuguese) Dario Fiorentini, que tem uma formação mista de matemática e educador, ele fez graduação e mestrado em Matemática, doutorado em educação, é professor da Unicamp e lá ele ensina tanto na pós-graduação quanto na licenciatura em matemática. Eduardo Vagner que é professor de matemática também e é editor da revista Eureka da SBM e também é membro do comitê editorial da revista do professor de matemática e é membro do comitê executivo das Olimpíadas Brasileiras de Matemática. O Paulo Cordano, que a maioria de vocês conhece, ele tem uma formação toda de matemático, aqui no IME e depois nos Estados Unidos e é presidente da SBM(Soc....)e o Rômulo Lins que também tem uma formação mista, ele é licenciado em matemática aqui no IME e é doutor em Educação em Matemática pela Inglaterra e foi presidente da SBEM (Sociedade....) e é professor da Unesp de Rio Claro e está envolvido em ensino de Graduação e Pós-Graduação em Educação de Matemática.

[4] Brazilian Indian tribe

[5] Aqui em São Paulo, antes de mais nada queria agradecer a presença de vocês aqui fazer uma grande introdução de como surgiu este debate. A idéia de organizar este debate surgiu de conversas que eu tive com a Ana Catarina, nossa colega aqui do IME, durante e depois de uma visita que nós fomos fazer lá no Mato Grosso. Nós fomos visitar lá um campus avançado da Universidade Federal. Nós fomos reconhecer o curso de licenciatura lá em Água Boa que é um território bem remoto. Há 30 anos atrás era um território xavante. Hoje em dia está se formando professores de matemática lá e lá nessa visita jantando com uma professora do curso ela fez uma pergunta assim num tom queixoso.

[6] E bom, é claro, digamos falando francamente, neutro nessa briga, eu sou secretário geral da SBEM. Eu acho que seria um avanço se nós conferíssemos, pelo menos, quais são as diferenças. Deixar claras quais são as diferenças e de uma forma cordial. Eu reconheço

que existe espaço para as duas sociedades, cada uma com sua característica, existem diferenças naturais entre as duas entretanto, não sei, talvez seja otimista demais achar que vai haver uma colaboração a curto prazo, mas pelo menos que sejam ditas quais são as diferenças. Eu acho que esse seria o avanço que este debate traria. Bom, esse não é um debate oficial entre as duas sociedades, que as pessoas que estão aqui presentes que eu vou apresentar representam informalmente as duas sociedades, mas não é uma coisa oficial.

[7] Derrida makes an X not a cross line

[8] De um lado eu trabalhava com análise e para esses mesmos alunos que eu trabalhava análise eu também acompanhava-os nas práticas de ensino tentando ensinar aos alunos do ensino fundamental e do ensino médio. E aí comecei a perceber contradições. Contradições nos dois lados. Eu estava formando um professor e eu estava de um lado, no curso de análise, tentando dar uma formação matemática sólida, que eu supunha sólida, (...) deficiências desses alunos estagiários ao tentar explorar a idéias matemáticas, a produzir um ensino de matemática significativo para esses alunos, eu percebia que eles tinham carência de um aprofundamento maior do conhecimento matemático e o conteúdo que eu estava trabalhando em análise não dava conta dessa formação necessária, dessa flexibilidade de pensamento matemático para dar conta a essa formação. ... Do outro lado, no trabalho de prática de ensino, o que eu encontrava? Uma ênfase muito grande no ensino tecnicista, generalista, principalmente da professora de didática que não conhecia o conteúdo, e portanto, um modo de ensinar, dissociado da natureza desse conhecimento, ... E é isso que me leva, então, a fazer leitura e estudos. ... Então, eu busco, a partir daí, discutir mais as idéias matemáticas, falar muito mais do significados historicamente produzidos dessas idéias matemáticas, ou seja, explorar as múltiplas formas de representação e significação da matemática, ou seja, um olhar diferente.

[9] um campo que eu vou colocar assim primeiro, a princípio assim, de ninguém , ou de todos, que é o campo do ensino da matemática.

[10] ...eu queria colocar alguns pontos, a minha fala vai ser super rápida, é que na realidade é mais voltada ao tema do debate, porque nós estamos diante de quê? Nós temos duas sociedades: a Sociedade Brasileira de Matemática e a Sociedade Brasileira de Educação Matemática, cada uma delas com a sua área específica de pesquisa, como bem lembrou o professor Dario, aqui. A Sociedade Brasileira de Matemática tem a sua área de pesquisa que é a pesquisa em matemática, matemática aplicada e a Sociedade Brasileira de Educação Matemática também tem sua área de pesquisa que é a pesquisa em educação matemática.

[11] O que a gente tem que discutir aqui é como essas duas Sociedades poderiam juntar esforços para se fortalecer e trabalhar num programa comum que é o problema do ensino.

[12] E outra questão final que eu queria colocar que é um outro ponto do debate aqui que eu acho fundamental é que nós devemos exercer uma forte vigilância e trabalhar muito nesses processos de avaliação de cursos superiores de formação de matemáticos. Tanto os cursos de licenciatura quanto os bacharelados. O governo, através do MEC, vem exercendo a avaliação desses cursos, através de provão etc, nós todos sabemos disso, mas acho que tem pontos muito importantes e eu acho que nós temos que discutir isso. Nota-se, claramente, atualmente, que os cursos, principalmente universidades particulares, eles estão fazendo muito esforço, para a capacitação do corpo docente, principalmente para que os professores obtenham o título de mestre ou doutores. Mas mestre, em especial, eles estão muito interessados. E tem uma discussão do que a gente deveria exigir nesses mestrados para um professor de matemática. Quer dizer, o professor de matemática do ensino do 3º grau tem que ter qual formação? E a SBM tem feito um esforço e tem lutado para que essa forma-

ção mínima seja em matemática. O mestrado seja em matemática para o professor do 3º grau e não em Educação Matemática.

[13] Há pouco tempo, talvez o Paulo saiba, houve uma tentativa, que eu não sei o quanto avançou, de se criar, a Educação Matemática está avançando muito na América Latina, avançando, que eu digo, crescendo, se fortalecendo, encontros fortes e produtivos, um Comitê Latino-americano de Instrução Matemática e numa das mensagens dizia uma coisa do tipo, no Brasil o problema é o UB, vocês sabem o que é o UB? Ubiratan Dámbrósio. O problema é o UB, estava numa mensagem oficial do grupo que tentava organizar. Então existe este conflito. Se a gente não admitir. A gente não vai conseguir avançar, porque tentar fazer de conta que a gente está trabalhando pela melhoria do ensino, que aliás é uma expressão que eu não uso, e aí é uma questão de conflito de posições mesmo, não é nada mais que isso. Mas ao mesmo tempo achando que existe um movimento do outro, e aí tanto faz quem é o um que diz o outro, para de algum modo, sabotar ou roubar espaço, ou alguma coisa, isto não funciona.

PINNING A PROBLEM IN MATHEMATICS EDUCATION
A Response to Batarce and Lerman

Una Hanley
Manchester Metropolitan University

The chapter by Marcelo Batarce and Stephen Lerman offers the reader a representation of a debate between mathematicians and mathematics educators. However, in choosing Derrida, the chapter presents a very interesting filter through which the debate might be read.

The debate presented in the chapter cannot be met in its own terms—an act of analysis on an act of analysis is bound to fail. It must do something else. This response is a 'supplement' to the original chapter which both adds (advertently and inadvertently) and takes away in some measure. By these means, I 'accumulate' a presence of a kind, which I bolster by employing visual supplements as an addition and which serves as a stand-in for the 'something else'. However, traces of the original are, I hope, visible in this response.

I enter the discussion by employing the metaphor of the asylum which was featured in a quotation employed by a colleague to describe the relationship between research and managing/teaching at my own institution. The quotation was used both seriously and playfully to draw attention to difference in terms of the 'insider'/'outsider' dichotomy, but carefully also, as it was not clear who belonged inside or outside the asylum.

> … One who desires to arrive at the best position in his calling will from the very first abstain from chattering outside the asylum about […] the curiosities of asylum life. Such a practice should be left to those who will never rise in the asylum world. (Campbell Clark, as cited by Stronach, 2007)

Both domains – insider and outsider – employ an internally coherent set of signs that do not, apparently, travel well across boundaries. Each finds it difficult to be heard by the other although each is implicitly present in the 'marking' of the other. There is, however, less to distinguish madness from sanity than the imposition of boundaries allows for. It is in the 'chattering' and silences outside the walls that traces of both sanity and madness are manifest.

So, I offer the notion of 'asylum' as a gesture of my intention to enter the discussion having already found myself in the middle of it and having already raised the notion of 'insider'/'outsider'— polarities to be soon abandoned as the identification of either emerges in far more complex ways.

The notions of insider/outsider offer broad brush strokes by which to consider mathematics and mathematics education. The authors of this chapter have created a more nuanced set of relations which jostle in between these points. Spurning a discourse of origins, the debate described in the chapter 'produces' both from an 'indefinite history' (p. 44). However, the authors acknowledge that this indefinite history, articulated 'in indeterminate locations' (p. 43), has already privileged mathematics, whilst positioning education as the entity which cleaves[1] to it – desiring intimacy of presence but also separate from it. The authors work to trouble mathematics as a transcendental signified (p. 45), but it is difficult to undermine the forcefulness which accompanies the internally coherent set of signs characterising mathematics. Following Derrida's (1976) notion of supplement (p. 152), mathematics appears to be self sufficient or at least, supplements like with like. By contrast, mathematics education affords a less determinate bag of disciplines, where the supplements 'education' 'ethno', 'critical' (p. 46) and 'psychology' (p. 48) which, while perhaps confounding mathematicians, are adjuncts that both support a need and say something else about mathematics 'which would be beyond mathematics itself' (p. 46).

At this point, I will explore the notion of supplement a little further. Derrida (1976) suggests: "Writing is dangerous from the moment that representation there claims to be presence and the sign of the thing itself" (p. 144). Language employed to represent the 'thing itself' brings with it a 'surplus', a supplement which enriches the gap between signified and that which describes it. However, alongside this presence there is an absence, 'a mark of emptiness' as the supplement works (but fails to) "fill(s) a void" (Derrida, 1976, p. 145). Taking a psychoanalytic turn, 'emptiness' or 'lack' is a state that we all work to cover up by employing a stand-in, but that stand-in will only work for a while as it cannot be equivalent to that which is lacking. Essentially, we are always in the act of re-finding that which is lost, in the substitutions we select for it. In Derridean terms, the stand-in is a sequence of supplements which substitute for that which is missing. Batarce and Lerman speculate that absent from 'mathematics education' is a mathematics that mathematicians both recognise and determine. Mathematics, on the other hand, does not appear to require a supplement from other disciplines - a notion alluring to mathematicians. It is of itself. Mathematics secure in a box.

The walls of the asylum come to mind. However this is my metaphor, pro-tem and one which is already creaky. The authors have their own.

Attempts to bring mathematics and mathematics education together are 'haunted' by the potential for mis-firings, back-firings, ricochets and reluctances that characterise a 'war' – a notion introduced in the title – and which profoundly hamper any accord (p. 49). It seems impossible, for example, to by-pass a 'structural kernel' (p. 51), re-calling the 'essential something' which the authors had earlier sought to trouble. However, boxes, walls, framings of any kind have certain features. Something from inside the frame eludes/escapes the framing and manifests as a presence on the outside. Similarly, what counts as 'fitting' on the inside is determined by the many discursive influences that frame the box from the outside - in.

Derrida's borders are always divisible (Royle, 2003).

Every metaphor has its effects upon other terms in its orbit. The term 'effacement' has a specific purpose in the discussion: "Mathematics education is the effacement of the sign mathematics, which, ironically, is what makes mathematics education legible" (p. 51). In crossing out the word, both the deletion and the word stand: "the mark of the absence of a presence" (Spivak, 1976, p. xvii). This is a nice move, but in the context of a war, deletion carries particular connotations. I would like to re-invoke the notion of hybridity, visible on page 45: "We are suggesting that *mathematics education* can be read at one go", rather than obliteration (p. 51) (this move is an example of to-ings and fro-ings by the authors perhaps). Mathematics education in its many guises as the multiple offspring of an ill sorted pair—mathematics and education engaging in a marriage of a sort.

The authors cannot and do not seek closure. Their discussion disturbs a discourse which privileges mathematics rather than education, reminding the reader that gaps between one and the other are played out at different times, in different contexts and in different ways. Theirs was a discussion of a relationship characterised by fluidity and movement, reflecting local as well as national concerns and where nothing can be finally pinned down. Any one framing has a permeable boundary. In 'doing something else' I offer a supplement to the discussion with some visual appeal. My choice emphasises comings and goings, to-ings and fro-ings where the porosity of boundaries is deliberately made clear.

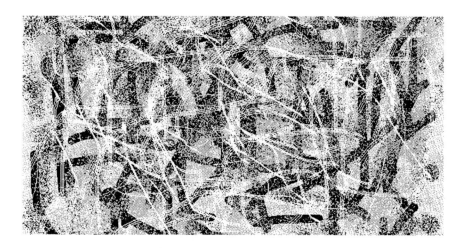

For this visual, I had Jackson Pollock's *Number 22,* (1949) in mind[2]. The painting has no name to guide the viewer toward particular representations. As with others of his 'drip paint' works, when my eye travels around it, the painting seems to have its own internal logic, there is not progress from one thing to another but there is movement and it is going 'somewhere'. That the logic is spatial rather than discursive is very refreshing. So, while incorporating earlier metaphors is unnecessary, there is a strong sense of the multiple as a play of difference between tone and form. If I pause to examine some sections more closely, where there is something 'suggestive' to view, there is an outcome of an indefinite history perhaps. The painting has no closure, no sense of happily ever after, but the possibilities for a fruitful liaison are evoked in different places, in different forms, and at different times.

ACKNOWLEDGEMENTS

With thanks to Gordon James for the use of his computer generated visual.

REFERENCES

Derrida, J. (1976). *Of Grammatology.* (Introduction and translation by G.C. Spivak). London: The John Hopkins University Press.

Campbell Clark, A., MacIver Campbell, C., Turnbull, A.,Urquhart, A.(1911). *Handbook for attendants on the insane.* Bangour: (6th edition, 1st published 1885) p.330, as cited by Stronach, 2007 (email communication: 18/04/07).

Royle, N. (2003). *Jacques Derrida*. London: Routledge.
Spivak, G. (1976). *Of Grammatology*, Translators Preface (pp. ix – lxxxvii). London: The John Hopkins University Press.

---

[1] This is an interesting word as it embodies a meaning and an opposite meaning.

[2] For copyright reasons it was not possible to include a copy of the print here. So, instead, I offer a computer-generated illustration which strives to resonate with Pollock's painting style sufficiently to interest the reader and to offer a cheeky supplement to the discussion.

WRITING AS THE INTRUSIVE THIRD SPACE
A Response to Batarce and Lerman

Elizabeth deFreitas
Adelphi University & University of Prince Edward Island

Consider the authors' question: "Is mathematics education any education at all?" This question has always been relevant. Always disturbing. Always already pointing to an aporia in our wisdom. Consider the Socratic method as a refusal to teach, as a testimony to the impossibility of teaching mathematics. Consider for a moment the meeting of Socrates and the slave boy in the Meno. The young boy is beckoned to crouch near the ground and enter into dialogue. This moment of learning is presented to Meno as though there was nothing else involved save the probing questions and the recollection of an eternal truth. "I shall do nothing more than ask questions and not teach him." (84c) He claims to be without motive or agenda, ready to engage in innocent dialogue, and to demonstrate that teaching is impossible, that no one can impart knowledge to others. Teaching is a negative act, an act of removal.

Socrates asks the slave boy to make marks in the ground. These inscriptions in the sand are guided by the Socratic words of instruction. The slave boy takes up the reed and scratches lines into the earth; his writing is the techne, the extension of the word, a scraping of his lost recollections, a preliminary trace of the mathematical truth he shall come to know.

But the act of writing is unwanted. The writing itself, the act of inscription in the sand, the diagrammatic, is never acknowledged as the significant third player in the learning process. Writing is the unwanted third in the dialogue. The drawing of the diagonals plays a crucial role in the slave boy's learning of the Pythagorean theorem, and yet Socrates would rather not attend to this imposition of writing. The writing of the mathematics, the movement and trace of the reed in the sand, this intrusion of otherness, other to both speech and objectivity, points to the contingency of the truth. The writing underscores a disturbing absence inherent in truth itself, pointing to the process of signification that actually constitutes the legitimacy of the truth claim.

Socrates must guide the slave through his ignorance, his fall into perplexity, forcing him to see the error of his initial steps. He turns to Meno, the slave owner who watches the moment of learning, and says "Do you think that before he would have tried to find out that which he thought he knew though he did not, before he fell into perplexity and realized he did not know and longed to know?" (84c)

And yet this is a demonstration, according to Socrates, that indicates how innocent the teacher is, how the teacher is not implicated in the knowledge; it is an attempt to demonstrate how mathematics is transcendental to the context of the writing.

But might the writing of mathematics be intrinsically embedded within mathematics, and thus the teacher implicated in the nature of the knowledge? Might the writing be the very condition of mathematical knowledge? And thus the teacher be the author of the mathematics in ways that are disruptive to the hierarchical structuring of the sciences?

> One can say, therefore, that mathematics is essentially a symbolic practice resting on a vast and never-finished language – a perfectly correct but misleading description, since by common usage and etymology "language" is identified with speech, whereas one doesn't speak mathematics but writes it. Equally important, one doesn't write it as one writes or notates speech; rather, one "writes" in some other, more originating and constitutive sense. (Rotman, 2000, p. ix)

Socrates would rather the boy learn without the mediation and disruption of some tainted form of inscription. He would rather that the absolute truths of mathematics be recollected in some more immediate way, but it seems that they always require these inscriptions in the dirt.

REFERENCES

Plato. (1981). *Meno*. Translated by G.M.A. Grube. Indianapolis, IN: Hackett Publishing.
Rotman, B. (2000). *Mathematics as sign: writing, imagining, counting*. Stanford, CA: Stanford University Press.

Chapter 4

OPENING THE MATHEMATICS TEXT

What does it say?

Paul Ernest
University of Exeter

Abstract: In this chapter, I consider the content and function of mathematical text. The term 'text' refers to written mathematical text, spoken text and texts presented multi-modally. I explore both the reading/listening and the writing/speaking dimensions of mathematical text in this broader sense. In addition to making the enquiry more extensive this necessitates the inclusion of a further vital dimension of written mathematical text in use, namely, the social context. Texts do not exist in the abstract, but are always and only present via their utterances and instantiations. Thus to open the mathematical text is to explore its social uses and functions, as well as its inner meanings and textures. To illuminate both of these dimensions, I sketch my theory of semiotic systems for mathematics and relate it both to the texts of research mathematics and school mathematics. In this chapter, I focus on the mode of address of the mathematical text and how this mode of address constitutes a complex form of agency for the learner. I explain how this form of agency is internally contradictory in being both an enactment of sign use within a powerful semiotic system and a social conformance to a highly regulative set of rules.

Key words: semiotics; theory; mathematics; mathematics education; signs; social context; mathematical text; agency; learners.

1.   WHAT IS MATHEMATICAL TEXT?

In keeping with modern semiotics I want to understand a text as a simple or compound sign that can be represented as a selection or combination of spoken words, gestures, objects, inscriptions using paper, chalkboards or computer displays, as well as recorded or moving images. Mathematical texts can vary from, at one extreme in research mathematics, printed documents that utilize a very restricted and formalized symbolic code, to the other extreme, multimedia and multi modal texts, such as those used in kindergarten arithmetic. These can include a selection of verbal sounds and spoken words, repetitive bodily movements, arrays of sweets, pebbles, counters, and other objects, including specially designed structural apparatus, sets of marks, icons, pictures, written language numerals and other writing, symbolic numerals, and so on.

The received view is that progression in the teaching and learning of mathematics involves a shift in texts from the informal multi-modal to the restrictive, rigorous symbol-rich written text. It is true that, for some, access to the heavily abstracted and coded texts of mathematics grows through the years of education from kindergarten through primary school, secondary school, high school, college, culminating in graduate studies and research mathematics. But it is a myth that informal and multi-modal texts disappear in higher level mathematics. What happens is that they disappear from the public face of mathematics, whether these be in the form of answers and permitted displays of 'workings', or calculations in work handed in to the school mathematics teacher, or the standard accepted answer styles for examinations, or written mathematics papers for publication. As Hersh (1988) has pointed out, mathematics (like the restaurant or theatre) has a front and a back.[1] What is displayed in the front for public viewing is tidied up according to strict norms of acceptability, whereas the back (where the preparatory work is done) is often messy and chaotic.

The difference between displayed mathematical texts, at all levels, and private 'workings' underscores the rhetorical norms that tidy texts into modes of public address. These norms concern how mathematical texts must be written, styled, structured and presented in order to serve a social function, namely to persuade the intended audience that they represent the knowledge of the writer. Rhetorical norms are social conventions that serve a gatekeeper function. They work as a filter imposed by persons or institutions that have power over the acceptance of texts as mathematical knowledge representations. Rhetorical norms and standards are applied locally, and they usually include idiosyncratic local elements, such as how a particular teacher or an examinations board likes answers laid out, and how a particular journal requires references to other works to be incorporated. Thus, one inescapable feature of the mathematical text is its style, reflecting its purpose and most notably, its rhetorical function.

Rhetoric is the science or study of persuasion, and its universal presence in mathematical text serves to underscore the fact that mathematical signs or texts always have a human or social context. I interpret signs and texts as utterances in human conversation, that is, within language games embedded in forms of life (Wittgenstein, 1953) or within discursive practices (Foucault, 1972). Texts exist only through their material utterances or representations, and hence via their specific social locations. The social context of the utterance of a text produces further meanings, positionings and roles for the persons involved. Thus, in any given context, a mathematical text or sign utterance, like any utterance, is indissolubly associated with a penumbra of contextual meanings including its purpose, its intended response, the positioning and power of its speaker/utterer and listener/reader. Such meanings are both created and elicited through the social context and are also a function of the meanings and positions made available through the text itself. Perhaps the most central and critical function (and hence meaning) of mathematical texts in the mathematics classroom is to present mathematics learning tasks to students.

Mathematical learning tasks are important because they comprise the bulk of school activity in the teaching and learning of mathematics. During most of their mathematics learning careers—which in Britain continues from 5 to 16 years and beyond—students mostly work on textually presented tasks. I estimate that an average British child works on 10,000 to 200,000 tasks during the course of their statutory mathematics education. This estimate is based on the not unrealistic assumptions that children each attempt 5 to 50 tasks per day, and that they have a mathematics class every day of their school career. A typical school mathematics task concerns the rule-based transformation of text. Such tasks consist of a textual starting point: the task statement.

The final transformational sequence of texts displayed by the learner, and the actual transformations derived during the work on the task may not be identical. The former may be a 'tidied up' version of the latter, constructed to meet the rhetorical demands of the context, rather than the working sequence actually used to derive the answer (see, e.g., Ernest, 1993). This distinction is most clearly apparent during the construction of a proof by a research mathematician, as in the distinction between the 'front' and the 'back' of mathematical activity (Hersh, 1988). Here the proof as first sketched and the final version for publication, both transformational sequences of texts, will almost invariably be very different. Lakatos (1976) and others have criticized the pedagogical falsification perpetrated by the standard practice of presenting advanced learners with the sanitized outcomes of mathematical enquiry. Typically advanced mathematics text books conceal the processes of knowledge construction by inverting or radically modifying the sequence of transformations used in mathematical invention, for presentational purposes. The outcome may be elegant texts meant for public consumption, but they also generate learning obstacles through this reformulation and inversion.

2.   SEMIOTIC SYSTEMS

The texts or signs, and the transformational rules applied to them in school or research mathematics can be described by the theory of semiotic systems. This provides a model that not only includes these public features of mathematical activity, but also of the underlying meanings that underpin the activity, especially the rules of textual transformation.

A semiotic system is defined in terms of three components, as follows (Ernest, 2005b, 2006):

1. A set of signs;
2. A set of rules for sign use and production;
3. An underlying meaning structure, incorporating a set of relationships between these signs.

The semiotic system of school algebra at the lower secondary school level has for its signs constants (numerals), variable letters (x, y, z, etc.), a 1-place function sign (–), 2-place functions signs (+, –, x, /), a 2-place relation sign (=), and punctuation signs (parentheses, comma, full stop).[2] These are typically represented as textual inscriptions on the chalkboard, in printed texts or worksheets or in student written work. In practice, the set of signs changes over the course of schooling. Early on, in the introduction to algebraic notions during the later primary or elementary school years, a blank space ' ', empty line '_' or empty box '□' may be used instead of a variable letter. Later, after the initial development of school algebra in secondary school including those listed above, further primitive function signs are introduced, including sin, cos, tan, x^c (a 1-place function sign, x raised to the power of a constant c), x^y (a 2-place function sign with variables x and y), etc. In school algebra at all levels, the formal signs may also be supplemented with written language (for example, in English or German).

Semantic rules concern the dimension of sign interpretation and meaning(s). Thus, for example, deriving '2x = 4' from '2x+3 = 7' in a semiotic system incorporating school algebra can be justified in terms of the meanings of the signs '2', '3', '4', '7', 'x', '+' and '='. In terms of significance, the dominant sign in these expressions is the binary equality relation '=' and this has an underpinning informal meaning of *balance* that must be respected to preserve truth. The import of this is that whatever operation is applied to one of the binary relation sign's arguments (one of its 'sides') must also be applied to the other. Another feature at play in this example is an implicit heuristic of simplification. This seeks to reduce the complexity of terms in an equation *en route* to solution.

Pragmatic rules include contingent and rhetorical rules and these are determined purely by social convention. Examples include classroom stipulations as to how answers to mathematical tasks should be presented. In the

past, sample rules that have been observed in use include teacher requirements that students label answers with the prefix '*Ans.* =', and double under-
line the answer. Likewise, in university and research mathematics the end of
a proof is commonly signified with the Halmos bar '□' (analogous to the
classical QED). Such pragmatic rules are socially imposed or agreed conventions which are immaterial to syntactic and semantic correctness.

The underlying meaning structure of a semiotic system is the most
elusive and mysterious part, like the hidden bulk of an iceberg. It is the re-
pository of meanings and intuitions concerning the semiotic system which
support its creation, development, and utilitization. For individuals it can
range from a collection of tenuous ideas and fleeting images, to something
more well defined, akin to an informal mathematical theory. The meaning
structure of a semiotic system can be described in three ways: as a set of
mathematical contents, an informal mathematical theory, or a previously
constructed semiotic system. In any of the three cases, the meaning structure
intersects, by necessity, with the performance norms of the social context.

An account of semiotic systems is incomplete without a discussion of
their social function, since this conditions the text-based activities. The social function and use of semiotic systems is primarily to represent and to
solve mathematical problems. As described above, solving problems and
working mathematical tasks is based on the transformation of texts. The
transformations employed are sign-based processes that follow the rules of
the semiotic system. These rules, whether explicit or implicit, are the key
operative mechanisms and principles through which new signs are formed
and composite texts are constructed and elaborated. The overt function of
these rules is to provide a technology for the transformation of mathematical
signs in a goal directed way[3]; that is, a means for bringing the signs closer to
some desired (and sometimes locally defined) canonical state, and in so doing preserving key invariants within the meaning structure. The two best
known types of transformations, corresponding to two dominant problem
solving activity types, are numerical calculation and proof, in which the invariants preserved are typically numerical value and truth value, respec-
tively.

The theory of semiotic systems provides a model for describing the
teaching and learning of mathematics in school. In learning any school
mathematics topic in the form of a semiotic system, learners are inducted
into a discursive practice involving the signs and rules of that system.
Teachers present tasks in the form of signs, and present rules for working or
transforming the signs for accomplishing the tasks. Most commonly the
rules will be exhibited implicitly through worked examples, particular instances of rule applications, rather than explicit rules stated in their full generality. Through observing the examples, working the tasks, and receiving

corrective feedback, learners internalize, build and enrich their personal meaning structures corresponding to the semiotic system.

Trying to teach rules explicitly rather than through exemplification can lead to what I have termed the 'General-Specific paradox' (Ernest, 2006). If a teacher presents a rule explicitly as a general statement, often what is learned is precisely this specific statement, such as a definition or descriptive sentence, rather than what it is meant to embody: the ability to apply the rule to a range of signs.[4] Thus teaching the general leads to learning the specific, and in this form it does not lead to increased generality and functional power. Whereas if the rule is embodied in specific and exemplified terms, such as in a sequence of relatively concrete examples, the learner can construct and observe the pattern and incorporate it as a rule, possibly implicit, as part of their own appropriated meaning structure. This is how children first acquire the grammatical rules of spoken and written language. Thus, the paradox is that general understanding is achieved through concrete particulars, whereas limited and specific responses may be all that results from learning general statements. This resembles the Topaze effect (Brousseau, 1997), according to which the more explicitly the teacher states what it is the learner is intended to learn, the less possible that learning becomes—for the learner is not doing the cognitive work (meaning making) that constitutes learning, but following surface social cues to provide the required sign (the desired response or answer).

The pattern whereby a learner first learns the use of signs through observation and participation in public sign use in discursive practices embodies the well known dictum of Vygotsky (1978): "Every function in the child's cultural development appears twice, on two levels. First, on the social and later on the psychological level; first between people as an interpsychological category, and then inside the child as an intrapsychological category" (p. 128). This Vygotskian scheme can be represented as a cyclic pattern for learners' appropriation of signs and the rules of sign-use through participation in a discursive practice (Ernest 2005b). In the development of a personal meaning structure a learner draws on diverse resources. These include existing meanings and the meaning structures of other semiotic systems already partly mastered, as well as meta-discussions of sign production and use.

The use of semiotic systems always takes place within a social context. Within social settings there are persons and their roles, positions, power relations, and relations with social institutions such as schools. An important dimension of social understanding as it relates to semiotic systems is the concept of school learning task and the aims, goals, and purposes of school work, which is presupposed by operating semiotic systems in school settings. The transformation of signs in semiotic systems is directional, and the understanding of directionality in general is socially acquired in a variety of social settings including home and school. Ultimately, directionality in activities results from directions given by a person in some powerful role. Conversation is a major channel for the communication of such matters. Where it concerns working matters pertaining to the semiotic system in use, i.e., the signs produced, the rules employed, and the accomplishment of mathematical tasks, I term this meta-discussion of the semiotic system. This plays an important role in correcting and shaping sign production and rule deployment, as well as enabling the development of the public meaning structure within the particular social context.

3. THE SOCIAL SEMIOTICS OF MATHEMATICAL TEXT

My claim is that the meaning of mathematical signs and texts are given by their social uses and functions rather than by their reference to some extra-textual domain of signification. Mathematical text is a peculiar form of text on account of its subject matter. Mathematical text does not refer to the embodied world of our experiences, with its frameworks of space and time. Instead it is understood to refer to a different realm, one in which time stands still or does not exist. Elsewhere (Ernest, 1998), I have critiqued the myth that this other realm is a Platonic universe beyond our social and material world. Instead, mathematics refers to a semiotic space, a socially constructed realm of signs and meanings. Human beings are sign using and sign making creatures, and most humans can participate in the semiotic space of mathematics, even if only to a limited extent. However, that participation involves the deployment of semiotic resources and tools and the assumption of certain identities. Entry to this semiotic space is via the texts of mathematics, but it is important to assert that it is not a timeless zone. While there is no universal timepiece ticking away in semiotic space, nevertheless individual and group engagement in mathematical activity is always over time. What this means is that accessing mathematical texts always has a sequential nature. Sequential development is the semiotic or logical analogue of time.

The linguistic theorist Halliday (1985) has developed the theory of Systemic functional grammar which provides an illuminating tool for the analysis of mathematics as a sign system. He distinguishes three metafunctions of text in use that can usefully be applied to mathematical text. These are the ideational, interpersonal and textual functions.

1. The ideational or experiential function concerns the contents of the universe of discourse referred to, the subject matter of the text, the propositional content. This includes the processes described and the objects or subject matters involved in the process. Morgan (1998)

relates this to mathematical questions such as "What does this mathematical text suggest mathematics is about? How is the mathematics brought about? What role do human mathematicians play in this?" (p. 78).

2.   The interpersonal function concerns the position of the speaker, the interaction between speaker and addressees, and their social and personal relations. The related mathematical questions suggested by Morgan (1998) include "Who are the author and the reader of this mathematical text? What is their relationship to each other and to the knowledge constructed in the text?" (p. 78).

3.   The textual function is about how the text is created and structured, and how it uses signs, and so on. Morgan (1998) relates this to mathematical questions such as "What is the mathematical text attempting to do? Tell a story? Describe a process? Prove?" (p. 78)

As Morgan (1998) points out, these three functions cannot be treated as wholly separate. In mathematical text, for example, the ideational function of representing the universe of discourse overlaps with the textual function of binding linguistic elements together into broader texts. Both treat the semiotics of mathematics, where subject matter and form are inescapably and indissolubly bound up together. For the purposes of this paper, I will be expanding on the first two categories of Halliday's typology, exploring how the ideational and the interpersonal are inscribed in different kinds of mathematical texts.

3.1   The ideational function

In exploring the ideational function of mathematical text the following questions arise. What is the propositional content of mathematical text, and what is mathematics/mathematical text about? What objects and processes are described? The answer from a semiotic perspective is that mathematics is about mathematical signs and the operations applied to them. The meaning of the signs of mathematics resides primarily in their uses and functions. Some signs, such as numerals, appear to represent objects, numbers in the case of numerals. Some signs represent operations on signs, and through them appear to represent processes applied to objects. The 2-place addition operation sign '+' is applied to numerals, and thus appears to act on numbers (objects). However, the classification of signs as representing objects or processes is relative. It depends on the function that is foregrounded and the perspective to which it gives rise. In fact, all mathematical signs represent both objects and processes.[5] A sign represents an object when viewed or used as a unified entity in itself, or as a single signifying entity. A sign represents a process when viewed in terms of its parts or in its actions on, or relations with, other signs. For the coordination or structuring of parts into a whole is a process.

Mathematics is constituted by semiotic systems, and by being made up of signs and sign-based activities it appears to be at once removed from its subject matter, the objects and processes of mathematics. For signs, by their nature, are always distinct from the objects they signify. Thus one might say that if the objects and processes of mathematics are to be found anywhere, it is in the underpinning meaning structures of semiotic systems. But this then raises again the question of the nature of the objects, processes and other entities that make up the meaning structures. What is this domain to which the signs of mathematics refer? Instead, my claim is that mathematical signs and texts do not represent or refer to some reality beyond our material world. Nor do they represent our material world itself. What mathematical texts and signs refer to is other mathematical signs, and these are cultural objects, not material objects. The vast array of mathematical semiotic systems created, communicated and sustained by human activity both make up the sign systems of mathematics and the subject matter to which these signs refer. Far from being a vicious, self-contradictory cycle, this is a virtuous cycle that creates and brings into being an ever growing universe of mathematical signs, objects and semiotic systems, as well as human understanding and creativity.

Thus the signs and texts in a mathematical semiotic system refer both to the signs of the semiotic system itself, and to objects and processes in the meaning structure of the system, which are themselves sign-based. The meaning structure draws on signs and meanings created in other semiotic systems, but also grows in meaning and complexity as the semiotic system develops and creates its own domain of signs during its development and use.[6]

Mathematics is a special subject matter in that its signs refer only to other signs and sign-based processes and operations. It is also unique in the depth and complexity of its sign formation operations whereby sign-based processes are condensed and reified into objects, and so transformed and constituted as further sign objects.[7] In most of the semiotic systems in mathematics these operations create a potentially endless supply of signs of increasing structural complexity and abstraction. Mathematical theories sometimes encompass these unending processes as a whole and in one bound turn them into new, yet more complex signs. By such processes the semiotic systems of mathematics can represent and incorporate infinite objects and processes.

3.2   The interpersonal function

The second metafunction of mathematical text according to Halliday's scheme is the interpersonal function. This concerns the positioning of the 'speaker', that is the author of the text, the positioning of the reader, and the relationships between the author and addressees as embodied in the text.

From the perspective of semiotic systems, there are two levels of language and text. First there are the signs or texts of a semiotic system, which is where mathematics is constructed, utilized or otherwise enacted. Second there is the metalanguage employed within the social context in which the semiotic system is utilized. This corresponds to actors discussing activities related to the semiotic system, or its social context, rather than enacting the mathematics itself. Rotman (1993) makes a comparable distinction between the Code and the MetaCode of mathematics.

In the school mathematics context, both of these two levels of text are involved in the setting of tasks, their performance by the students, and commentary on and the evaluation of the texts produced. Classroom texts spoken by the teacher, often in conjunction with other supporting modes of representation, position the actors in a number of reciprocal and pairwise defined roles including task setter – task performer, work manager – productive worker, assessor – assessee, knowledge giver – knowledge applier, knowledge owner – knowledge requester. In each case the student is in the second of the two roles, the less powerful position. This reflects that the teacher has two interrelated roles, namely as director of the social organisation and interactions in the classroom, i.e., social controller, and as director of the mathematical tasks and work activity of the classroom, i.e., task controller.

In written classroom texts only some of the listed personal positions and roles are embodied in the text, including task setter – task performer, knowledge giver – knowledge applier, with the student/addressee adopting the second of the two roles, as before. Most of the roles prescribed for students, whether in spoken or written texts, are to a large extent implicitly embodied and encoded at the level of semiotic system texts, i.e., at the Code level.

Halliday has argued that positionings in the text become a surrogate for social regulation. They stand in for and reproduce social structures and power differentials as experienced by children. Thus there is a "chain of dependence such as: social order – transmission of the social order to the child – role of language in transmission of the social process – functions of language in relation to this role – meanings derived from these functions" (Halliday, 1975, p. 5). Thus social structures and power relations are embodied in language uses (in discursive practices), and in particular, in the uses of texts.

Post-structuralists like Henriques *et al.* (1984) assert the potency of the constitutive triad of power-knowledge-subject. They challenge the concept of unitary human subject and argue that that through the confluence of power and knowledge embodied in socially located texts not only positions but subjectivities are formed. In place of the human subject as unitary agent, they see the "subject as a position within a particular discourse" (Henriques *et al.*, 1984, p. 203).[8]

The formative import of text and discourse in the construction of subjects and selves can be traced back to the works of G. H. Mead and Vygotsky, via such processes as are mentioned above (see also Ernest, 1998, 2003, 2005b). More recently such views are stressed by discursive psychologists including Gergen (1999), Harré (1979), Harré and Gillett (1994), and Shotter (1993), who see distinct identities being constructed for an individual within differing discursive practices, according to the linguistic and social positionings in play.

More broadly, the strong impact of attitudes and beliefs on the formation of mathematical identity is well known through a variety of studies. The social construction of mathematical ability (and inability) is multiply theorized by psychological, sociological, educational and feminist researchers (see, e.g., Burton, 1988; Buxton, 1981; Diener and Dweck, 1978; Ernest, 1995, 2005a; Evans, 2000; Fennema and Leder, 1990; Walkerdine, 1998). There is currently a growth of interest in research on mathematical identity within the mathematics education research community (e.g., Boaler *et al.* 2000, Lerman 2005). Little of this work as yet, however, treats the role of mathematical text in positioning its readers (and writers) and the impact of this on identity construction.

Semiotics offers some tools that further this project. In analyzing the role of texts on readers Eco (1984) theorizes the Model Reader presupposed by and produced by the text.

The author has to foresee a model of the possible reader (hereafter Model Reader) supposedly able to deal interpretatively with the expressions in the same way as the author deals generatively with them.

At the minimal level, every type of text explicitly selects a very general model of possible reader through the choice (i) of a specific linguistic code, (ii) of a certain literary style, and (iii) of specific specialization-indices. ...

Many texts make evident their Model Readers by implicitly presupposing a specific ... competence. ... But at the same time text ... creates the competence of its Model Reader (Eco, 1984, p. 17)

This raises the question: how do mathematical texts impact on their readers, and what is specific about these texts (and readers)? Do these texts take for granted certain competencies and address the reader in modes that demand she enact those competencies? The deepest analysis that promises answers to these questions is the semiotic theory of mathematics due to Brian Rotman. As part of his project on the semiotics of mathematics Rotman (1988, 1993) analysed the language of published research mathematics texts. He identified sentences to be the main linguistic units, and these to be made up of symbols, terms (nouns) and verbs.[9] Following the traditions of literary and grammatical analysis, he takes the type of verb case in mathematical sentences to be the main indicators of the roles of author and addressee. He finds these verb cases to be of two main sorts.

First, there are verbs in the indicative mood, concerning the communication or indication of information. In this case, "the speaker of a clause which has selected the indicative plus declarative has selected for himself the role of informant and for his hearer the role of informed" (Berry, 1975, p. 166). Thus, the speaker/author asserts to the hearer/addressee some state of affairs that obtains (or more commonly in mathematics where texts describe mathematical actions and processes) the outcomes of these processes. Such sentences not only describe the outcome of past, contingent sequences of actions and procedures—a particular transformation of signs—but also claim that when operating within the rules of the language game, the outcome described is what always must happen. The descriptions of these outcomes resemble logical predictions, taking place in a timeless realm but describing the logical outcomes of the processes involved. Thus, indicative propositions might be said to describe thought experiments which persuade us to accept the validity of their assertions.

Second, there are verbs in the imperative mood, asking for an instruction or action to be carried out. There are two forms:

(i) the inclusive imperative (e.g. "Let us define ... .", "Consider a language L ..."), in which the addressee is required to cooperate or collaborate in following the speaker or carrying out the instruction in some imposed shared realm of discourse jointly, and

(ii) the exclusive imperative (e.g. "Add...", "Count the cases...", "Integrate the function...") which asks or demands that an action be carried out by the hearer alone in a presupposed shared frame.

In both cases "the speaker of a clause which has selected the imperative has selected for himself the role of controller and for his hearer the role of controlled. The speaker expects more than a purely verbal response. He expects some form of action." (Berry, 1975, p. 166)

These findings are echoed in Shuard and Rothery's (1984) analysis of school mathematics texts. They found several types of text, each with its own purpose: Exposition, Instructions, Examples and exercises, Peripheral writing, and Signals. These go beyond Rotman's analysis, presumably because the function of the texts goes beyond that of describing mathematical results. These authors found expository writing utilizing the indicative mood in school mathematics texts, although these typically provided exposition of concepts and methods, including explanations of vocabulary, notation, and rules, rather than fully fledged proofs.

Another type of language in school mathematics texts utilizes the imperative mood. This includes instructions to the reader to write, draw or to perform some action, typically utilizing direct imperatives. It also includes examples and exercises for the reader to work on. Often these are routine problems involving the application of specific procedures to symbols, but they can also include word problems, non-routine problems and investigative work requiring the use of general heuristics to guide solutions. These tasks may be expressed with direct imperatives, but can also utilize implied imperatives if they are in question form or contain the substance of imperatives without the appropriate verb.

Beyond these two types of text, Shuard and Rothery also found that peripheral writing—including introductory remarks and meta-exposition encouraging the reader, giving clues, and so on—although they utilized the indicative mood, were metalinguistic. Finally, they also found signals, such as headings, letters, numbers, boxes, logos. These are not assertions but meta-signals to the reader to give the text structure and emphasis.

There is thus a good correspondence between the types of language employed in school mathematics and research mathematics, as indicated by the verb forms. However, the roles of reader and writer and the social power relations they embody are more sharply distinguished in school mathematics text than in research mathematics text. This reflects the clear cut role and power relation differentiation in the social context of schooling, where the teacher and pupil roles are not interchangeable. The teacher is almost invariably the writer of the task text (or their surrogate, its presenter), while the pupil is the reader/enactor of the text. In research mathematics texts although the author role controls that of the reader, it is expected that mathematicians will assume the roles of both reader and writer according to whose text is being read.[10] Furthermore such readers can also adopt the meta-role of critic of research mathematics texts, in a way that is not normally encouraged in the context of the mathematics classroom. However, Walkerdine (1998) argues that classroom indicators of mathematical success include both rule-following and rule-challenging:

> To be successful, children must follow the procedural rules. However, teachers perceive breaking set as the challenging of the propositional rules. They read it as 'natural flair'. ... To challenge the rules of mathematical discourse is to challenge the authority of the teacher in a sanc-

tioned way. Both rule-following and rule-breaking are received—albeit antithetical—forms of behaviour. (p. 90)[11]

Thus, the positioning of the reader of school mathematics text is a complex and contradictory one if the reader is to both develop the powers that are available through the text and be perceived by the teacher as so doing.

Opening the mathematics text, including both research and school texts, with the tools of semiotic theory, reveals the complex layers of the social encoded in these texts, contrary to the traditional myth of their objectivity and impersonality. In contrast, this analysis reveals how important these texts are in the construction of the personal, the identity of the mathematical learner and, ultimately, that of the mathematician.

REFERENCES

Berry, M. (1975) *Introduction to Systemic Linguistics I*, London: Batsford Books.

Boaler, J., Wiliam, D. and Zevenbergen, R. (2000) The Construction of Identity in Secondary Mathematics Education, consulted 24 July 2006 at 1210, location <http://www.kcl.ac.uk/education/papers/construction.pdf>.

Brousseau, G. (1997) *Theory of Didactical Situations in Mathematics: Didactique Des Mathematiques, 1970-1990* (Translated and edited by, N. Balacheff, M. Cooper, R. Sutherland, V. Warfield), Dordrecht: Kluwer Academic Publishers.

Burton, L., Ed., (1988) *Girls into Maths Can Go,* London: Holt, Rinehart and Winston.

Buxton, L. (1981). *Do you Panic about Maths? Coping with Maths Anxiety,* London: Heinemann Educational Books.

Diener, C. I. and Dweck, C. S. (1978) An analysis of learned helplessness: Continuous changes in performance, strategy and achievement cognitions following failure. *Journal of Personality and Social Psychology*, Vol. 36, 451-462.

Eco, U. (1984) *The Role of the Reader*, Bloomington: Indiana University Press.

Ernest, P. (1991) *The Philosophy of Mathematics Education*, London: Falmer Press

Ernest, P. (1993) Mathematical Activity and Rhetoric: Towards a Social Constructivist Account, in I. Hirabayashi, N. Nohda, K. Shigematsu, F. L. Lin, Eds, *Proceedings of PME-17 Conference*, Tsukuba, Japan: University of Tsukuba, Vol. 2, 1993: 238-245.

Ernest, P. (1995) Values, gender and images of mathematics: a philosophical perspective. *International Journal of Mathematics Education, Science and Technology*, Vol. 26, No. 3, 1995: 449-462.

Ernest, P. (1998) *Social Constructivism as a Philosophy of Mathematics*, Albany, New York: SUNY Press.

Ernest, P. (2003) 'The Epistemic Subject in Mathematical Activity', in Anderson, M, Saenz-Ludlow, A. Zellweger, S and Cifarelli, V. V. Eds. *Educational Perspectives on Mathematics as Semiosis: From Thinking to Interpreting to Knowing*, New York, Ottawa and Toronto: Legas Publishing, 81-106.

Ernest, P. (2005a) *Gender and Mathematics: The Nature of Mathematics and Equal Opportunities,* Exeter: School of Education and Lifelong Learning, University of Exeter.

Ernest, P. (2005b) 'Agency and Creativity in the Semiotics of Learning Mathematics', Hoffmann, M., Lenhard, J. and Seeger, F., Eds, *Activity and Sign – Grounding Mathematics Education*, New York, Springer, 2005: 23-34.

Ernest, P. (2006) 'A Semiotic Perspective of Mathematical Activity: The Case of Number', *Educational Studies in Mathematics*, Vol. 61, 2006: 67-101.

Evans, J. (2000) *Mathematical Thinking and Emotions in Context: Adults, Practices and Numeracy*, London: Falmer Press.

Fennema, E. and Leder, G., Eds, (1990) *Mathematics and Gender*, New York: Teachers College Press.

Foucault, M. (1972) *The Archaeology of Knowledge*, London: Tavistock.

Gergen, K. (1999) *An Invitation to Social Construction*, London: Sage.

Goffman, E. (1971) *The Presentation of Self in Everyday Life*, London: Penguin Books.

Halliday, M. A. K. (1975) *Learning How to Mean*, London: Edward Arnold.

Halliday, M. A. K. (1985) *An Introduction to Functional Grammar*, London: Edward Arnold.

Harré, R. (1979) *Social Being*, Oxford: Basil Blackwell.

Harré, R. and Gillett, G. (1994) *The Discursive Mind*, London: Sage Publications.

Henriques, J. Holloway, W. Urwin, C. Venn, C. and Walkerdine, V. (1984). *Changing the Subject: Psychology, Social Regulation and Subjectivity*. London: Methuen.

Hersh, R. (1988) Mathematics has a Front and a Back, paper presented at *Sixth International Congress of Mathematics Education*, Budapest, July 27 - August 4, 1988.

Lakatos, I. (1976) *Proofs and Refutations: The Logic of Mathematical Discovery* (Eds, J. Worrall and E. Zahar), Cambridge: Cambridge University Press.

Lerman, S. (2005) *Learning mathematics as developing identity in the classroom*, consulted 24 July 2006 at 1201, location <http://publish.edu.uwo.ca/cmesg/pdf/Lerman.pdf>.

Machover, M. (1983) 'Towards a New Philosophy of Mathematics', *British Journal for the Philosophy of Science*, Vol. 34, 1983: 1-11.

Morgan, C. (1998) *Writing Mathematically: The Discourse of Investigation*, London: The Falmer Press.

Restivo, S. (1992) *Mathematics in Society and History*, Dordrecht: Kluwer.

Rotman, B. (1988) 'Towards a Semiotics of Mathematics', *Semiotica*, Vol. 72, No. 1/2, 1-35.

Rotman, B. (1993) *Ad Infinitum The Ghost in Turing's Machine: Taking God Out of Mathematics and Putting the Body Back in*, Stanford California: Stanford University Press.

Sfard, A. (1987) 'Two Conceptions of Mathematical Notions: Operational and Structural', in J. C. Bergeron, N. Herscovics and C. Kieran, Eds, *Proceedings of PME 11 Conference*, Montreal: University of Montreal, Vol. 3, 1987: 162-169.

Shotter, J. (1993). *Conversational Realities: Constructing Life through Language*. London: Sage.

Shuard, H. and Rothery, A., Eds, (1984) *Children Reading Mathematics*, London: John Murray.

Vygotsky, L. S. (1978) *Mind in Society: The development of the higher psychological processes*, (Edited by M. Cole *et al.*), Cambridge, Massachusetts: Harvard University Press.

Walkerdine, V. (1998) *Counting Girls Out* (second edition), London: Falmer Press.

Wittgenstein, L. (1953) *Philosophical Investigations* (Translated by G. E. M. Anscombe), Oxford: Basil Blackwell.

---

[1] Hersh draws his analogy from Goffman's (1971) work on how persons present themselves in everyday life.

[2] Technically I should put, e.g., '=' for =, in this account, but instead I am following common usage to allow = to stand, ambiguously, both for a 2-place relation sign in the object lan-

guage and for the metalinguistic sign that names it in the metalanguage, where my discussion takes place.

[3] These rules, whether implicit or explicit, embody in operative form the structural meanings of objects, relations and processes in the meaning structure of the semiotic system.

[4] This also applies to any general item of knowledge that is applicable in multiple and novel situations, such as a mathematical concept, rule, generalised relation, skill or strategy.

[5] Several authors have remarked on the dual nature of mathematical objects from philosophical, psychological and sociological perspectives, and stressed the role of reification in the construction of objects from processes in mathematics (Ernest, 1991, 1998; Machover, 1983; Restivo, 1992; Sfard 1987).

[6] Semiotic systems have a dual nature, both public/collective and private/individual (Ernest, 2005b). Culturally semiotic systems grow and develop historically as their creators develop them as human socio-cultural artefacts. For educational purposes these are reconfigured, re-contextualized, and presented to learners for them to meet on the interpsychological plane and internalize and appropriate on the intrapsychological plane (Vygotsky, 1978). Through such processes learners reconstruct private/individual meaning structures, although their sign utterances and rule applications are primarily public.

[7] Elsewhere I argue for the importance and prevalence of the reification in the semiotics and philosophy of mathematics (Ernest, 1991, 1998). See also note 4.

[8] Henriques *et al.* (1984) go on to problematize of the tensions between different subject positions, and the production of human subjectivity. However, my concern here moves in the opposite direction. Backgrounding a temporarily unproblematized concept of a person, the question I wish to address is: How are new (subsidiary) subjectivities or identities constructed through engagement with mathematical texts/contexts?

[9] Rotman defers a discussion of what terms and symbols signify, namely the nature of mathematical objects, because of the unavoidable philosophical and ideological controversies that are raised by their consideration. Traditional philosophy of mathematics categorises the three possible viewpoints concerning mathematical objects as conceptualism, nominalism and mathematical realism, thus discounting the possibility of advancing a socially constructed semiotic account of the nature of mathematical objects, and hence requiring a reconceptualisation of the field before such a position can be advanced philosophically.

[10] Indeed mathematicians, certainly in Anglophone countries such as USA and UK, are loathe to bestow the title 'mathematician' on anybody who is not a writer of research mathematics texts, irrespective of whether they routinely read research mathematics texts, or work professionally with mathematics in other ways.

[11] Walkerdine goes on to argue there are gendered presuppositions about the appropriateness of rule-breaking, and that it was valorised by teachers for the boys that she studied in the 1980s and pathologised for the girls.

HUH?!
A Response to Paul Ernest

Brent Davis
University of British Columbia

"1:2 :: 4:8," I write on the paper between us.

"Yep," Christine nods.

"So how would you explain why that's true," I ask, adding, "without reducing it to a rule or procedure?"

"Simple. Taking one of every two items is the same as taking four of every eight. Or one doubled is two, and four doubled is eight. Basically, when the value goes up in one pair, the value in the other pair has to go up by the same proportion."

"Okay, then how would you help someone understand 1: ⁻1 :: ⁻1:1?"

"Huh? ... Well, that's something totally different. It's not really a proportion in the same sense, because one ratio goes down and the other goes up. ... I'd explain this one in terms of following the rule."

This excerpt is from an interview with a middle school mathematics teacher with more than 20 years of teaching experience. The interaction was organized around what I call "Huh?! moments"—a term offered in contradistinction to the "Aha! moments" used by educators to flag moments of clarity, coherence, and smoothed associations.

In contrast to *Ahas*, *Huhs* suggest turbidity rather than clarity; inconsistency rather than coherence; jarring breaks rather than tidy connections. *Huhs* are those instances when you realize that something is amiss ... in which a rule or interpretation that has always seemed to work suddenly comes up short—and not because the interpretation is wrong. In fact, as Christine demonstrates, it's likely still "correct", so long as it's applied appropriately.

For example, Christine has announced a few distinct images that frame her understanding of proportionality. One is based on sets of objects, another on inclines (or, perhaps, ramps that are resting on top of sets of objects). I'd speculate that notions of pattern, order, multiplication, and slope are also tangled up in this network of associations. Evidently, however, it's not a web that can accommodate a negative operator. Hence the *Huh*.

Huhs aren't unlike the "cognitive obstacles" proposed by Brousseau (1983) or the "discrepant events" described by Strike and Posner (1985). They're moments in which what is immediately conscious can't be fitted with established and embodied associations. They are sequences of experiences that lead to surprising results, but the reason for that surprise might not be immediately available for interrogation. Christine, for example, knows there's a conflict between her rationalization and the rational process. She knows she's correct in her explanation at the same time she knows that her explanation is lacking.

It would seem that a *Huh* is an occasion to be attentive to what is being taken for granted—and, if appropriate, to reject, elaborate, or otherwise revise one's frame of reference. These are moments in which, if we could bear to look, we would be presented with the convoluted networks that constitute our personal understandings. Unfortunately, school mathematics has provided us with an "out": the "explain this one in terms of following the rule" escape hatch.

It is for this reason that I believe semiotics may be a great boon to research on mathematics understanding. Semiotics seeks to pry open the black box of collective knowledge to reveal that shared webs of association can be as tangled, as muddled, as arbitrary, as accidental, and as fragile as those of the individual. That is, it's not just *my* idiosyncratic associations that prompt the *Huhs*; the collective construal is as messy and chaotic as that of the individual (cf. Lakoff & Nunez, 2000). Deconstructionist readings of domains like mathematics reveal that *Huhs* don't flag errors; they don't point to interpretations that need to be corrected or replaced. Rather, they announce interpretations that seem to be calling for elaboration—to be blended with a new image, a novel metaphor, a broader analogy.

Indeed, there was a time when research mathematicians had to grapple with the very example that stopped Christine in her tracks. In the 17th century, Antoine Arnauld asked: "How can a smaller be to a greater as a greater is to a smaller?" (cited in Sanderson, 1996, p. 57). This question makes perfect sense if the concept of proportionality is framed in terms of parallel growth.

This conceptual conflict around the nature, uses, and implications of negative numbers lingered among mathematicians for at least a century beyond Arnauld's query, until a broad agreement began to emerge among mathematicians that the multiplication of signed numbers could be characterized in terms of stretching and rotating a number line (Mazur, 2003). In effect, the statement $1:-1 :: -1:1$ was re-imaged not in terms of climbing (or descending) ramps, but of spinning them.

This isn't a small point. The suggestion from semiotics is that what is deemed valid in mathematics has everything to do with the transparent backdrop of activity; that is, not with the ability to present logical argument, but with the ability to fit new suggestions with a mostly nonconscious weave/web/network/text of bodily based, culturally situated, and linguistically effected associations.

So, what might this mean for mathematics pedagogy? To my reading, Ernest responds to this question in the following passage:

> Lakatos (1976) and others have criticized the pedagogical falsification perpetrated by the standard practice of presenting advanced learners with the sanitized outcomes of mathematical enquiry. Typically advanced mathematics text books conceal the processes of knowledge construction by inverting or radically modifying the sequence of transformations used in mathematical invention, for presentational purposes. The outcome may be elegant texts meant for public consumption, but they also generate learning obstacles through this reformulation and inversion. (p. 67)

It's the final sentence of this passage that most catches my attention. In it I hear a powerful claim that I'm not convinced is developed in adequate detail. What, exactly, are the elements of "mathematical invention" that are concealed, inverted, or otherwise modified?

To my mind, at least part of the answer to this question is to be found in *Huh* moments. A major trigger in these conceptual hiccups seems to be the sudden and unexpected realization that a trusted figurative frame no longer cuts it. And so, pedagogy is falling short around a failure to be conscious of the need for new metaphors or images when concepts are elaborated. For example, the mantra: "Multiplication is repeated addition" is one that must be troubled and extended when we ask young learners to multiply fractions or integers or imaginary numbers or vectors or matrices. To fail to be explicit about new images—or worse, to gloss over the centuries of personal struggle and collective contestation through which new images were proposed, debated, embraced, and so thoroughly embodied in cultural knowledge—is to abdicate teacherly responsibility. It is to engage, as Ernest describes, in a pedagogical falsification.

The grand irony here is that much of mathematics pedagogy seems to be completely oblivious to the discipline's figurative substrate—the metaphors, analogies, images, gestures, applications, examples, and so on that are invoked to give shape to concepts and procedures. And so, for example, multiplication of signed numbers is treated as an extension of multiplication of whole numbers, rather than a moment of recursive elaboration through the incorporation of a new metaphor.

In the desire to pull learners along a smooth path of concept development, we've planed off the bumpy parts that were once the precise locations of meaning and elaboration. That is, we have created obstacles in the effort to avoid them. What's worse is that these inadvertent barriers operate more like concealed pits than obvious boulders. We don't realize they're there until we find ourselves groping instead of coping.

So, how do we get to the pretexts and the subtexts that are concealed in the presented-as-pristine text of *school mathematics*—especially when part of the power of mathematics resides in the concealment of pretexts and subtexts? Perhaps we might begin by unraveling the web of images and associations that coalesces into the notion of *text*, which, as is so often noted, derives from the Latin *texere*, "to weave"—rendering *pretext* a disguise or cover (i.e., something *pre* or "in front of" the weave) and *subtext* a lining of knowledge (i.e., something *sub* or "under" the weave).

That's interesting enough, I suppose. But Bringhurst (2002) points to a prior metaphor that must be literalized and transparent before notions of text, pretext, and subtext can start to make sense:

> An ancient metaphor: thought is a thread, and the raconteur is a spinner of yarns—but the true storyteller, the poet, is a weaver. The scribes made this old and audible abstraction into a new and visible fact. After long practice, their work took on such an even, flexible texture that they called the written page a *textus*, which means cloth. (p. 118)

We knowers, and we who seek to prompt the knowing of others, are storytellers, poets, weavers. Our shame is in our vanity, in our eagerness to display the artfulness of our finished weaves/texts. It is a shame that prompts frustration when a mumbled *Huh?* reveals a flaw in the cloth. It is a shame that's manifest in the too-common response: "I'd explain this one in terms of following the rule."

Huh?

REFERENCES

Brousseau, G. (1983). Les obstacles épistémologiques et les problèmes en mathématiques. *Recherches en Didactique des. Mathématiques*, 4(2), 165–198.

Bringhurst, R. (2002) *The elements of typographic style*, 2nd edition. London: Hartley and Marks.

Lakoff, G., & R. Nunez. (2000). *Where mathematics comes from: How the embodied mind brings mathematics into* being. New York: Basic.

Mazur, B. (2003). *Imagining numbers (particular the square root of minus fifteen)*. New York: Farrar Straus Giroux.

Sanderson, M.S. (1996). *Agnesi to Zeno*. Emeryville, CA: Key Curriculum Press.

Strike, K.A., & and G.J. Posner. (1985). A conceptual change view of learning and understanding. In L.H.T. West & A.L. Pines (eds.), *Cognitive structure and conceptual change* (pp. 211–231). New York: Academic Press.

OPENING UP THE TEXT - STARTING IN THE MIDDLE

A Response to Paul Ernest & Brent Davis

Tara Stuckless
University of Regina

How do texts facilitate learning? Ernest states that in the case of mathematics, rhetorical norms hide the messiness of the text, and in fact act as a gatekeeper. Davis' response is an elaboration on the dangers of hiding the mathematical processes behind the tidied final text, and asks how it is we might "get to the pretexts and the subtexts that are concealed in the presented-as-pristine text of school mathematics" (p. 84).

I think that the problem of 'tidied texts' is not unique to mathematics. My experience in writing this response illustrates this point. How many passes over the text before I got a feeling for the connectedness of the whole? How many readings before I thought I understood where the author was coming from? Why did parts of the text present themselves differently during different readings - sometimes as a gem of wisdom, and other times as merely a structural element connecting two thoughts? Even as I constructed my response, I realized that the text presented here would be a tidied version of the understanding I had gained from the text. By presenting this tidied version, am I doing just what Ernest says mathematicians do, and what Davis says teachers train their students to do, and what Walkerdine says is detrimental to learning?

Rather than present a tidied version of what I eventually came to glean from the texts, I stopped to think about how I might present the learning I experienced along the way as I read the two pieces. Learning is a transformational process, and so I wonder if it can actually be adequately captured in language? How do I use language to write about how I came to find the language to express what I have learned? It seems to me that learning is a precondition for being able to articulate an understanding. That is to say, interpellation into a way of seeing comes before (and again after) one begins to see in that way.

It was in wrestling with the 'huhs' of the papers that I gained access to the discursive frames that would help me make sense of each piece individually, as well as tackle the two pieces in relation to each other. While I agree that this 'turbid' and 'inconsistent' land of confusion has to be acknowledged in teaching and learning, and that to mask it poses some serious critical issues, I don't think I can put into words the experience of turning a 'huh' into an 'ah ha'. As I read and reread these papers I learned something about the authors' understandings of the teaching and learning of mathematics, but I can't capture the transformational process that I went through to get there. In-between spaces are rich spaces for exploration but they are dense, like the real number line. Between any two rational points there is always an infinite number of other rational points, each of which might be called to our attention.

In what follows, I describe the actions that lead me to new understandings of what Ernest and Davis wrote. I read each piece multiple times. On the first pass, I wrote short notes in the margins to mark the places where I found 'Ah ha!'s or 'Huh?'s. During subsequent readings, as I developed a stronger feeling for how the texts connected as a whole, I began to journal more elaborate thoughts that emerged. I share excerpts of these two 'raw' elements of my learning process to illustrate how I made sense of my engagement with these authors' words, hoping that these 'signs' might be meaningful to other readers, or at least assist in 'opening the text'.

Part 1: Taken out of context

In his paper, Ernest states that school mathematics texts discursively position the student at the mercy of these texts. This is in large part, he says, because of rhetorical norms that encourage a tidied presentation that hides the messiness of the mathematics. Davis elaborates on this, pointing out the importance of encountering and attending to the bumps in the road. Challenges to traditional forms of textual representation, I think, provide a tool for doing just that.

Obviously, I start from a different discursive frame than either Ernest or Davis, and the points I reflected on, taken out of context, do not enable the same kinds of meanings these authors found in their own discursive frames. In short, I may be missing their points. I could read and read again until all the questions I have about the two pieces fade— until I find a discursive frame in which all of the pieces fit together for me (no more bumps in the road). In doing so, however, I would be masking the transformational realizations that brought me to the point of being able to write with **author**ity.

Instead, I present here a few isolated passages of reflection that I typed as I wrestled with the texts:

As I re-read the points, I find myself skimming over the familiar words as if they no longer have meaning... the struggle is a change in me. How can I put a change in me into words on a page? This is the place where I see a crack in the rhetorical norms of 'research text'. Here is where it becomes possible for me to value poetry and art and music - forms of representation that are arguably better at attending to the in-between spaces in our experience that exists without being named. But I don't think that way (yet?). I've never been encouraged to think about the space between. I've always found it easy to find the words to represent what I see, and so I've never turned my glance to try and see how I come to see it.

Language games: illustrated by the differences in meaning between different passes of the text. On one pass, one thing appears significant, and another meaningless. But another pass fills in more highlighted sentences, while I try to remember why previous highlights were meaningful. Signs enable certain understandings, which in turn cause the signs to be read differently.

Ernest says: "teachers present tasks in the form of signs, and present rules for working or transforming the signs for accomplishing the tasks"; thus, "rules" are a necessary element of his theory of semiotic systems. Is it possible to imagine a time when teachers present tasks in the form of signs, and then initiate a conversation about how these signs are used, thus de-essentializing the 'rules', which can become a singularity or black hole for students and teachers, sucking them in and preventing each from thinking in the web of connections from which the rules emerged? The rules are but a sample of what can be thought, and only really become meaningful as further mathematical experience fills in the 'space between'.

Essentialization of the 'rules' gives them weight, and can distract from other learnings that can make the signs more meaningful. For example, one of the key questions (I think) in the learning of mathematics is "why is this rule necessary?" It was a question I was encouraged to ask in some of my undergraduate mathematics classes, but not in school mathematics - in that environment the 'rules' are essentialized. It didn't make sense to question them. In fact, in some classes it seemed that there was nothing else; to question a rule was to refuse to participate in the mathematics. Yet now I see such questioning as an entry point to a rich kind of mathematical understanding.

Part 2: Getting more or less particular

As the road bumps were smoothed out through readings and re-readings of the texts, I could not remember what many of my early 'mis'-understandings were. My initial 'marginal' thoughts—presented below as isolated 'signs' or utterances—would not show up in a 'tidied' response meant to reflect my *final* understandings. I include them here in an effort to notice and embrace the process of learning. Each line below was taken from the margins of my copies of Ernest's and Davis's chapters. A few expressions, written in bold font, are taken directly from the chapters. I invite the reader to engage the signs in whatever order they wish – perhaps starting in the middle?

social uses and functions
TEXT
inner meanings and textures

sanitized outcomes
Victorian ideals?
Spic and span!
gleaming white bathroom full of …
Shiny white text.

Why can't I see this now?
discourse, I think

Look what I've discovered!
like an archaeologist digging up
  meaning
… or is it constructed in the shape of
  the hole that's left?
… or does the meaning come from
  the way the author arranges the
  dirt?
I like embedded, rather than concrete
Neat!
Okay… I'm starting to see his point

big assumptions in here?
is this an assumption?
The semiotic function has a
  particular social function?

is this obtuseness just an illustration
  of what he means?
Is he doing this on purpose?
trying not to smooth the bumps?
my bumps, not his.
Am I looking for meanings outside
  the text? should I stick to the
  language game?
But texts don't exist in isolation.
Is there an 'outside of the text?'
But this then raises again the
  question of the nature of the
  objects, processes and other
  entities that make up the
  meaning structures.
But what if the meaning structures
  are not made of entities?
Or too many entities to count?
so is there meaning outside meaning-
  in-use?
I can't figure his position on this
interpretations that seem to be
  calling for elaboration
what else is there?
Why meta?

YES!!!

Don't the 'transformational rules'
  apply to only particular kinds of
'signs'?
not *where* is there meaning? but
  HOW is there meaning?
does meaning come from the
  discourse in which these signs are
  used?
is the discourse determined by the
  signs?
which came first.... ?

This is how I see it now, but not how
  I saw it in elementary school.

Are we opening the text? Or are we
  fixing it?
Can *more* words ever open the text?
  (*yes*) or is fewer better? (*yes*)
Language enables and constrains

acquisition instead of participation
  can I rewrite this paragraph to be
  clearer?
are we still talking about inherent
  meaning?
huh? This is obtuse. Thanks.
... criticizing a representational form

There seems to be a positioning of
  different discourses here.
many intersecting subjectivities
is there only one Code to
  understand?
is interpretation an artificial
  generation?
wtf? obfuscated much?
This is a harsh way of saying it I
  think?
I find this hard to believe...
a bit of a stretch I think

I need more to 'get' why this is
  undesirable
turbidity rather than clarity;
inconsistency rather than
  coherence
Are these the in-between spaces?
A discourse perspective makes this
  easy to talk about...but does it
  help me to see what to **do**?
so long as it's applied
  appropriately
from within a particular language
  game
A link to meaning-in-use?
bumps in the (dis)course?
Huhs point toward new discoveries?
Ernest's semiotics seems to
  acknowledge...
lost my thought.

TIMELESS PLEASURE[1]
A Response to Paul Ernest

Elizabeth de Freitas
Adelphi University & University of Prince Edward Island

In mathematics, Agnes discovered the ultimate act of timeless pleasure. She relished how austere, selfless, and careful it claimed to be. The peaceful and private deductions of mathematics—and the transparent logic of her purpose—only underscored the bumbling awkwardness of everyday language. Mathematics became a domain where she felt more and more at home. It was a safe domain, a place where mistakes were easy to identify, where assumptions were spelled out, and where statements were necessarily true, not just true here and now, but true in some timeless way.

Mathematics brought rule and rhythm to the silent world. Each silent algebraic operation was infused with pattern and rhythm, each quiet calculation laid out in metered fashion. Math was the ultimate unspoken art. It was always already a form of writing. It seemed to emerge on the page, a graphical form of thinking, its meaning rendered through the process of writing itself. Writing, scripting, scribbling. Scratching the page with a silent enthusiasm. The peacefulness of deduction, the lack of dissent or debate, allowed for austere moments of meditation. Agnes indulged in that quiet hard work. She developed a passionate attachment to the symbolic world of mathematics. She saw beauty in mathematics. But the beauty captured in a mathematical proof was a purist's beauty that despised the messiness of the world. Agnes embraced this purist beauty and this method so completely that it crippled her will. She became possessed by reason; her body, emotions, and actions inscripted by logic. What began as tolerance and respect for the truth, devolved into a defensive self-abnegating disposition, a retreat from risk and adventure. An erasure of voice.

> "While there is no universal timepiece ticking away in semiotic space, nevertheless individual and group engagement in mathematical activity is always over time." (Ernest, *this volume*, p. 71)

Self-denial became her second nature. Food and water and time itself were rationed and apportioned and denied until her desire and need grew intense. Denial, she decided, was the best way to magnify her desires and give herself purpose. She lived by the clock. Every act was quantified in terms of potentially deferred gratification. She filled her hungry mind with yearning, and was driven by the hunt. The outcome or aim, the little reward at the end of her trial, was ultimately irrelevant. What distinguished her from other girls pursuing literature and art, or so she imagined, was this lack of consequence. She imagined the others as victims of desire, incapable of resistance, subjected to their own indulgence. She watched them with both envy and righteous indignation, alternating between the two as only the self-perceived virtuous can do.

Agnes removed herself from the messy world, and watched it from without, applying her sword-like discrimination to the everyday moments of each day. She used her fine-honed reason to evaluate other kinds of knowledge, always despairing at the lack of rigor others exhibited. Like a hammer used to plant a soft seed, her tools were inappropriate to the task of interpretation. Even her father, who had touted reason and logic above all other forms of intelligence, was surprised when his littlest girl derived her beliefs from a set of axioms. He had hoped that she might become the perfect classless creature, like a beautiful mind unattached to its position in the world. She tried to live his ideal, to extrapolate from perfect to imperfect, to cross the fuzzy border between herself and all the rest, but her mental acuity was too awkward for any reasonable form of interpellation.

Agnes began to feel as though she were inviting destruction down upon her. She studied mathematics for four long years, increasingly anxious about the unruliness around her. Each human encounter seemed to presage her immanent deletion. She fiddled with proofs, inscribing and re-inscribing a lexicon of semiotic purity, a mapping of textual de-ontology, a mathematics of self-erasure. Outside amidst crowds of strangers, she suffered severe paranoia, projecting her nihilism onto others, who then seemed all too eager to witness her undoing. She carried the negation on the outside, pasting it onto her body, inviting erasure of all kinds. "You don't look like a math major," said a Humanities professor, "You don't have food stains all over your clothes." She heard these little prohibitions all the time. Others said the same; she didn't look like a math major. She looked like something else. Something other.

She delved deeper and deeper into the esoteric ontology of arithmetic. There seemed to be a sort of vengeance that now drove her towards the cracks in mathematics. She strove to expose the weak foundations of all argument and proof. Then, one rather momentous day, a day when it rained and rained, and the streets were flooded, and her clothes wet, she attended a lecture on the history of mathematics and found warmth and dryness in the classroom auditorium. Professor Larek spoke with a harsh Russian accent, smiling with apparent pure joy as he recounted the story of Gödel's discovery of incompleteness. Agnes listened with avid interest. She forgot her umbrella and walked home in the rain, deeply satisfied to learn that reason had finally surrendered. She felt a sense of justice, or perhaps vengeance, as she explored the scandalous history of mathematics. It seemed as though uberrationalism had finally given up the ghost in 1931. She enjoyed the thought that Whitehead and Russell and all the other aspiring logicians had rolled over and surrendered to the unknown. She relished the thought of Frege humbled by the news.

Equally discomforting was her introduction to the highly debated axiom of choice. The axiom seemed, at first sight, a fairly innocuous assumption: from an infinite set of bins, one element from each bin can be selected, without specifying the rule for selection[2]. But conflating the infinite with the embodied act of choice caused many of the contradictions that troubled the dreams of positivists. Critics felt that it should be abandoned. The axiom was blamed for all the foundational problems arising from incompleteness. Individual choice and the infinite were unhappy bedmates, despite the fact that the axiom of choice was implicit in much of the incredible developments in eighteenth and nineteenth century calculus.

Agnes found the axiom of choice hugely satisfying. In it she recognized the paradox of mathematical agency. She saw how it posited a mathematical agent interfering with an abstract realm. As a young female mathematics student, dangerously detached from voice and conviction, she was drawn to the axiom of choice, as though subliminally aware of how it might help her to discover an embodied mathematics. She started exploring the scandalous axiom, pleased to see how crucial it was in constructing the very concept of number. She began to write papers on how the axiom of choice was both necessary and problematic, how it furnished essential theorems while undermining the certainty of mathematics. She devoted her time to troubling the authority of the discipline, celebrating all trickster proofs that belied the "reasonableness" of mathematics. Until finally, content that she had thoroughly explored the frailty of its authority, she began to invest in her own autonomy and her own agency, and she found herself more at home in the ambiguity of everyday language. She grew to love the messiness of rain. She luxuriated in wetness, dragging her rubber boots through puddles wherever they appeared. On the radio, in the evening, she listened to Leonard Cohen, his voice that of an old man, "Forget your perfect offering. There is a crack in everything. That's how the light gets in."

---

[1] This narrative is taken from the paper "Mathematics and its other: (Dis)locating the feminine", published in *Gender and Education* (in press).

[2] This is only one of the many equivalent forms for the Axiom of Choice.

Chapter 5

COMFORTING NARRATIVES
OF COMPLIANCE

Psychoanalytic perspectives on new teacher responses
to mathematics policy reform

Tony Brown
Manchester Metropolitan University

Abstract: Despite a history of ambivalence towards the subject of mathematics, a recent
study shows that many trainee primary school teachers did not continue to present themselves as mathematical failures once they had become teachers. This
chapter considers some psychoanalytical aspects of that recent U.K. study,
with a focus on the trainee teachers as they progress through university into
their first year of teaching mathematics in primary schools. The research set
out to investigate the ways in which such non-specialist students conceptualised mathematics and its teaching and how their views evolved as they progressed through an initial training course. The study suggests that trainee
accounts of themselves are produced at the intersection of their personal aspirations of what it is to be a teacher and the external demands they encounter *en
route* to formal accreditation.

Key words: initial teacher education; psychoanalysis; mathematics; policy reform.

1.   INTRODUCTION

Mathematics is a subject that filled many trainee primary teachers with
horror in their own schooling. Yet, despite a history of ambivalence towards
the subject of mathematics, a recent study in the U.K. shows that trainees did
not continue to present themselves as mathematical failures once they had
become teachers. Instead, they offered an account of themselves that omitted
to mention the issues that had previously troubled them. This chapter considers some psychoanalytical aspects of the study that has been reported in

full in Brown and McNamara (2005). The wider study examines how initial training students make this transition and concludes that such trainees 'story' themselves so as to sideline mathematics and to present their own perceived qualities in a positive light. It also suggested that a governmental regulative apparatus provided a language that could be readily embraced; a set of rules that could be loved. This chapter focuses on the trainee teachers as they progress through university into their first year of teaching mathematics in primary schools. It suggests that trainee accounts of themselves are produced at the intersection of their personal aspirations of what it is to be a teacher and the external demands they encounter *en route* to formal accreditation. It also suggests that participation in the institutions of teaching results in the production of discourses that serve to conceal difficulties encountered in reconciling these demands with each other. It urges caution in inspecting the trainee accounts of this experience, by suggesting that the accounts mask anxieties emerging in a difficult transition. The chapter commences with an introduction to the empirical studies from which data is drawn. It then proceeds to consider a theoretical reading of this study, using an approach derived from psychoanalysis, on how trainees produce accounts of their experience. The final section discusses how these accounts are woven into the discourse of government regulation.

2.   THE EMPIRICAL STUDY

This chapter draws on two government-funded studies (Economic and Social Research Council) undertaken within the B.Ed. (Primary) program at Manchester Metropolitan University. The empirical material produced provided a cumulative account of student transition from the first year of training to the end of the first year of teaching. The specific interest in the discussion which follows is on how the students'/teachers' conceptions of school mathematics and its teaching are derived. In particular, it explores the impact that government policy initiatives relating to mathematics and Initial Teacher Training, as manifest in college and school practices, have on the way in which primary students and first year teachers describe themselves.

The first study spanned one academic year (Brown, McNamara, Jones and Hanley, 1999). The team interviewed seven or eight students from each year of a four-year initial training course from a total cohort of approximately 200 students. Each student was interviewed three times at strategic points during the academic year: at the beginning of the year, whilst on school experience, and at the end of the year. The study took the form of a collaborative inquiry between researcher and student/teacher, generating narrative accounts within the evolving students'/teachers' understandings of mathematics and pedagogy in the context of their past, present and future lives. Only one member of the research team was involved in teaching the trainees (Hanley). The second study followed a similar format, but without any teaching staff, and spanned two academic years. In the first year of the study, a sample of thirty seven 4th year students was identified. Each student was interviewed three times during this year. The sample included seven students involved in the earlier project, five of whom were tracked for a total of four years. In the second year of the study, eleven of these students were tracked into their first teaching appointment. Each of these students was interviewed on two further occasions. These interviews monitored how aspects of their induction to the profession through initial training manifested itself in their practice as new teachers.

Specifically, students involved in the research were those who were training to be primary teachers and who, as part of their professional brief, would have to teach mathematics. Significantly, whilst all the students who were interviewed held a 16+ mathematics qualification as required for entry to college, none had pursued mathematics beyond this. Nor had any of the students elected to study mathematics as either a first or second subject as part of their university course. The research set out to investigate the ways in which such non-specialist students conceptualised mathematics and its teaching and how their views evolved as they progressed through an initial training course.

These studies took place at a time of great change in English schools. This change comprised a major program of curriculum reform in which new regulative policies for the teaching of mathematics took centre stage. The *National Numeracy Strategy* (Department for Education and Employment (DEE), 1998), for example, offered a radical re-conception of classroom practice in mathematics in which specific guidance was offered and checked through rigorous school inspections. The studies pointed to this strategy being seen in a positive light by new teachers in primary schools, since it provided clear guidance in an area where many such teachers experienced their own anxieties in relation to the subject (Brown et al, 1999; McNamara and Corbin, 2001).

3.   NARRATIVES OF RECOVERY

For the trainee teacher building a sense of self, there is inevitably a gap between how she 'is' and how she 'might be'. In this chapter, I shall suggest that a resolution between supposed and desired states is not easily achieved without compromise in which certain desires will be re-routed. There are multiple stories of what it is to be a teacher to be negotiated. These stories do not necessarily lend themselves to final resolution in relation to each other. Conceptions may be both idealistic and unachievable in themselves and impossible to reconcile with other conceptions. The teacher, however, may nevertheless experience this apparent need for reconciliation as a requirement being made of her in a school setting. That is, images of what constitutes a 'competent' teacher may be circulated and influence the teacher's understanding of the multiple demands she needs to meet. She may feel obliged to respond to this requirement with some account of her success in achieving reconciliation, or otherwise feel disappointed as a result of failure. But in which ways would this account be offered? As Convery (1999, p. 139) suggests "identity is created rather than revealed through narrative" (cf. Gergen, 1989). Convery continues (p. 142) by suggesting that perhaps teachers

> feel that they are deficient in relation to their stereotype of how teachers behave, and conceal this inadequacy... by reconstructing a morally prestigious self-description that they can use for public display. However, in so doing we reinforce an unrealistic stereotype and become complicit in our own alienation. Such reconstructions may act as short term therapy for the individual, whilst contributing to a collective repression, to which the only response is this ultimately disabling palliative of further self reconstruction.

In other words, the failure to reconcile is understood as a personal failure to achieve a particular image of teaching and activates a perceived need to change oneself yet again.

At the commencement of the study, the trainees were asked to recount their mathematical experience during their school days. According to the majority of the interviewees, mathematics was a subject that caused many difficulties, sometimes real emotional turbulence. The interviewers followed them through transitions from school to university training courses and from thence to attaining their first teaching appointment as a new teacher and 'supposed' mathematics authority. The study then considered how their understandings of themselves shifted in response to the different positions they adopted, as trainee/new teacher, and the different roles they assumed (learner, teacher, assessor, assessed, employee). The trainee/new teacher may feel the need to attempt a reconciliation of these various roles in order to have some account of her achievement and satisfy her need to narrate a coherent narrative of self (cf. Harre, 1989; Sokefeld, 1999).

What does the sort of account described above look like in the data? Consider this question in relation to some typical comments from fourth year students about the skills they feel they need in order to be a teacher of mathematics: 'I like to give as much support as possible in maths because I found it hard, I try to give the tasks and we have different groups and I try to make sure each group has activities which are at their level. Because of my own experience.' Another student commented: 'The first one that springs to mind which I believe that I've got and which I thinks very important particularly in maths as well, would be patience'. A recently qualified teacher was more expansive:

> Well I'm sensitive towards children who might have difficulty with maths because I know how it might feel and I don't want children to not feel confident with maths ... I use an encouraging and positive approach with them and ... because I think if you're struggling in maths the last thing you want is your confidence being knocked in it, you want someone to use different strategies in trying to explain something to you and use a very positive, encouraging approach and not make the child feel quite - Oh they can't do maths never ... you know, so, yeah, I think my own experience in maths has allowed me to use a certain approach with children.

Such happy resolutions to the supposed skills required to teach mathematics (being 'sensitive', 'patient', 'supportive') it seems, can provide effective masks to the continuing anxieties relating to the students' own mathematical abilities. The evidence in the interviews pointed to such anxieties being side stepped rather than removed since they were still apparent in relation to more explicitly mathematical aspects of the enquiry, such as mathematical concept mapping exercises carried out, or, to a lesser extent, in relation to government mathematics skills tests for teachers.

4. THE TRUTH OF THE TRAINING EXPERIENCE

There is a need, however, to be cautious in relation to how data is being read. Which truth are the interviewees telling? In an informal conversation, Rom Harre described how he often asked a lot of neutral questions in the first half-hour of any interview he was conducting since he felt the interviewees did not really relax until later. However, can we be sure that the state of being relaxed would produce a better truth? Lacan (to be discussed shortly) thought the reverse, and so conducted short consultations of undefined length to keep his clients on their toes. Perhaps the state of being more relaxed might enable the trainee to move more easily into her habitual mode of describing herself. That is, she might merely occupy the depictions of self with which she has learnt to live, which may, or may not, paint her in a positive light ('shy', 'bad at maths', 'caring towards children'). By inspecting the previous interview extract it might be suggested that there are various forms of concealment evident. Apart from the masking of mathematical anxiety that I have already identified, there is an uneasy mix of moral and causal explanations. These have been combined to produce a "preferred identity" (Convery, 1999, p. 137) that uses moral platitudes to endorse a style of operation that the trainee has been obliged to choose as result of her mathematical shortcomings. This sort of strategy has been discussed more fully by Harre (1989). For Convery (1999), responding to Harre's work, "individuals use metaphors of struggle to create an impression of an essential self" (p. 137). The 'truth' of experience is processed through a story frame in which the individual portrays herself as struggling. This story provides the subjective fantasy through which reality is structured (Žižek, 1989). But how might the truth beneath be accessed? Clearly such a notion of a singular truth is problematic. And is it concealed? In Žižek's account, we live the fantasy, where the Real sometimes interferes.

The content of our interviews clearly touches on some personal stuff yet the media through which this is accessed precludes any sort of neutrality. The unconscious is pressing upon the things the interviewees say yet there can be no definitive manifestation of this unconscious (Lacan, 1977). Successive stories are tried out for size as the interviewees negotiate the trust they feel able to offer to others and the preparedness they have to accept a particular version of themselves. Yet as indicated, identity is constructed rather than revealed through such narrative processes. There is not an innate truth to locate. But the question remains of how interviews enable access to versions of reality and what those versions reveal. Žižek (2001) has explored the difficulties in identifying and accessing this sort of 'truth' or 'reality'. In his analysis of the Polish film director Krzysztof Kieslowski, he touches upon what Derrida has called 'fictive devices' (Derrida, 1994). Kieslowski started out his career as a social documentary filmmaker, examining the lives of people in Poland in the politically turbulent nineteen eighties. Yet, in touching on the emotional lives of his subjects, Kieslowski was uneasy about the portrayal of these lives on film. Insofar as genuine emotions were revealed, his work as filmmaker became intrusive. Such emotions need to be recast and read as fictive material and in a sense be made unreal to work in the filmic medium. Kieslowski's resolution was to move into fiction films rather than documentaries as the former enabled him to get at a better truth of the emotional content of lives that he wished to explore. Žižek (2001) argues, regarding an actor in Kieslowski's documentaries, "he does not immediately display his innermost stance; it is rather that, in a reflective attitude, he 'plays himself' by way of imitating what he perceives as his own ideal image" (p. 75). In the case of our study (Brown & McNamara, 2005), the emotional content of personalities was only partially accessed in interviews and that element then further needed to be fitted within a discourse (story frame) appropriate to the research domain. The study found itself obliged to retain the limitations of the documentary form and there is a necessary distancing of the story told from the life it seeks to capture. The reality of that life can only, Žižek argues, be mediated through a subjectively produced fantasy of it. And as Žižek (2001) further advises "the only proper thing to do is to maintain a distance towards the intimate, idiosyncratic, fantasy domain – one can only circumscribe, hint at, these fragile elements that bear witness to a human personality" (p. 73). Personalities can only be read against certain backdrops where researchers and perhaps the personalities themselves seek to understand how personalities, research perspectives, backdrops, discourses, external demands and personal aspirations, all intermingle in the accounts offered of this process.

5.   REGULATING CONSENSUS

Trainee teachers in the study were unable to synthesise all of the demands encountered. A Lacanian perspective on how a human constructs his or her self as a subject rests on the inevitability of mis-recognitions resulting from attempts at achieving resolution of disparate concerns. In meeting the impossibility of a full reconciliation between conflicting demands faced in the early stages of teaching, it would appear that the trainee or new teacher presents an unachievable fantasy of her own personal and professional identity or, at least, she remains content with a partial picture. In this section I shall suggest that this cover story is often expressed through a language provided within the official training discourse. The discourse provides a camouflage for issues that seem to remain complex and irreconcilable. The trainees subscribe to various social programs relating to the classroom. These, I suggest, can be seen as being governed by mis-recognitions of effective participation that enable the trainees to suppress some of the more difficult issues arising in their training. Whilst they do identify with many of the external demands that they encounter, their articulation of their engagement often seemed to build the very gap that keeps them away from 'antagonistic' discourses (Žižek, 1989), or conflicting stories. Any attempted resolution of the conflicting demands cannot be achieved without some compromises. It is not possible to achieve a unifying structure upon which everyone will agree. Certain desires will always be left out, no matter how pluralist or attentive to diversity we may be. The only consensual frameworks that seem to claim a unifying agenda in English mathematics education at present are governmental policy instruments. Such instruments succeed in hegemonic control, in that they appear to achieve governance through fairly widespread common consent (McNamara and Corbin, 2001).

As a key example in the study, the *National Numeracy Strategy* seemed to provide a pragmatic approach to facilitating the trainees' participation in the professional enterprise of teaching. Some trainees found it over-prescriptive with its tight guidelines (e.g. Numeracy Hour), but relatively few seemed to be wholly opposed. It was accepted as a centralised unifying structure given the relative weakness of any other frame. It had also become a generally popular social programme to which many could subscribe. Delusional or not, the trainee teacher perceived himself or herself as part of some social program designed for the common good (Althusser, 1971). This seemed to be based on some faith that if the *National Numeracy Strategy* were to be administered effectively then children would learn mathematics more effectively. As one final-year student put it:

> I think maths was one area where it did prepare us well, better than other subjects ... we spent a lot of time in maths ... making the links between the different areas and we had quite thorough training about the numeracy strategy, about mental maths, getting children to talk about maths, so maths and literacy were probably the areas where I was most prepared.

The Strategy provided practical guidelines for effective participation in a collectively conceived social programme. Participation in such a programme was seen as a key aspect of professionalism. The supposition seemed to be that the programme had become a benchmark of 'effective practice'. If you followed the *National Numeracy Strategy* you bought into a specific trajectory that supposed a particular approach to improving mathematics for children. The trainees' conception of mathematics was then a function of how they understood their social participation. Their conception of being a teacher was shaped by perceived expectations of this participation and one's success in complying with its demands.

Trainees were tugged in many different directions along the way as there were many agencies (e.g. university tutors, schools) seeking to mediate their agenda through the broader governing programme. Trainees, for example, were required to inhabit other government constructions of teachers and of mathematics, in which personal discourses and practices were squeezed into shape: 'I thought OK, just for the sake of argument, and say for the next three weeks, I would do as she asks but I know that that is not right' but also by their perception of how they are living up to these expectations: 'we are being (inspected) in maths, we are scared that if they come and see us and we are not, this, this and this'. This also arose through prescriptive curriculum documentation regulating the training process:

Where gaps in trainees' subject knowledge are identified, providers of ITT must make arrangements to ensure that trainees gain that knowledge during the course and that, **by the end of that course**, they are competent in using their knowledge of mathematics in their teaching (DEE, 1998, p. 48, DEE emphasis).

University tutors concerned about their own inspections further added to this. One student made some observations of her tutor:

She [the tutor] was probably exceptionally nervous, just like teachers are, I mean, you're being watched and, you know you're being observed and you're going to have comments made upon your teaching approach or teaching style, the level of teaching, ... inspections are the same in schools, it's just completely false, you don't get a proper idea of the school and it's like when we were on school experience and the planning that we had to do for maths for numeracy and it was like rigorously checked and we weren't allowed to go into schools unless the plans were good enough and that was all for the benefit of [the inspectors].

There was considerable evidence that students who were still in university demonstrated a keen awareness of the frameworks governing the course and their imminent accreditation. There was an air of a strongly regulatory climate with a host of government initiatives supplementing the demands students faced in university and on school placements. The trainee's professional identity seemed to be a function of a partial reconciliation anchored in some assumption about what constituted correct behaviour, or practices that would result in their accreditation. As such there was a sense of having to get it right according to official agendas, although the data suggested that the partiality of the students' perspectives resulted in immediate tasks being privileged over any broader reconciliation. The data, unsurprisingly, pointed to trainees being more anxious about the various requirements they faced prior to their accreditation and being more concerned with achieving what was expected of them. Certainly for such students the external demands ensured a compliant attitude, but a compliance with an approach that was generally seen as supporting the common good, namely the generally accepted need for mathematics to be taught: 'it's something we need to participate fully in life from a very early age'. The apparent hegemonic grip of government policy would not appear to be easily displaced. It was offering one version of governance supported largely through popular consent.

6.   THE MYTH OF EMERGENT AUTONOMY

Meanwhile, however, once released from university in to the relative responsibility of being a teacher in school, there was a greater sense of autonomy expressed with the individual teacher in the driving seat governed more by personal motivations and ideals. Here the new teacher might more readily have recognised that the antagonisms were irreconcilable but at the same time also recognised that looser interpretations could be sufficient as a more pragmatic attitude evolved. This offered more scope for making individual decisions. Once work as a teacher had begun, he or she recognised that the various demands could be met and integrated more with his or her own personal aspirations ('you have more autonomy'). As another new teacher put it: 'you can be more spontaneous ... even though you've got to follow the demands of the ... numeracy hour'. This then might be seen as a frame privileging the teacher seeking to recover his or her 'own voice'. Although a harmonious and complete social perspective may not easily be achieved, the individual – having negotiated entry in to the profession—could now seek to juggle the external demands from a position of greater assumed personal control.

A Lacanian reading of the induction process, I suggest, contests the assumption that teachers make a transition from compliance with external demands to a more autonomous state of affairs. As they shift from pre-service to in-service, teachers continue to embrace cover stories of compliance. It seems more realistic to suggest, instead, that in both environments the demands are so great that reconciliation is not possible in any actual sense. The trainee or new teacher's account provides a cover story for a situation that is complex and does not lend itself to clear representation. For example, it seems unlikely that the new teacher could juggle the various demands (e.g. meeting government requirements, enabling children to find mathematics interesting, maintaining classroom control, reconciling school and university demands, fitting into school structures, being liked by the children, etc.) into a clear story. It is just that the demands on teachers to do this are less pressing once employed. As a new teacher put it: 'what you teach and how you teach it and the actual set-up of the lesson is restricted to sort of government requirements and school requirements and local education authority requirements and [school inspectors'] requirements and everyone else but you can still fit in your own style in that'. Despite the optimism of this quote it seemed impossible for this new teacher to appreciate fully and then reconcile all of the alternative discourses acting through her. The statement might be seen as an image that the new teacher wants to have of herself. The teacher might buy into official story lines and see (misguidedly or not) her 'own' actions in those terms. This does not have to be seen as a problem. But it may mean that new teachers like her subscribe to intellectual package deals laid on for them rather than see the development of their own professional practice in terms of further intellectual and emotional work to do with re-solving the contradictory messages encountered.

Professional development was more broadly seen, it seems, in terms of better achieving curriculum objectives such as those framed within the *National Numeracy Strategy*— a strategy that the new teachers seemed comfortable with as a framework for organising practice. It seemed to be that the Strategy provided the consensual frameworks that could claim some sort of unifying agenda, at least partly because it had become the new orthodoxy: 'I find the numeracy and literacy strategies quite useful but I've never known any different'. It appeared to succeed in hegemonic control where a trainee's capacity to be critical was limited by her need to comply.

> The thing with government policies is really whether you agree with them or not and you think they're beneficial or not, you've got to adapt and change to go with them, so it's just a case of experimenting with them, trying them out and then adapting them to suit you, so ... I mean, you've got to use them, so if you can adapt it to suit you then it's going to be beneficial.

The Strategy seems to have provided a language that can be learnt and spoken by most new teachers interviewed. In this sense, the official language spanning the *National Numeracy Strategy* and the inspectorial regulation of it seemed to have been a success. Many trainees, it would seem, saw the Strategy as a pragmatic approach that facilitated their participation in the professional enterprise of teaching a subject where previously many trainees had some uncertainties. One new teacher commented:

> I think largely it's the way that it's structured rather than my own - my own personal experience of maths since I left primary school has not been good, ... it was never my most enjoyed subject so I definitely think it's the way that it's structured.

Meanwhile, another new teacher states: 'I quite actually quite like the structure of the numeracy, the mental maths, the section at the end, the plenary I quite like that structure because it's quite sort of easy to follow'. Any ambivalence towards the Strategy seems measured with an acceptance that others know better. After all, as one stated, 'obviously somebody somewhere with a lot of authority has actually sat down and written this Numeracy Strategy, well a number of people, so they ... it's not like they don't know what they're talking about'. It has thus become a generally popular social program with which many can identify.

This does, however, point to a perceived need to find ways of adopting a critical attitude in relation to the parameters of this discourse in that certain difficult issues are being suppressed rather than removed. For example, when confronted with mathematics of a more sophisticated nature from the school curriculum the new teachers remained anxious. Mathematics had been masked by the administrative performances that shaped it. The *National Numeracy Strategy* and university training had, between them, provided an effective language for administering mathematics in the classroom in which confrontation with more challenging aspects of mathematics could be avoided. If true, this points to certain limits in a teacher's capacity to engage creatively with the children's own mathematical constructions. The *National Numeracy Strategy* hints at the 'ready-made' or 'fast-food' fantasy of teacher training which is preferred to the more difficult task of responding creatively to children's individual fantasies of mathematical constructing. The problem is that the *National Numeracy Strategy* presents a clearly inscribed object, whereas the task of responding to the individual fantasies of mathematics that might arise in more student-centred conceptions of education would place the teacher in a much more unstable position. Yet, whilst for so many of the trainees interviewed this instability was an element to be ejected, this is not necessarily in the interests of valuing children's emerging thinking.

REFERENCES

Althusser, L. (1971) Ideology and ideological state apparatuses. In *Lenin and philosophy and other essays*. London: New Left Books.
Brown, T. and McNamara, O. (2005) *New teacher identity and regulative government: the discursive formation of primary mathematics teacher education.* (New York: Springer).
Brown, T., McNamara, O., Jones, L. and Hanley, U. (1999) Primary student teachers' understanding of mathematics and its teaching. *British Education Research Journal*, 25(3), 299-322.
Convery, A. (1999) Listening to teacher' stories: are we sitting too comfortably? *International Journal of Qualitative Studies in Education*, 12(2), 131-146.
Department for Education and Employment (DEE) (1998) *Initial teacher training National Curriculum for primary mathematics, Annex D of circular 4/98.* London: Department for Education and Employment.
Derrida, J. (1994). Deconstruction of actuality: an interview with Jacques Derrida. *Radical Philosophy, 68*, 28-41. Reprinted in Derrida, J. (2002) *Negotiations: interventions and interviews, 1971-2001.* Stanford; Stanford University Press.
Gergen, K. (1989) Warranting voice and the elaboration of self. In J. Shotter and K. Gergen (Eds.), *Texts of identity* (pp. 70-81). London: Sage.
Harre, R. (1989) Language games and texts of identity. In J. Shotter and K. Gergen (Eds.) *Texts of identity* (pp. 20-35). London: Sage.

Lacan, J. (1977) *Ecrits: a selection.* London: Routledge.

McNamara, O. and Corbin, B. (2001) Warranting practices: teachers embedding the National Numeracy Strategy. *British Journal of Educational Studies, 49*(3), 260-284.

Sokefeld, M. (1999) Debating self and culture in anthropology. *Current Anthropology,* 40(4), 417-447.

Žižek, S. (1989) *The sublime object of ideology.* London: Verso

Žižek S. (2001) *The fright of real tears: Krzysztof Kieslowski between theory and post-theory* London: British Film Institute.

THE PROMISES OF DISRUPTING COMFORTING NARRATIVES OF COMPLIANCE
"A Handful[1]" of Responses to Tony Brown

Kathleen Nolan, Brent Eidsness, Shana Graham, Kathy Lawless, Devona Putland and Tara Stuckless
University of Regina

There are many different ways in which the world can be experienced and represented... some human experiences are so complex and intensely emotional, that creative forms of representation can reflect their texture more evocatively than traditional academic text. Creative forms invite us to develop insights that would otherwise be inaccessible and they invite us to see more clearly and feel more deeply. (Brearly, 2000)

If increasingly the seductive power of our texts and utterances is to be enacted, it will not happen by reigning in our analyses or by excessive throat-clearing and textual gesturing toward ideological safety. It is not more timid or paralyzed performances we need but more adventurous ones. We need adventures that allow us to perform knowing in ways that are pleasurable to ourselves and a larger audience of others. (McWilliam, 1997, p. 230)

Figure -1 The Adventures of Super Teacher by Brent Eidsness

Exploring 'Gaps' Through Brown's Chapter
by Shana Graham

This visual image portrays themes I discerned while reading Tony Brown's chapter. The themes weave, interconnect, and overlap with undefined boundaries - extending/expanding beyond web-like linear connections. This response only focuses upon the 'GAPS' theme. I invite the reader to consider how potential research opportunities might be identified when 'gaps' are noticed and explored.

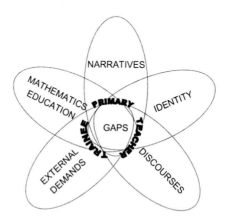

Brown suggests school discourses, prescriptive curricula, and government initiatives afford, perhaps unintentionally, inappropriate means for primary teachers to teach mathematics without developing deeper/connected understandings of mathematical concepts. [*I agree with Brown because my past mathematics teaching experiences are filled with stories of my procedural compliance in curriculum coverage without deeper understanding of mathematical connections.*] Likewise, (perhaps unintentionally although not inappropriately) Brown's chapter affords opportunities for the reader to reflect on research ideas by considering the potential of 'in-between spaces' (Fleener, 2004), openings, or gaps. I explain this interpretation using my favorite quote as an example.

"For the trainee teacher building a sense of self, there is inevitably a gap between how she 'is' and how she 'might be'." (Brown, *this volume,* p. 99)

This statement suggests to me that it may be valuable for educational researchers interested in the concept of identity formation to further explore the gap between current and future self perceptions in pre-service primary teachers. Exploration might lead to investigation of possible issues/aspects usually hidden, masked or ignored during transition from pre-service to employment. Brown discussed one such aspect - unsuccessful past mathematics education experiences - but likely there are other aspects worthy of reflection. I invite the reader to identify other 'gaps' within the article and to consider the research potential in exploring these possibilities. Perhaps such 'gaps' could be used in 'occasioning' (Davis, Sumara & Luce-Kaplar, 2000) future/new research.

The 'gaps' I found are presented in the illustration on the previous page (p. 114), but I leave the reader to ponder the potential research value of each gap and supplementary linked concepts. The circular abyss-like image portrays an opening for exploration. Broken line segments suggest that - although connections between two concepts are made in Brown's article - there are hidden, masked, or ignored aspects/issues that are not discussed. Written on each broken segment are words reflecting incompleteness/in-between spaces/openings—words that leave room for multiple interpretations and expressions. The broken segments cross over to suggest a complex interweaving of identified connections and hidden, masked or ignored aspects/issues. Consider how the identified connections are not line-arly/directly related since there are gaps in the connections—gaps that could be researched/explored, and presented through multiple perspectives.

Figure 2 illustrates how I imagine 'occasioning' future/new research through my interpretations of Brown's writing – opening a dialogue with the reader. When I shared this response and figure with Dr. Nolan, her interpretation further enriched my learning experience (as opening dialogue with others can do). Her comments follow:

I tried a few other connections... that is, I applied angles other than 180 degrees (straight line) to connect the concepts. For instance,

<u>Understanding of self</u> *shifts* **(turn 35°)** *through* <u>external images of</u> <u>'competent teacher'</u>.

<u>Capacity to be critical</u> *limited* **(turn 70°)** *by narrative* <u>cover story.</u>

What will you choose to explore?

Figure -2 Occasioning Future/New Research

METAMORPHOSIS?
by Kathy Lawless

The influences that shape teachers' lives and that move teachers' actions
are rarely found in research studies, policy reform, or institutional mis-
sion statements. They are more likely to be found in a complex web of
formative memories and experiences. (Ellsworth, J. & Buss, A., 2000)

```
I don't like math.  Why do I have to take it anyway?  It
is so boring, not fun like reading or science where we
get to do experiments.  I am no good at memorizing.  The
teacher says I need extra help because I am not keeping
up with the rest of the class.  I hate going for extra
```

help.   The other kids tease me about being stupid.   I
don't want to go for extra help.   I hate math.   Why do I
have to take it anyway?

Math class is so boring. We copy notes everyday from the board. And I
don't always get what it is I am copying down in my notebook. No one
seems to care about that. The important thing is that I just write it down
as fast as I can to get through it. Why do I have to take math anyway?
My dad says I am no good at math because he wasn't any good at it either. He says it runs in the family. Mom says girls usually aren't good at
math and I probably won't need it when I grow up anyway.

*We have this most amazing teacher in math this year. We get to work in groups and
solve problems together. She wants us to talk to each other and share our ideas. I
am much better at doing math this way. She explains things really well and I am
actually understanding it. She is awesome. She says I am good at math. She said
that it is a ridiculous idea that girls aren't as good at math as boys. It must be true
because she is really good at math.*

I am not sure I should have signed up for this class. What if I can't handle math at this
level? If I can just pass this math class I won't take anymore. I don't need anymore math
classes for my degree anyway. But I should finish this one. I want to be a better math
teacher than the teachers I had at elementary school.   Math would be so much easier if
I had been born with natural ability. I just don't think logically enough or have a good
enough memory to memorize all those rules and formulas. If I could find the right answer by being creative or using my gut feeling I would do much better. I have never
learned the magic key to doing math.

*I think the mathematics methods class I just finished is really going to help me be a good
math teacher. I don't want any of my future students to hate math like I did. I am going to
teach math in such a way that my students will like it. I want them to experience math in
ways I never did. I like the idea that students should be allowed to discover mathematics on
their own without the teacher always showing them how to find the answer. I will be able to
give my students lots of different activities too. And I want to provide my students with
hands-on materials like those manipulatives that the prof had in class the other day. I think
I am really well prepared to teach math now.*

**Gosh, I didn't think teaching three classes of fourth-grade math was going to
be so busy or I wouldn't have agreed to take on this assignment. I was thinking
that there would be less preparation time needed but, as it turns out, I am bus-
ier than ever with large classes and all the marking I have to do. And on top of
it all I think this year's groups of students are more difficult to handle than last**

year's. Putting their desks in rows has certainly helped. I certainly won't be doing much group work with them though; they just can't handle it. Just imagine if the Superintendent or Principal had been in my class that day I brought out the manipulatives. It was chaos! A complete waste of 45 minutes. If I am going to get these students ready for the math assessment tests by next month, I need to make the best use of every minute I have. I don't want them doing badly on those assessments – it wouldn't make me look very good. Next *year I am going* to ask for less math to teach.

Confronting Narratives of Compliance: A Poetic Response
by Devona Putland

Student in the classroom, math period nears
Usually competent, but now filled with fears
Student survives, although instruction lacks meaning
University bound towards teacher training
    Student to teacher, the chosen path
    Experiencing limited successes in school-based math
    Foundational attitudes formed in public education
    Masked as adults as teaching sensations
        Desires rerouted, too idealistic, unachievable
        How could such dreams be so inconceivable?
        Deficient teachers, math inadequacy
        Whose later self perceptions ill reflect reality
            Government policy, curriculum reform
            National Numeracy Strategy, the classroom norm
            Adding a routine with rigorous school inspection
            Secured the inadequate faceless self-rejection
                Teacher training completed, now a math teacher
                A transition from failure to exceptional creature
                Masking anxiety with façade of ability
                Does the image reflect the present reality?
                    Could teacher training result 'in-competent' teachers
                    With such daunting tasks as a main feature?
                    Deficiencies reconstructed, public identification
                    Reinforce teachers' self alienation
                        Failure to reconcile personal failure of the past
                        Create contradictions, in self that will last
                      How one is, and how one might be
                      Defining aspirations from base reality

Disappointments resulting from past failure, no less
False reconciliation leads to apparent success
One's image in comfort, a preferred identity
The truth beneath, your failure to see
The habitual living of the desired description
Life in a fantasy will be the inscription
No innate truth to locate or define
How to access the layers, will there be time?
Revealing oneself as an attitude reflective
Gives the fictional image of the ideal perspective
The backdrop defining personality perspective
From student to teacher, where was the directive?
Circumscribe the discourse of personal imitation
Intermingles with accounts of research observations
Practical guidelines, key aspects of professionalism
Benchmarks of effective practice, the presupposition
Mathematics now an aspect of social participation
Meeting the demands of teaching expectations
Lessons for the benefit of the school inspector
Take on a difference from trainee to instructor
Spontaneous lessons, reflecting own voice
Result in teachings that are teacher's own choice
Speaking the language, National Numeracy Strategy
The language of experts inscribed on trainees
Limited capacity for engaging in math meaning construction
Emerging thinking for children, meeting destruction
Fast food fantasy for teacher training
Math without thinking practices remaining
Inscribed mathematics, lock-step instruction
Hinder the practice of meaning production
Instability of emergent thinking ejected
Teacher creativity, also rejected
Teachers engaged
Student-centered connections
Future for math
New meaning and perceptions

Reflections on Reflections on Reflections…
by Tara Stuckless

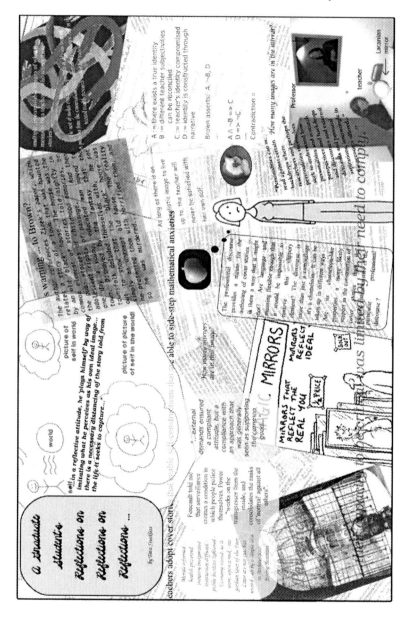

REFERENCES

Brearley, L. (2000). Exploring the creative voice in an academic context. *The qualitative report, 5*(3-4). Available: http://www.nova.edu.libproxy.uregina.ca:2048/ssss/QR/QR5-3/brearley.html. Retrieved April 18, 2007.

Davis, B., Sumara, D. & Luce-Kapler, R. (2000). *Engaging minds: Learning and teaching in a complex world.* Mahwah, NJ: Lawrence Erlbaum Associates Ltd.

Ellsworth, J. & Buss, A. (2000). Autobiographical stories from preservice elementary mathematics and science students: Implications for K-16 teaching. *School Science and Mathematics, 100*(7), 355.

Fleener, M. J. (2004). Why mathematics? Insights from poststructural topologies. In M. Walshaw (Ed.), *Mathematics education within the postmodern* (pp. 201-218). Greenwich, CT: Information Age Publishing.

McWilliam, E. (1997). Performing between the posts: Authority, posture, and contemporary feminist scholarship. In W.G. Tierney & Y.S. Lincoln (Eds.), *Representation and the text: Reframing the narrative voice* (pp. 220-232). New York: State University of New York Press.

---

[1] This 'handful' of five responses presented in these few pages were created by graduate students enrolled in a mathematics curriculum class during the fall of 2006. The instructor for this graduate course was K. Nolan and she writes her own response/reflection to this one in a piece that follows. Her response attempts to 'trouble' the promises, and to understand the (com)promises, of assigning such arts-based writing assignments in her classes.

THE (COM)PROMISES OF DISRUPTING COMFORTING NARRATIVES OF COMPLIANCE
"More Than A Handful" Response to Tony Brown

Kathleen Nolan
University of Regina

In the fall of 2006, I taught a graduate course in mathematics curriculum and instruction. One of the course assignments involved writing personal responses (entitled, "What I'm thinking is…") to two articles discussed in class. Since I already had a reputation for attempting to disrupt traditional notions of academic text in my classes, it likely came as no great surprise to my students to read the following on the course outline…

"WHAT I'M THINKING IS…?"

This assignment involves writing personal responses to articles/issues discussed in class. Each written response should focus on how the article/issue and discussion has had an impact on you and your thinking, the struggles you anticipate (or already face) in 'living out' the implications of the article/issue, an argument for/against the ideas being presented, questions being generated for you, etc. You are required to write <u>two</u> of these responses— one on a research article of your own choosing and one on an assigned research article. The assigned piece is a book chapter written by Tony Brown entitled, *Comforting narratives of compliance: Psychoanalytic perspectives on new teacher responses to mathematics policy reform*. Alternative formats are supported and encouraged for these responses. For example, one can respond through collage, poetry, image-based writing, conversational text, etc. More information will be forthcoming on format suggestions and opportunities within this assignment.

There is really nothing unusual in this assignment description to startle or provoke students into a *"what do you want for this?"* frenzy. (These days, the more I attempt to disrupt traditions in mathematics, curriculum, and/or school practices in general, the more this question triggers my retreat back into familiarity!) In this assignment, students were given a choice to respond through an alternative format, or NOT. Simple. What was unusual for the students, however, was the additional assignment feature (or, opportunity, as I called it): "… if you choose a format that attempts to demonstrate your learning through an arts-based representation or disruption of the text, then you are invited to submit your assignment for publication consideration."

I was excited about the assignment. The students were intrigued by my list of possible formats *through* which they could express their ideas and learnings. And I was thrilled when the assignments came in—ten out of the twelve students in the course chose to "take up the challenge" of alternative formats and respond to Tony Brown's chapter through a graphic story, a poetic rendering, an autobiographical narrative, a photographic projection, or other arts-based approach.

But then it hit me. What do I do now? How do **I** respond (as an instructor? a colleague? an evaluator?) to this work? Isn't the most important aspect of the assignment now complete, that is, the student learning? I recently wrote (Nolan, 2005) that we should embrace different ways of knowing (in) academic writing because this will, in turn, enable us to imagine and embrace different ways of knowing (in) mathematics. I wrote:

> My desire [is] to not only write the research text *about* different ways of learning and knowing (in) mathematics… but to actually write the research text *through* different ways of learning and knowing. The meaning behind the prepositional choice of 'through' over 'about' highlights the intimate connections between research, learning, and knowledge, proposing a paradigm shift for understanding and realizing the possibilities of a performative text. (Nolan, 2005, p. 120)

Yet here I was, providing opportunities for students to write *through* not *about* other ways of knowing, and I found myself feeling like an impostor. In my mind, it is one thing to draw on arts-based approaches in my own research and then dissuade the critics; it is quite another to *be the critic* of arts-based approaches! What do *I* know about arts-based writing? More specifically, what do I know about *evaluating* arts-based writing?

And there's the rub. *Evaluation.* I intentionally resisted resorting to a rubric, even though I knew that, properly designed, a rubric can quash even the most diligent mark-protesters in a class. No, I decided to be more creative and open, and go with a qualitative response for each student that focused on the strengths of the piece, but also included a critique which was cleverly embedded within a few questions for the student to consider. I was concerned about being overly critical—partly because of my own inexperience with judging such formats but also because the last thing I wanted to do was to discourage the students from ever stepping out of their academic writing comfort zone again.

The following two examples illustrate my approach to providing evaluation and feedback to the students:

A (*nolan*) **Response to a** (*brown*) **Response for Kathy Lawless...**

I followed right along on your METAMORPHOSIS path, either identifying with the text myself as a learner or with students' expressions of math learning through my various research projects. I do find myself wondering... is this you from start to finish or are you morphing the learners also? My reading of your piece was not off to a great start because the first two narratives/paragraphs did not easily connect to the rest of the *growing text* that emerged for me. As you revisit the piece now, would you change anything about it? Is the metamorphosis complete? Has the first year teacher come full circle, back to her stark reality of math as memorization and notes, or is their still hope for her? Thanks for seizing the opportunity to write a response that endeavours to open up the text so the reader may engage in her/his own personal learning experience.

A (*nolan*) **Response to a** (*brown*) **Response for Brent Eidsness...**

Your humour is an engaging feature of this piece... but this does not mean that I missed the underlying messages while chuckling at your comic strip pals and puns. The connections that can be made to Brown's chapter in *The Adventures of Super Teacher* are many. For me, one critical aspect highlighted in the comic strip was that many interns and new teachers can quite easily identify what is boring and not working in mathematics classrooms, but it is far more difficult to propose ideas for what *might* work and *might* be worth trying. Somehow, there is still a loud cry for someone else to do the problem solving on this one—for someone else to come up with a "manual" (or, *National Numeracy Strategy*) that can be followed to do it right. Interesting.

Sounds fine, right? But then, seemingly out of nowhere, I plopped down a real number **x**, where $0.0 \leq x \leq 10.0$. (Well, actually, because this was a graduate studies course, it was more like $7.0 \leq x \leq 9.5$. Don't ask me why.) (At least) one student was confused. That one student e-mailed me. The back-and-forth written exchange (speaking of (dis)comforting narratives of compliance...) went something like this:

Subject: What I'm Thinking Is...
Message no. 94
Date: Tuesday, November 7, 2006 1:19pm
Kathy –
I'm confused! I don't normally do this, but... I'm confused as to how marks were arrived at for our responses. I appreciated the comments, and I am not trying to argue that my marks should necessarily be higher (well, maybe a little...), but the way that a mark out of ten was given baffles me. I completely understand the conundrum when trying to compare apples to automobiles (some people's work is not even within the fruit family - and that's wonderful to see).

I have included the [assignment] as an attachment and would ask for a second read of it. If I am losing marks because I am having a conclusion being ascribed to my work that simply tries to respond to the points raised in the article, I am a little uncomfortable. If I am losing marks because the quality of this work is an 8.8/10, I would like to know why.

I know I am quibbling about very little in the grand scheme of things, but I am a product of the way I was taught and marks and assessments were an important part of that process.
Brent

Subject: Re: What I'm Thinking Is...
Message no. 95 [Reply of: no. 94]
Date: Wednesday, November 8, 2006 11:46am
Brent,

It's November. I'm doing my best to stay on top of (perhaps in the middle of?) my marking pile. I simply do not have the 6-8 hours of extra time that would be required to re-mark the class assignments (re-marking one assignment in isolation is not acceptable if one takes into consideration both norm and criterion-referenced evaluation).

I will, on the other hand, be happy to meet with you to discuss what's on your mind. It will also give me an opportunity to express more clearly my meaning behind my written comments and the strengths and shortcomings of your assignment that made me decide that your response was 'just shy' of 90%.
Kathy

Subject: Re: What I'm Thinking Is...
Message no. 96 [Reply of: no. 95]
Date: Wednesday, November 8, 2006 6:32pm

Kathy –
I have no problem with the 8.8/10 standing as a 8.8/10 (I completely understand the time issue and the fact that there were comparisons made with the
other assignments - so a rereading is not possible nor fair). I am fine with
that. I was trying to ask for clarification as to the way that this grade was
arrived at. Sorry, it came off so ham-fistedly.

Some of this can be addressed face-to-face, but here are some of my questions (and I am not asking these questions about this assignment in particular,
but about any such non-traditional work):

- What makes one response better or worse than another?
- What constitutes an 80%? a 75%? a 95%?   (In effect, what does the
  mark signify?)
- How do you compare a photographic response with a written response
  with a combined written and visual response?

Part of the reason I have these questions are the discussions we've had in
class about constructivism and alternate teaching methods and how to assess
learning and other topics. I would like to try using some of these alternative
project ideas, but I am obviously uncertain as to how I would assess them
(and in a high school setting, as in a university one, marks are important).

I'm flattered that my work earned the second highest mark in the class - but
that doesn't help me understand why it earned that mark. I would have similar questions about a 9.5/10 or a 7.0/10.
Brent

Subject: Re: What I'm Thinking Is...
Message no. 97 [Reply of: no. 96]
Date: Tuesday, November 14, 2006 4:16pm
Brent,
In short, your questions about alternative formats are important ones, mainly
for the reason (I think) that they are common ones and feed into a big reason
why teachers don't want to try new things. Actually, I **cannot** compare a
photo to a comic strip to an online dialogue, etc. in the same ways as I might
think I can compare one linear text to another (even then I think we have an
illusion of objectivity, which is further supported by an illusion of numbers as
absolutes). This sort of assessment is so subjective and yet there are things to
look for... creativity with ideas (I saw that in yours); originality of response (I
saw that in yours), clarity of communication given the style adopted (also in
yours), depth of engagement with the ideas (in yours, but not to a level that
might be possible). I never had a question about your response's relationship

and connections to Tony Brown's chapter... I believe I was aware of most (but certainly not all) of the connections you were alluding to. Still, I kept asking myself if this could be taken further, deeper, into the ideas of identity and 'becoming' a teacher.

In retrospect, I wish I had written the critique of the level of your reflection on your comment sheet; you deserved this constructive feedback along with the positive. I guess that I wanted to encourage alternative approaches while still working within the confines of our system of marks... and (naively, I think) thought that the students were accepting that I too am just figuring this out.

Kathy

Subject: Re: What I'm Thinking Is...
Message no. 99 [Reply of: no. 97]
Date: Wednesday, November 15, 2006 8:30am
Kathy –
Thank you for your thoughts. Your listing of some of the things you were looking for was very helpful and I could see teachers (myself included) taking them and developing a rubric for assignments such as these with rating scales for each of the elements (creativity with ideas, originality of response, clarity of communication given the style adopted, depth of engagement with the ideas) that could be used to compare the wide variety of work that this type of 'non-traditional' format would encourage. In high school classes, as in university, we are tied to the idea of a number used as a rating scale or mark.

I think part of my frustration when I sent my first e-mail was a system one (not directed at either of my profs this semester). In this, my first semester in graduate studies, it seems that these marks are only allowed to range from 70% to 90% and the difference between an okay mark (say low 80%) and a good mark (say high 80%) involves a lot of hours and effort. I have been in a few conversations with colleagues who have resigned themselves to this. Anyway, this is a conversation for another time.
Brent

Subject: Re: What I'm Thinking Is...
Message no. 101 [Reply of: no. 99]
Date: Wednesday, November 15, 2006 3:07pm
Brent,
Thanks for your reply. I must say that I intentionally declined to use an already developed rubric that I have often used when teaching [a different

course]. The rubric outlines those (or similar) criteria and **exactly** what each level looks like. I'm still not comfortable with such rubrics because they take very subjective criteria and make them look like they can be objectively evaluated. It's as if each of the words 'thoughtful' or 'creative' or 'original' has one possible understanding, not to mention further qualifiers like 'slightly' thoughtful, 'fairly' thoughtful, 'very' thoughtful... what do these words mean?

Ok, so I've clearly been in 'this business' for too long? :-)
Kathy

And that, in a nutshell, is the conundrum I face at the moment. Do I not 'know enough' about arts-based research to judge its validity (or, "believability" (Eisner, 2006)) and then convincingly straddle the line between the seemingly incompatible paradigms of non-traditional assignments and traditional evaluation? *Likely.* Can I buy into the notion that arts-based research "harbour[s] a penchant for ambiguity, openness, a playful consideration of alternatives, a generation of viewpoints alternative to the current regime of truth" (Barone, 2001, p. 26) but then attempt to judge/assess it in the context of educational settings (well-known for their lack of ambiguity and playfulness when it comes to evaluation)—a place where students tell me: "I am a product of the way I was taught and marks and assessments were an important part of that process". *Not likely, not at the moment anyway.*

> Issues of power and control emerge when boundaries are stretched in this way. If we challenge the conventions of representation and engagement with text, then where does the authority to evaluate it reside? Who guards the gate of the academy? Is it possible to reframe the paradigm of exclusivity and adversariality so that it is possible to question dominant forms of long-revered paradigms? (Brearley, 2000)

I am reminded of something I read recently: "Any attempted resolution of the conflicting demands cannot be achieved without some compromises. We cannot easily aspire to a unifying structure upon which everyone will agree. Certain desires will always be left out, no matter how pluralist or attentive to diversity we may be." (Brown, *this volume*, p. 103) Is "buying into the *National Numeracy Strategy*" (an issue on which Brown deliberates) a very different trajectory than the one I'm on?

Eliot Eisner (2006) asks, and then answers, the pertinent question in my mind: Does arts-based research in education have a future?

> ... my answer to my own question is that arts-based educational research will have a future depending upon our ability to reach for the heavens by crafting research that reveals to us what we have learned not to see and on the public's willingness to accept what we have made visible as one

useful way to understand and renew schools. In opening our eyes, arts-based educational research may become something of a revolution in awareness, epistemology, and in method. But it will not be without its battles. (Eisner, 2006, p. 17)

As a mathematics education researcher and teacher, I ask myself if arts-based educational research has a future in my own practice—in my own graduate and undergraduate course classrooms. I am tempted (at the moment anyway) to shy away from making life more challenging than it already is in the academic world of balancing research, teaching, and life in general. I firmly believe, however, that well-entrenched notions about knowledge (what counts and who decides) and evaluation paradigms need challenging, disrupting, and re-imagining. And *that*, my colleagues, my students, will not be without its battles. But can I take on those battles? Is the cause worth it? What mark will **I** get?

Because we are embarking on a new journey,
I have no clear-cut method for evaluating these texts...
(Tierney, 1997, p. 33)

REFERENCES

Barone, T. (2001). Science, art, and the predispositions of educational researchers. *Educational researcher, 30*(7), 24-28.

Brearley, L. (2000). Exploring the creative voice in an academic context. *The qualitative report, 5*(3-4). Available: http://www.nova.edu.libproxy.uregina.ca:2048/ssss/QR/ QR5-3/brearley.html. Retrieved April 18, 2007.

Eisner, E. (2006). Does arts-based research have a future? *Studies in art education, 48*(1), 9-18.

Nolan, K. (2005). Publish or cherish? Performing a dissertation in/between research spaces. In R. Barnett (Ed.), *Reshaping the university: New relationships between research, scholarship and teaching* (pp. 119-135). Great Britain: Open University Press.

Tierney, W. (1997). Lost in translation. In W.G. Tierney & Y.S. Lincoln (Eds.), *Representation and the text: Reframing the narrative voice* (pp. 23-36). New York: State University of New York Press.

Chapter 6

POWER DISTRIBUTION IN THE NETWORK OF MATHEMATICS EDUCATION PRACTICES

Ole Ravn Christensen, Diana Stentoft and Paola Valero
Aalborg University, Denmark

Abstract: The importance of mathematics and mathematics education in current societies is associated with them being seen as "powerful". The meaning of power is, however, not always explicitly expressed or easy to define in a clear-cut way. In this chapter, we trace three different perspectives on thinking about power in relation to mathematics education, as they are expressed in the network of mathematics education practices. The intrinsic perspective, the technical perspective and the structural inequality perspective represent three different ways of seeing what power is and how it is distributed. Highlighting these perspectives helps us investigate the constraints and potentials of different ways of conceiving mathematics education and of constructing new imaginaries for the future.

Key words: power in mathematics education; intrinsic perspective; technical perspective; structural inequality perspective; power distribution; research discourse; network of mathematics education practices.

1. INTRODUCTION

Educating people in mathematics is considered a powerful enterprise. 'Mathematics is at the core of Western culture'. 'Mathematics is a powerful tool to reinforce and secure access to the material, economic and the social world'. Statements of this nature frequently appear in discussions on the role of mathematics in the construction and consolidation of a modern, industrialized and democratic society. Even though modern societies have entered into a post-industrial era, such statements are still at the core of justification for allocating funds for mathematics education and for improving the teaching of mathematics at all educational levels. Where mathematics used to be a tool for building infrastructure and developing industry, it has gradually become a tool for building the informational infrastructure and advanced communication technologies. In this sense, mathematics is continuously perceived as a prerequisite for progress and wealth.

Thinking in terms of *mathematics* as powerful immediately grants power to *mathematics education* as a privileged social practice through which children and adults alike will come to know about mathematics. But what is the meaning of the term power when connected with mathematics and mathematics education? How and by whom is this power exercised? What are the consequences of power for participants in mathematics education? On the following pages we will address these questions with a view to demonstrate that it is not a straightforward issue to talk about power in relation to mathematics education. Instead we argue that power is complexly distributed across the entire *network of mathematics education practices*. By this term we refer to the network of language games that, intertwined by family resemblances, constitute mathematics education—from social interaction at a micro level, such as classroom interactions, to practices at macro levels of society at large, such as political decision making, labor market needs and even mathematics education research[1].

In this chapter, we focus on three perspectives on power found in the network of mathematics education practices and often addressed in mathematics education research: an intrinsic perspective, a technical perspective, and a structural inequality perspective. The exploration of these three perspectives serves as our analytical lens through which we observe the enactment and distribution of power in the network of mathematics education practices. These different perspectives set the scene for constructions of distinct imaginaries about what mathematics and its educational practices are about. Furthermore, the perspectives are not limited to one particular type or level of practice where 'proper' mathematics education practice resides. Rather, these perspectives on power in the network of mathematics education practices also serve as a framework for connecting practices across micro and macro levels, where they may not traditionally be thought of as interrelated.

2.   THREE PERSPECTIVES ON POWER IN MATHEMATICS EDUCATION PRACTICES

Researchers' perceptions of power and power distribution in mathematics education are not always explicit. They remain implicit parts of the fundamental assumptions about mathematics education with its objects and subjects of research and their justifications and contributions to particular studies. However, researchers' perceptions are of extreme relevance since, to a considerable extent, they determine how a researcher constructs and presents mathematics education and its achievements, shortcomings and development to society, politicians and education practitioners. A deeper understanding of power as it is distributed and enacted in the web of everyday practices surrounding mathematics education is therefore needed.

Traditionally, many scholars in mathematics education have applied a structuralist perspective when examining power. The source of power of mathematics and its learning have traditionally been seen as residing in one of three places: in the logical structures of mathematics, in cognitive structures of the learner, or in the traditional social and cultural structures and categories such as gender, class and race[2]. Such a perspective emphasizes a view of power as a monolithic entity which individuals may/may not possess according to their own personal attributes or their relation to surrounding structures, and which individuals may/may not decide to exercise. In recent explorations of power in mathematics education, the researcher is challenged to deconstruct the existing practices in a way that will reveal how power operates in various educational practices. Through this approach, researchers wish to demonstrate the way in which participants in various practices create different ways of relating to and with mathematics and mathematics education for achieving different goals. From this approach, power is seen as rooted in social interactions, as being in constant movement and as being distributed among the participants in social practices constituting the network of mathematics education practices. This perspective can be termed post-structural and is concerned with power distribution, not power possession[3].

We will now clarify the three perspectives on power in mathematics education practices, and how they are acted out and distributed in people's everyday involvement with mathematics education. The three perspectives on power have emerged from our examination of ways of talking[4] about power in mathematics education research literature and in mathematics education practices outside the research environment. We choose to present the main features of these discourses by playing with a mix of fictional narrative constructions and our supplementary analysis. Such an approach allows us to bring ideas about power and power distribution in mathematics education research in close contact with educational practices and to illustrate through a variety of scenarios the constant interplay between micro and macro levels of practices that characterize the network of mathematics education practices.

2.1   The intrinsic perspective

It is a hot summer day in the northern hemisphere. In a high school mathematics classroom, pupils are doing trigonometry and it's difficult. Only a few seem to engage with the assignment that has just been handed out by the teacher. He is waiting to see how they cope with it before throwing a helping hand to those in trouble. Most of the students are not making much progress. They are having a hard time dealing with the sine and cosine functions and actually only a fraction of them has really understood what the assignment demands. Instead, they are focusing on each other and on people that are not in the classroom right now...

Teacher (thinking): I have to remember to leave the car keys behind for Line, otherwise she won't be able to pick up the kids tomorrow...

Ali (a pupil) is on the verge of texting from his mobile phone....

Teacher: Ali STOP THAT right now or I will confiscate your mobile!

Ali (thinking but saying it all aloud with his eyes): Fuck you, man! Can't you see I'm busy? I have to find some way to join the party on Friday. I won't let Maria be there alone... Ken will be there and...

Teacher (thinking): He is totally and utterly lost when it comes to mathematics. He will never pass the course no matter how much time we put into him from now on. He only disturbs the others. He will never be able to learn mathematics; he's just not got what it takes...

Meanwhile Louise (another pupil) is almost done with the assignment.

Teacher (thinking): But Louise... she has got it right as the first one once again. I should persuade her to do the advanced mathematics next year. Quite unusual for a girl to put this effort into math...

Louise (thinking): Piece of cake! I can't believe the others are so lazy. They don't do anything and exams are just around the corner. I wonder if the exam will have this topic. It's easy!

Ali succeeds in sending his text to the proper destination. He still has no clue about the assignment. It doesn't even enter his mind that it would be possible to solve one single problem with a couple of minutes of hard effort because he tried that years ago and didn't succeed at all; he has never experienced a "well done" or "correct", only red ink on returned assignments that clearly reads *"you just can't do it"*.

Louise finishes, looks around at her classmates, most of whom are still not showing any signs of doing mathematics. She fiddles her pencil around and flips through her textbook to see if she could find some more entertainment. She is also thinking about the party on Friday and whether she will be able to persuade her mum to buy her that cool blue top she so desperately wants.

The teacher walks around and patiently assists the few students showing a bit of interest in the assignment. He then takes a look at Louise's assignment and is once again surprised at her precision and speed.

Later that summer Louise receives yet another set of top grades and decides to continue with advanced mathematics. She has a dream of becoming a medical doctor so she needs the good grades. She wants to be like her dad and continue the family tradition of going through university. Ali gets one of the lowest term grades in the class and it will only add to a number of grades that are equally low in other subjects, reinforcing his experience of being incapable of learning anything. Just like his siblings and parents. This boy was born with the wrong genes...

One widespread perception of the intrinsic positioning of people in relation to mathematics education concerns the idea that, from the outset, different individuals have different capabilities in learning mathematics. Consequently, it is easy to see how power may be distributed in the setting of a mathematics classroom based on the intrinsic capacities of the students. The cards are, so to speak, already dealt before the educational system enters into operation and as a result the role of the educational system can be seen as simply reinforcing what has already been decided by nature.

The intrinsic perspective can be traced back to one of the most famous interpretations of mathematics, namely Plato's (Plato) conception: All individuals have had a glimpse of the world of ideas—including the mathematical ideas—but not everyone has received the same skills from birth to explore it. Most are born with bronze in their soul and they are therefore best suited for the work of the hand. Some have silver-souls and they best fit the organization of the State as warriors. Few are born with gold in their soul and these are the ones who should do the work of the mind in the State. These people should contemplate mathematical ideas and, after training their thinking with mathematics, they should proceed to the even more difficult areas of work in philosophy such as organizing the State and deciding what justice is.

Considering distribution of power from a perspective of intrinsic capacity has much in common with Plato's thoughts. This power distribution is found in the ongoing constructions of who can learn mathematics and who cannot. Actors in mathematics education practices may consciously or unconsciously adhere to these ideas and engage with the students accordingly. They may base their choices of teaching strategies and how to relate to students on grounds of gender, race or intelligence. For example, actors operating from an intrinsic perspective could believe that each human being is born with a specific gene-structure which determines his or her capacity to learn mathematics. The resemblance to Plato's conception is quite obvious and in constructing mathematical practices based on perceptions of intrinsic capacity, teachers, parents, politicians and other decision-makers design and carry out mathematics instruction according to differentiated ideas about students' capabilities. Politicians might want to propose elite schools, believing that less able pupils may hinder the progress of the stronger pupils. Mathematics education, a privileged means of making "the gold in the soul shine", thus becomes a clear arena for the empowerment of some students, thereby contributing to the inclusion and exclusion of individuals in society based on their perceived mathematical capabilities.

Although rarely addressed openly, the perception of power as an intrinsic capacity in mathematics education is not limited to micro relations between teachers and students but can also be located at a political macro level. Shocking examples are found in different places in different historical times. In Nazi Germany mathematics education was organized by the Mathematics Society as an important factor in training the "new powers" for managing the new regime in an appropriate way[5]. In apartheid South Africa, African students were not perceived as being apt for learning mathematics and were therefore systematically excluded. Mathematics education was used as a tool for the "occupation of the mind" of African students[6]. Another contemporary and less dramatic example is the placement of so-called "elite students" in either separate classrooms or special elite schools for what is considered to be the "geniuses" of a generation. In these examples, mathematics education opens/closes doors to the right/wrong groups of students, based on particular traits deemed compatible/incompatible with the learning of mathematics.

This perception of mathematics education practices seems blind to deeper and more contextual explanations about how, and especially why, some pupils and students are incapacitated with regard to the learning of mathematics. It closes the research on mathematics education off from a number of social and cultural perspectives by assuming a power distribution that is natural and pre-existent; for example, the children in a given socio-economic class became acquainted with numbers or engaged with the educational system. This perspective on power distribution in mathematics education removes, to a large extent, real responsibility for students' learning of mathematics from the teachers and other decision makers. The cards are, so to speak, already dealt.

2.2   The technical perspective

We now shift our focus to a Western European television station. A debate program is running live and we listen quietly from the entrance of the studio – right behind the running cameras.

The Minister of Science and Technology: Unless we modernize and restructure our educational system and particularly the technical and scientific subjects in the years to come we will severely damage the nation's competitiveness. We face two major threats in the very near future. One is the increasing number of elderly citizens who will need support and services even though the workforce is reduced. And secondly, increased globalization places new demands on the workforce which has to be educated to compete with the cheap labor in other parts of the world. In the future there just won't be room for uneducated people in the labor market. Work that can be carried out without a higher education will eventually flee the West and be outsourced to countries where wages are lower. So we really need young people to go through higher education, preferably half of the population should have a higher education, and as many as possible within science, technology and engineering.

Interviewer: Globalization will mean high unemployment rates unless we act now?

Minister: We have to evaluate what can be done to ensure that we remain competitive in state-of-the-art science and technology. And we can only ensure this by training our youth in the basic scientific skills. We need to get away from the 1968's small-talk pedagogical methods and start getting serious about teaching our youth the basic skills that can secure our own future as a welfare society with a sound economy and a leading position when it comes to producing and utilizing information and communication technology.

Interviewer: What will become of the young people who have no interest in science and technology?

Opposition leader: As was just mentioned, it is unquestionably necessary to focus on the organization of the educational system. However, with the Government's proposals only the elite will benefit. It will not be possible to educate more young people at universities if entry requirements are continuously increased and the range of different educational offers limited. Not everybody can have an interest in science and technology and it seems crucial not to forget the contributions of the social sciences and the humanities to our welfare state.

Minister: We are simply scoring too low in the international tests on mathematics and science year after year. Unless we strengthen the focus on these subjects our competitiveness and ability to be in the forefront of technological advances will simply disappear.

We quietly leave the studio and head back home. Undoubtedly the educational system is headed for yet another reform strengthening subjects like mathematics and science in the primary schools and technology in higher education in an attempt to secure a sound economy for the State and a high standard of living in the years to come.

In the technical perspective, mathematics is considered a tool or technique for enhancing our lives both as individuals and as members of a society that strives to become richer, and possibly happier too. Mathematics is believed to be an important ingredient in the rational construction of modern societies, an important tool for the control of threats of nature on humans, and a fundamental piece in the advancement of high-tech production in a global market economy. This view is not new. It has been on the go in the Western world —and is expanding to the rest of the globe—since the time of the Sputnik Shock in the 1960's.

Mathematics is powerful and the role of mathematics education is to transfer that power to as many citizens as possible. In this technical perspective, power distribution occurs at both a micro and a macro level. At a micro level, power is distributed through the individual's conscious or unconscious choices and priorities in relation to their educational portfolio. Individuals are continually presented with possibilities and limitations when it comes to learning mathematics. Very often mathematics is not something the individual chooses out of interest but rather because the educational system demands mathematical capacity to pursue a particular prestigious line of education, for example, to be allowed to study medicine, science or engineering[7]. Students are continually encouraged by parents, teachers and through the media about how they could gain from learning mathematics, how mathematics opens up opportunities and how not learning mathematics will inevitably close some important doors.

At the macro level, politicians and educational researchers and planners consider the technical skills of the workforce as a whole. As was illustrated in the narrative above, politicians often point attention to the need for the workforce to be molded and shaped to cope with social needs, such as, in our present time, the rapid changes in the global market economy. To know about mathematics is to be in a powerful position, both for the individual and for society as a whole. Not knowing about mathematics, on the other hand, is considered a less advantageous position whereby power is surrendered to other actors, for example, people, companies or societies with greater technical capacity in mathematics.

In mathematics education research the idea of power being distributed according to technical skills is widely supported. Here we present an example that clearly reflects these views. In the *Handbook of International Research in Mathematics Education,* English (2002) invites contributing authors to think about the issue of access to powerful mathematical ideas. In the book, English gives meaning to the term powerful, in the following way:

> [...] the lack of access to a quality education—in particular, a quality mathematics education—is likely to limit human potential and individual economic opportunity. Given the importance of mathematics in the ever-changing global market, there will be increased demands for workers to possess more advanced and future-oriented mathematical and technological skills. Together with the rapid changes in the workplace and in daily living, the global market has alerted us to rethink the mathematical experiences we provide for our students in terms of content, approaches to learning, ways of assessing learning, and ways of increasing access to quality learning. (p. 4)

She supplements her explanation in the following manner:

> Students are facing a world shaped by increasing complex, dynamic, and powerful systems of information and ideas. As future members of the workforce, students will need to be able to interpret and explain structurally complex systems, to reason in mathematically diverse ways, and to use sophisticated equipment and resources. [...] Today's mathematics curricula must broaden their goals to include key concepts and processes that will maximize students' opportunities for success in the 21st century. These include, among others statistical reasoning, probability, algebraic thinking, mathematical modeling, visualizing, problem solving and posing, number sense, and dealing with technological change. (p. 8)

In these extracts, English highlights the power of mathematics in relation to technology and development. The power to ensure such technical capacity lies with the practices of mathematics education. The issue of exclusion is brought forward: Not all individuals have access to quality mathematics education and, consequently, they do not have the same life opportunities as others who have received appropriate mathematics education. The former will simply lack the skills—the mathematical know-how and techniques—that are essential for being able to cope with working in a highly technological society. This is micro-level reasoning about the powerful skills an individual can obtain through mathematics education. The workforce as a whole, however, is also addressed with a special focus on the connection between a global market economy and the mathematical skills required to succeed in it.

Following this line of reasoning, mathematics education is directly linked to competition. Through mathematics education, power is distributed to individuals who battle to acquire the best skills in mathematics with the aim to succeed in life. Who can finish the assignment first? Who has the best mathematical (technical) skills for the job? The competition among individuals, however, is mirrored by a fierce competition among schools and even among nations. Schools are, to an increasing extent, being graded according to the level of mathematical skills their students demonstrate on exams and national tests. Nations use test results to compete in the international arena and political decisions about the educational structure are often based on this competition. International tests on mathematical skills are frequently linked to the economic wellbeing of the nation. Poor test results are interpreted as a clear sign that educational reforms are needed. Governments invest money in various developmental initiatives and in more research with the hope of improving a situation perceived to have potentially catastrophic economic consequences for a country[8]. These scary scenarios influence the distribution of power at all levels, including decision-making regarding mathematics education from the perspective of politicians in parliament to the organization of school resources and teaching capacities.

It can be seen that the technical perspective on power distribution in mathematics education practices is clearly different from the intrinsic perspective. It does not see mathematics as something in which only some human beings were predestined to excel. Rather it suggests that, in principle, everyone can and should learn and acquire mathematical skills, thereby obtaining the power that lies inherently in these trainable competencies. It is often forgotten, however, that not everybody can win when power is distributed through competition. Some individuals will eventually lose and some nations most certainly will too.

2.3   The structural inequality perspective

A teacher is in a three-day seminar on mathematics and social equity. The main issue being addressed is whether pupils' social background plays a role in determining their performance in mathematics and their advance and participation in the educational system in general. This is considered to be a challenge for democracy and society.

Mathematics education researcher: Mathematics functions as a vantage point in to-day's society. It is not like some were born good mathematicians and some were born bad mathematicians. And it is equally false to assume that the main purpose of mathematics education is to support our competitiveness in the global economy. If we made that our goal we would need education which is much more focused on the business world and not so much on the generation and regeneration of our cultural fundamental values, beliefs and customs. No! Mathematics education plays the role of maintaining a clear stratification between social classes: working class, middle class, upper class etc. Why does this pose a problem to society? It is a problem be-cause we believe ourselves to live in a democratic society where every citizen is given equal rights and opportunities to live out their ambitions and desires. In class divided societies, people from social A teams and B teams will have their social class reinforced by the educational system—in particular through the most abstract and speculative discipline: mathematics. They will only, under very special circum-stances, be able to break with their social inheritance. We will not obtain equity in the mathematics classroom until we obtain it in the surrounding society!

Teacher (thinking): That's true but we always try to work with the parents in order to ensure the inclusion of the children from under-privileged homes. What else can we do?

Other teacher (discussing): I can see your point about the classes but I think it is a bit old fashioned? One of the challenges I face in my daily work is dealing with im-migrant students. They are often the students who need special attention in everyday mathematics education. They have trouble with language, with the learning style; we try to encourage them, and so on.

Mathematics researcher: There may be different types of lower classes in today's society as compared to the 20th century division of classes according to socio-economic status. People coming from different cultural backgrounds—I can only begin to imagine the implications of this in the classroom, but unless these students are also given access to mathematical knowledge and skills, they will have funda-mental problems with participating in a democracy on equal terms with other citi-zens, I should say.

The structural inequality perspective on power distribution addresses the issue of the participation of large segments of the population in mathematics education practices in relation to the larger social structures in which such participation takes place. The activity of giving meaning to mathematics education practices, in different sites and scenarios and by different actors, is connected with broader social processes through which people are classified as included or excluded. The power associated with the possession of mathematical competencies is distributed—willingly or unwillingly—following existing social divisions on the grounds of class, gender, culture, ethnicity, race and religion, among others. This perspective is often concerned with how researchers, teachers, policy makers, students themselves and other actors within the network of mathematics education practices construct new (or reinforce old) structures of exclusion in and through the teaching and learning of mathematics.

The work of Marilyn Frankenstein exemplifies some of the main characteristics of this perspective. Frankenstein (1995) writes:

> So, I argue that mathematics education in general, and mathematics in particular, will become more equitable as the class structure in society becomes more equitable. Since I also contend that working-class consciousness is an important component in changing class inequities, developing that consciousness during teaching could contribute to the goal of ensuring equity in mathematics education. [...] I think that mathematical disempowerment impedes an understanding of how our society is structured with respect to class interests. (p. 165)

In this passage, Frankenstein acknowledges social class divisions and how mathematics education is immersed in it. Mathematics and mathematics education cannot be equitable practices since they are implicated in class stratification. The role of adopting a critical stance towards this situation, which is not frequently recognized by, for example teachers or researchers adhering to the intrinsic or the technical perspective, is promoting class-consciousness and awareness in students. Mathematical knowledge and competencies are essential to unraveling deep structural inequalities. Students can be empowered through mathematics teaching and learning that promotes such awareness.

Another example of the structural inequality perspective is to be found in the political challenge posed by ethnomathematics to the reign of Western, white mathematics. A fundamental critique by D'Ambrosio (1993) is the uncontested imposition of mathematics as the privileged form of human thought. Because of its high status in the Western world, mathematics "is positioned as a promoter of a certain model of exercising power through knowledge" (D'Ambrosio, 1993, p. 24, authors' translation). Through the historic development of the West—which has a well-documented impact on the transformation of people in other parts of the world—mathematics has imposed the rationality of the dominant power over other ways of thinking and expression in non-Western, indigenous, colonized cultures. Powell (2002) also highlights how ethnomathematics departs from forms of thought that privilege "European, male, heterosexual, racist, and capitalistic interests and values" (p. 17). This important critique of mathematics as a tool of ideological domination is incorporated into research and into the pedagogical proposals derived from it.

As exemplified above, the structural inequality perspective assumes a divided society based on unequal gender, race, ethnicity, ability, culture and class positioning—which differs from the kind of global, market society to which English (2002) refers. At a macro level, the general inequalities in society are reproduced through the ideological apparatus of the State. At a micro level, inequality is maintained in and through several practices and sites, particularly in schools and, within them, mathematics classrooms. Power is seen as the capacity of the owners of productive, social or cultural resources to promote their interests through the alienation of other groups from such resources. As a result, a situation of oppression and dispossession of the latter is created. The "excluded", however, may resist in an attempt to regain control over resources in order to pursue their own interests. The initiatives of critical people to help the excluded break their alienation and, in doing so, demand a space in the distribution of power are also important.

In the arena of mathematics education practices, empowerment through mathematics can be seen as the capacity that an individual gains, via the learning of mathematics, to see the way in which mathematics operates in society and perpetuates an unequal class distribution. Learning mathematics can be an element in breaking with injustice. Mathematical disempowerment, on the other hand, contributes to the general alienation of people as part of the operation of the capitalist system. Empowerment, though, is not a result of an individual enlightening process but rather a social process in which the disempowered are assisted by others in order to gain consciousness.

Although the technical and structural inequality perspectives view society and the misdistribution of resources in different ways, their views on power do not seem to differ significantly. The idea that the learning of mathematics provides students with a capacity to act in the social world is shared between these two perspectives, although the justifications for the relevance and the utility of mathematics are quite different. These two perspectives also differ in their view of the kind of actions that can be undertaken with the use of mathematics. While in the technical perspective mathematics is seen as a positive constructive tool, the structural inequality perspective views mathematics as a tool that is used in destructive, but also constructive (as a result of resistance) ways.

3.   THE THREE PERSPECTIVES IN RESEARCH

In this chapter, we have shown how power and power distribution can be viewed from three different perspectives in the network of mathematics education practices. Each of these perspectives sheds light on the dynamics of power distribution at both micro and macro levels and each perspective contains its own narrow scope for analyzing practices of mathematics education. In these concluding remarks we wish to point to the way in which each perspective can be linked to the practice of research in mathematics education. Each perspective leads to different research possibilities and consequently distributes particular powers and responsibilities to the researchers involved.

From an intrinsic perspective, mathematical skills are strongly linked to the individual as something one may or may not be able to acquire depending on particular traits and characteristics. Mathematics education here provides the framework for nurturing these skills for different groups of people. In this perspective, mathematics education research would naturally focus on understanding the difference in conditions offered by nature in acquiring mathematical skills. This could be, for example, research on intelligence or genetics.

In the technical perspective, the learning of mathematics can be considered not only as the individual's acquisition of a particular skill for his/her own use, but also as a skill residing in society. At a national level, mathematical skills contribute to improving competitiveness and economic interests of the nation. This view naturally leads to research on teaching strategies and learning environments, with a direct obligation to contribute to the enhancement and effectiveness of these strategies and environments.

In the structural inequality perspective, it is emphasized that mathematics education can play both a constructive and destructive role in society. This is evident when mathematics education is utilized in order to promote equality or, on the contrary, when it favors particular social groups with the consequence of marginalizing other groups. Research from this perspective revolves around inclusion strategies of groups who are perceived to be marginalized; for example, students of poor socio-economic backgrounds, women and immigrants.

Research in the three perspectives can, each in their own way, be related to the distribution of power in the network of mathematics education practices. Research will promote certain perspectives on mathematics education and downscale other perspectives. In doing so, research is directly contributing to the continuous reshaping of the landscape of power distribution in mathematics education practices.

The question remains, however, whether the three perspectives cover the landscape of power distribution. Do these perspectives merely represent traditional research paradigms and, therefore, are rarely challenged? Is the landscape already being challenged, albeit indirectly, by the setup of this chapter? And what would alternative perspectives for viewing power distribution in the network of mathematics education and research practices look like if not the intrinsic, technical or structural inequality perspectives?

REFERENCES

D'Ambrosio, U. (1993). *Etnomatemática. Arte ou técnica de explicar e conhecer.* Sao Paulo: Ática.

de Freitas, E. (2004). Plotting intersections along the political axis: The interior voice of dissenting mathematics teachers. *Educational Studies in Mathematics, 55*, 259-274.

English, L. D. (Ed.). (2002). *Handbook of international research in mathematics education.* Mahwah, N.J.: Lawrence Erlbaum.

Frankenstein, M. (1995). Equity in mathematics education: Class in the world outside the class. In E. Fennema & L. Adajian (Eds.), *New directions for equity in mathematics education* (pp. 165-190). Cambridge: Cambridge University.

Johansen, L. Ø. (2006). *Hvorfor skal voksne tilbydes undervisning i matematik? – en diskursanalytisk tilgang til begrundelsesproblemet.* Unpublished PhD Thesis, Aalborg University, Aalborg.

Khuzwayo, H. (2001). *Selected views and critical perspectives: An account of mathematics education in South Africa from 1948-1994.*, Aalborg University, Aalborg.

Mehrtens, H. (1993). The social system of mathematics and national socialism: A survey. In S. Restivo, J. P. Van Bendegem & R. Fischer (Eds.), *Math worlds. Philosophical and social studies of mathematics and mathematics education* (pp. 219-246). Albany (USA): State University of New York Press.

Mellin-Olsen, S. (1987). *The politics of mathematics education.* Dordrecht: Kluwer.

Plato. The Republic (Vol. The Classics Archive): MIT Media Lab http://www.classics.mit.edu/plato/republic.html.

Powell, A. (2002). Ethnomathematics and the challenges of racism in mathematics education. In P. Valero & O. Skovsmose (Eds.), *Proceedings of the third international conference on mathematics education and society* (pp. 15-28). Copenhagen: Center for Research in Learning Mathematics.

Skovsmose, O., & Valero, P. (2002). Democratic access to powerful mathematical ideas. In L. D. English (Ed.), *Handbook of international research in mathematics education. Directions for the 21st century.* (pp. 383-407). Mahwah, NJ: Erlbaum.

Valero, P. (2002). *Reform, democracy and matahematics education. Towards a socio-political frame for understanding change in the organization of secondary school mathematics.* Unpublished PhD Thesis, Danish University of Education, Copenhagen.

Valero, P. (2007). A socio-political look at equity in the school organization of mathematics education. *Zentralblatt fur Didaktik der Mathematik.*

Walshaw, M. (2004). *Mathematics education within the postmodern.* Greenwich, Conn.: IAP Information Age Pub.

---

[1] The notion of network of mathematics education practices has been discussed in Valero (2002, 2007)

[2] For details on the discussion of different views of powerful mathematical ideas see Skovsmose and Valero (2002).

[3] For examples of this trend see de Freitas (2004) and the different chapters in Walshaw (2004).

[4] The expression "ways of talking" refers to the set of ideas and constructed meanings that different actors in the network of mathematics education practices express, implicitly or explicitly, about what mathematics education is and what it involves.

[5] See Mehrtens (1993).

[6] See Khuzwayo (2001) for an analysis of the role of mathematics education in South Africa from 1984 to 1994.

[7] Mellin-Olsen (1987) presents a discussion of instrumental reasons for choosing to engage in mathematical learning.

[8] Just as an example, the results of international comparative studies such OECD's Second International Adult Literacy Survey (SIALS) motivated the reform of the vocational training of adults in Denmark with the aim of providing a better chance for adults with a short, basic education to improve their numeracy skills (Johansen, 2006).

A LANDSCAPE OF POWER DISTRIBUTION
A Response to Christensen, Stentoft & Valero

Ole Ravn Christensen, Diana Stentoft and Paola Valero
Aalborg University, Denmak

Diana: Three perspectives on power have been outlined but they don't quite qualify as the full story about this issue. I think the best way to put it is to say that they are analytical constructions. We could have chosen many other perspectives that would have presented different aspects of the distribution of power in the network of mathematics education practices.

Ole: For example we could have structured the article from the perspective of different types of agents involved in mathematics education: a teacher, a pupil, a researcher, an educational policy maker, a curriculum designer etc.

Diana: All in all, they are three somewhat arbitrary perspectives but, nonetheless, not chosen out of the blue. They are grounded in very strong narratives about power distribution in the network of mathematics education practices and they are often found in contemporary mathematics education research. The first one—the intrinsic perspective—could be considered as a kind of anti-contextual perspective that basically interprets the actual power distribution among individuals based on non-social mechanisms. The philosophy inherent in this perspective raises deep issues about our cultural perception of mathematics and the practices of mathematics education. It favors a perception of mathematics where the world of mathematics is distanced and independent of the human social sphere. Hence, the mathematics education practices need not be too concerned with the social or cultural background that students bring with them into the classroom, or the micro processes that take place in the classroom. I think this perspective dramatically limits the potential for understanding why some people have an easy time doing mathematics and why some struggle all their lives.

Paola: I agree. In contrast, it is interesting to see how the technical and the structural inequality perspectives are less static in their portrayal of who can learn mathematics and who cannot. They both present the idea that anybody could ideally become fluent in mathematics and, in their dynamic approach, they rely on the idea of progress. Both perspectives adhere to the idea that mathematics can be a liberating tool for humans when faced with threats from nature or suppression; that mathematics as part of the technological core of our society will ensure a better society all together. 'Better technology equals a better social sphere.' This is questionable to say the least. It is the idea that von Wright has termed "The Myth of Progress"[1].

Ole: The technical and the structural inequality perspectives could be thought of as modern frameworks for understanding mathematics education practices. Either one believes that through mathematics people can be given a tool for bettering their lives or one believes that some are given this tool while others are excluded from acquiring it. I could imagine an alternative perspective characterized by less reliance on the progress followed by acquiring this tool. It would transparently reflect the goals of mathematics education and favor an interpretation of mathematics that focused on its social origin.

Paola: Thomas Popkewitz[2] has offered some interesting insights relating to a postmodern position for thinking about mathematics education. He talks about the mathematics curriculum as an ordering practice analogous to creating a uniform system of taxes or developing a uniform system of measurement that works as an inscription device, making the child legible and administrable. From this position, the mathematics curriculum embodies rules and standards of reason that order how judgments are made and conclusions drawn so that the fields of existence are made manageable and predictable. Also, Popkewitz quite agrees that mathematics education carries the narrative of progress in a global knowledge society.

Diana: One could say that from Popkewitz' position, mathematics education is a social practice which, together with other sets of practices, contributes to the governance of citizens and their possible participation, or exclusion from participation, in the social world. This governance is carried out through the instauration of systems of reason, which are socially constructed and accepted forms of characterizing and organizing the world. These systems frame what is possible, desirable and appropriate and therefore what constitute the basis of classification of individuals in a society. The teaching of mathematics and the mathematics curriculum are not exclusively devices and processes in charge of the transmission of mathematical knowledge.

Mathematics education operates as part of broader mechanisms which determine what is valued, what is right and what is normal in society.

Ole: Popkewitz' formulations, then, can be characterized as being representative of an alternative perspective on the distribution of power, namely one that emphasizes the social dimensions of mathematics education. This perspective could be supported by the later Wittgenstein's conception of mathematics when he talks about mathematics as measure, not thing measured[3]. He persistently pursues the idea of mathematics as normative rules – mathematics is on a pedestal because it outlines ways of reasoning that cannot be rationally questioned once they are accepted as proved. In this Wittgensteinian framework, there is only our use of the signs of mathematics that determines their meaning. Mathematics is a language game; one we are gradually socialized into over many years as we train in both in-school and out of-school practices.

Diana: I think Wittgenstein's concept of language game is a possible framework for understanding the distribution of power in the network of mathematics education practices. We could think about 'mathematics education' as a network of language games that overlap each other in a complex pattern – they share family resemblances in Wittgenstein's terminology[4]. The language games inherent in the field of 'mathematics education' all share the condition that they are open-ended scenes for social interaction. A fundamental aspect of a language game is the continual development and power struggle through every utterance about how the game is to be played. Every utterance or action is a move in the game that changes the game – sometimes only infinitesimally and at other times the change is radical. We play with the rules of the language games of which we are part. People position themselves in the game, with power eventually being distributed among the players.

Paola: If we return to Popkewitz' perspective, his ideas are actually highly inspired by Foucault's analysis of the microphysics of power in modern societies[5]. I think this supplements Wittgenstein's basic arguments about how our language and interaction works well by focusing more directly on the notion of power. In this view, power is a relational capacity of social actors to position themselves in different situations, through the use of various resources. Such a definition implies that power is not an intrinsic and permanent characteristic of social actors; instead, power is *relational* and in constant transformation. The transformation does not necessarily happen directly as a consequence of open struggle and resistance, but through the participation of actors in social practices and in the construction of discourses. In this sense, power is not openly overt but subtly exercised.

Ole: This also means that power is both a constructive and a destructive force, and that this duality is always present in any social situation. When power is defined in these terms, it becomes possible to enter into a very fine-grained analysis of how mathematics and mathematics education are used in particular discourses as well as the effects of those discourses on people's lives. This definition could possibly bring new insights to research because it finds resonance not only with the advance of postmodern ideas in education[6], but also with new possibilities for reinterpreting many of the theories that have been at the core of the discipline of mathematics education.

Paola: In the book *Mathematics Education within the Postmodern*[7], there is a series of articles adopting similar perspectives on power. Hardy, for example, presents a toolkit (a series of notions coming from Foucault[8]) which has helped her see how power is exercised in mathematics classrooms in the relationship between students, teacher and school mathematics activities. Through the examination of a video excerpt from teacher training materials published by the UK government as part of the *National Numeracy Strategy*, she presents an interpretation of the interaction between teacher and students in which the teacher's pedagogical techniques are in operation.

Diana: Ahh, I remember that one. From Hardy's perspective, the teacher creates a situation of surveillance in which students' actions are exposed to the control of the teacher, who publicly approves and disapproves their answers to calculations. Students are not only "answering" to the teacher's demands, but they are being identified with an answer and are learning to identify themselves with an accepted (or rejected) behavior and thinking. The teacher's way of managing the classroom discourse plays with the double strategy of individualizing (that is, making noticeable in public an individual action) and totalizing (that is, hiding individuals within a collectivity) through her constant distinction between particular students (with proper name) and the collectivity of the class (the "we" referring to "all" in the classroom). This strategy is used in systematic ways. Individualization is used to publicly correct wrong answers and to reward right answers, thereby creating a clear differentiation between those who cannot and those who can do the mathematics. Totalization, on the other hand, is used to give a collective legitimacy to what the teacher considers to be appropriate behavior. I think Hardy's analysis illustrates that the power dynamics of a classroom go deeper than the expected mathematical empowerment assumed by the views of power found in the intrinsic, the technical and the structural inequality perspectives that we have presented in our analysis.

Diana: Well, now we have discussed some general perspectives on power distribution in mathematics education practices, but we still have not addressed how the landscape of power distribution affects our practice as mathematics education researchers and how mathematics education research is related to other practices of mathematics education. If we cannot depart from only one perspective exclusively such as the intrinsic, the technical or the structural inequality perspective, and if we are to maintain an active acknowledgement of the complexity of power distribution in the landscape of mathematics education practices, how do we engage in research and how can we interpret our own roles as researchers as part of the complexity of power distribution?

Ole: From a postmodern position, research and the researcher can never be neutral or detached, standing outside the mathematics education practices peering inside. Power is inevitably distributed one way or another when the practice of mathematics education research meets with the practices of, for example, teaching or curriculum design. Tamsin Meaney[9] has used Foucault's idea of power as embedded in the relationships of social actors in order to analyze her role as a white expert consultant developing mathematics curriculum while working with a Maŏri community, socially positioned as a disadvantaged community. In her analysis of the changing positions that both her and the community acquired during the inquiry process, she highlights that what came to be considered as valid knowledge and truth was deeply dependent on the way in which the relationship among the project participants evolved. She argues that power fluctuated among participants in their differential use of strategies to argue for, and give meaning to, the knowledge being constructed in their relationship.

Paola: Actually, several scholars[10] have recently argued that an analysis of power in these terms is not restricted to the practices of teaching and learning where school mathematics is implicated. The analysis should also extend to the way in which research is produced. Researchers, in their privileged position as active constructors of knowledge (and with it, of discourses about what is valid) participate in the consolidation of certain systems of reason. As Popkewitz argues[11], "intellectual traditions of research construct ways of thinking and ordering action, conceive of results and intern and enclose the possibilities imagined". In this sense, researchers' discursive practices are not a neutral search for truth but an active engagement in opening/closing possibilities for phrasing and giving meaning to the social world. Therefore, this view opens for an examination of the way in which researchers are also implicated in the social distribution of power.

Diana: When considering how research and researchers are part of the web of power distribution in the network of mathematics education practices, I cannot help thinking about how we can easily be instrumental in establishing specific perspectives and imaginaries about mathematics and mathematics education. For example, if we only address power distribution from a technical perspective, we perpetuate a perspective that does not address the destructive powers that are also associated with mathematics education. Simultaneously, we can be influenced in our research by other mathematics education practices and social constructions. We should never underestimate our own roles in influencing mathematics education practices through our research. Is it not exactly a tool for that purpose—to influence practice?

Paola: So in other words, we're sitting here now—three researchers of mathematics education talking to other researchers in the field—and it appears crucial to always remember that we too are part of the network of mathematics education practices. Take for example this response: what is it we wish to achieve? Are we not trying to influence the way in which others think about mathematics education and the distribution of power? More specifically, are we not trying to influence the way in which others 'read' and interpret what *we* think about mathematics education and the distribution of power?

Ole: I think this is what every researcher is trying to do. Mathematics education research is about constructing standpoints or perspectives on power distribution. In a way, this is an ethical challenge that is always part of the research agenda. It could be thought of as always taking seriously the rather philosophical question: Why is mathematics considered a powerful enterprise in Western culture?

REFERENCES

Cotton, T. & Hardy, T. (2004). Problematising culture and discourse for mathematics education research. Defining the issues; tools for research. In P. Valero & R. Zevenbergen (Eds.). *Researching the socio-political dimensions of mathematics education: Issues of power in theory and methodology* (pp. 85-103*)*. Dordrecht: Kluwer.

Foucault, M. (1972). *The archaeology of knowledge* ([1st American ed.). New York: Pantheon Books.

Foucault, M., & Faubion, J. D. (2000). *Power.* New York: New Press; Distributed by W.W. Norton.

Meaney, T. (2004). So what's power got to do with it? In M. Walshaw (Ed.), *Mathematics education within the postmodern* (pp. 181-200). Greenwich, USA: Information Age.

Popkewitz, T. (2002). Whose heaven and whose redemption? The alchemy of the mathematics curriculum to save (please check one or all of the following: (a) the economy, (b) democracy, (c) the nation, (d) human rights, (d) the welfare state, (e) the individual). In P. Valero & O. Skovsmose (Eds.), *Proceedings of the Third International MES Conference,* 2nd ed., Copenhagen: Centre for Research in Learning Mathematics.

Popkewitz, T. (2004). School subjects, the politics of knowledge, and the projects of intellectuals in change. In P. Valero & R. Zevenbergen (Eds.), *Researching the socio-political dimensions of mathematics education: Issues of power in theory and methodology* (pp. 251-268). Dordrecht: Kluwer.

Popkewitz, T. & Brennan, M. (Eds.) (1998). *Foucault's challenge. Discourse, knowledge and power in education.* New York: Teachers College.

Valero, P. (2004). Postmodernism as an attitude of critique to dominant mathematics education research. In M. Walshaw (Ed.), *Mathematics education within the postmodern* (pp. 35-54). Greenwich, USA: Information Age.

von Wright, G. H. (1994). Myten om fremskidtet. Munksgaard-Rosinante, Copenhagen.

Walshaw, M. (Ed.) (2004). *Mathematics education within the postmodern.* Greenwich, USA: Information Age.

Wittgenstein, L. (1978). *Remarks on the Foundations of Mathematics* (3rd edition). Oxford: Basil Blackwell Oxford.

Wittgenstein, L. (1997). *Philosophical Investigations.* Oxford: Blackwell Publishers, Ltd.

---

[1] See von Wright (1994).

[2] Popkewitz (2002, p. 35).

[3] Wittgenstein (1978).

[4] Wittgenstein (1997).

[5] See for example Foucault (1972) and Foucault and Faubion (2000).

[6] See for example Popkewitz and Brennan (1998).

[7] Walshaw (2004).

[8] Foucault (1972).

[9] Meaney (2004).

[10] Meaney (2004), as well as Cotton and Hardy (2004) and Valero (2004).

[11] Popkewitz (2004, p. 259).

LIVING THE LANDSCAPE WITH/IN A THRICE-TOLD TALE
A Response to Christensen, Stentoft & Valero

Kathleen Nolan
University of Regina

In high school mathematics class-rooms, I could always do a math problem **justice**, and then carry on talking so as not to appear too nerdy and 'mathy' to the other students in the class. It was as if I had this **intrinsic** ability to do math, almost without thinking.

In fact, I used to doodle in the margins a lot, as a way to pass the time once my assigned work was done in math class. My rather displeased math teacher felt it her duty (as a nun guiding the spiritual well-being of all Catholic girls I suppose) to inform me that such doodling in my books indicated that I would grow up to be a **destructive** person. **How does she know?**

As a high school mathematics teacher, I encountered substantial resistance when I gave problem solving challenges to my students. "It's **just us**, Ms. Nolan, and we're not very good at math."

If I focused on problem solving in context, students often felt they were missing the necessary **technical** skills and would give up, frustrated. If I focused on the skills, students would ask: "When will I ever **use** this?"

How can I answer such a question? Which is more **destructive** to their image of math and their interest in learning the subject: to

My preservice high school mathematics teachers think they are, indeed, very good at math. Transformations of their image of math and what it means to know (in) math are generally not on their minds; they experienced success (in math) and they are certain they know how to help others experience success (in math).

"Teaching Math for Social **Justice**" (as the curriculum course is entitled) has become a meaningless catch-all phrase, serving only to baffle students as they bemoan the **usefulness** and relevance of social issues in math lessons. After all, they say, mathematics is a socially and politically neutral

That wasn't my take on things. I thought I was quite adept at balancing my mathematics class life— I could execute procedures mindlessly *and*, at the same time, doodle. I knew exactly *what* rule or procedure to apply and *when* (following along with the appropriate page in the textbook, of course). And that's **more** than I could say about most of my friends and fellow grade 12 classmates. For them, it seemed the cards were, so to speak, already dealt.

Anyway, I thought the doodling was a sign that I had an artistic side to me, since I yearned to become a photographer. In grade 12, however, my guidance counselor confidently guided me elsewhere, saying: "You have such high marks in math and physics... why not put them to good **use** in university?!" I did not **resist** his advice and even began to believe myself that my ninety-something average in math and physics would surely "go to waste" if I did not use it. It is as if I thought I would be taking photographs of the ink fading on my report cards.

say 'well, actually, never' or to say 'oh, everywhere'? **How do I know** where/if they will ever use it?

I spent so much time and energy trying to dismantle the image that math was all about memorizing procedures that I don't think I even noticed that most students preferred the procedural approach. It was what they were used to. Until now, their math experiences were mainly characterized by being told exactly *what* rule or procedure to apply and *when* (following along with the appropriate page in the textbook, of course). They **resisted** my efforts to turn it into something **more** than that. To them—like it or not, able to do it or not—this is what it was to do math.

Perhaps even more disheartening to me was the realization that they were buying into the notion that as long as they could perform the math procedures, doors would be open for them. The knowledge market is competitive, with both winners and losers, but if they can

subject. Studying **structural inequalities** belongs elsewhere, not in math class. Perhaps, if there is time left over once the curriculum is covered, they will **resist** less— but for now there are more important content matters at hand.

Maybe it is my **de(con)structive** tendencies that drive my desires to empower them to start questioning and doubting our mark(et) driven society. How can I get them to think more deeply about the oppression that is experienced by so many students who face the oppressive discourses inherent in preaching math-for-all yet teaching math-for-the-few? But really, **how do they know** about what they have not experienced?

How many of my white, mostly middle class students have experienced, first hand, alienation and exclusion from the interests of the dominant group? *Not many.* But how many of these same students have experienced the invisible and subtle hand that reaches

In retrospect, I wonder if this guidance counselor (along with my math and science teachers who supported his 'guidance') had read Plato... surely they saw 'gold in my soul', as they banished this doodling artist to the margins.

And there,
all around me,
are the haves/have-nots
caught in dichot...
o my
how to (re)solve this one?

show their 'I-took-math' card at the door, they could begin a journey toward becoming richer... and possibly happier too.

And there,
before me,
are the haves/have- nots
caught in dichot...
o my
how to (re)think this one?

into classrooms to shield their eyes from seeing the destructive role that mathematics can, and does, play? *Many more, I'm thinking.*

And there,
with/in me,
are the haves/have-nots
caught in dichot...
o my
how to (re)view this one?

Chapter 7

MATHEMATICS EDUCATION
IN A KNOWLEDGE MARKET

Developing functional and critical competencies

Ole Skovsmose
Aalborg University

Abstract: In this chapter, I address some of the conceptual uncertainties related to the
              field of mathematics education. First, I discuss the notions of mathematics and
              knowledge in action. Next, I discuss mathematics in action as a particular ex-
              ample of knowledge in action. Mathematics in action plays a particular role in
              the knowledge society. This brings me to consider mathematical competencies
              in the knowledge market. I raise the question of what it could mean for compe-
              tencies and action to be functional or critical. Had I been able to answer this
              question, I would have provided a clarifying characteristic of what could be
              the meaning of critical mathematics education. However, my chapter ends
              with me being in doubt, as throughout the whole analysis, I have drawn heav-
              ily on unstable, run-away concepts.

Key words: mathematics in action; knowledge market; prescription readiness; functional
              competencies; critical competencies.

1.   INTRODUCTION

Concepts run away in all possible directions. When one tries to get hold
of concepts like knowledge, action, and learning, it appears that the notions
through which we try to provide clarification are at least as complex as those
concepts we are attempting to clarify. Thus, an exploration of the meaning of
empowerment easily brings us into an exploration of equality, equity, citizenship, dialogue, etc.[1] We could try to avoid dealing with run-away concepts, but I find it important to address such concepts.[2] The point is not to try

to keep them on a short leash through a simplifying and apparently manageable definition, but to deal with them in their vitality.

When grappling with the purpose and substance of mathematics education, it is important to recognise that each attempt to grasp the relevant concepts must also acknowledge their run-away nature. In this chapter, I address some of the conceptual uncertainties related to the field of mathematics education. I try to indicate ways in which these run-away notions coalesce to constitute particular subject positions or competencies in learners. I focus on the evolving connections between mathematics as a school discipline and mathematics as a form of agency. I use the term *mathematics in action* to characterize the latter, and I trace the ways in which this form of action is taken up and re-iterated in the knowledge market.

The issues discussed in this chapter are framed by the distinction between being functional and being critical. One could suggest that a student with functional competence would almost 'automatically' fit into a given work practice. A student with critical competence, on the other hand, might raise questions about the particular practice and reflect on the practices in which he or she participates. In general, reflection is a characteristic of being critical, while rule following is a characteristic of being functional. But what does 'reflective' mean, and how can one think of 'rule following'? The meanings of these expressions are rapidly running away from us, especially as the distinction itself between functional and critical is in play. Furthermore, actions and competencies intersect in both the critical and functional field, and in our understanding of the notion of *mathematics in action*, we must grapple with the political context of all educational discourse.

Many others have struggled with the distinction between being functional and being critical. Paulo Freire, for example, contrasted a functional 'banking education' with an education oriented towards 'conscientização'.[3] He wanted to propose what it could mean for an educational process to become critical and political. Throughout this chapter, I will struggle with the notions of 'being functional' and 'being critical' in the context of mathematics education.

2. MATHEMATICS

We are accustomed to thinking of mathematics as a well-defined term. Many clear-cut definitions of mathematics have been formulated: It is a set of tautologies, as suggested by logicism; or it is the science of formal systems, as suggested by formalism. A clear delineation of mathematics was also basic to the form of structuralism inspired by Bourbaki, who pointed to certain 'mother structures' of mathematics.[4]

Despite an ongoing attempt by some to formulate an ultimate definition of mathematics, many educators and researchers have more recently turned to ethnomathematics, pointing out the mathematical features in a wide variety of possible work practices: house construction, carpenter work, weaving, accounting, banking, etc.[5] With this new understanding comes an awareness that mathematics might be defined differently in different contexts. Mathematics can be found in diverse procedures for decision making, whether the procedures have to do with medicine, management, economy, or war. Mathematics can be integrated with tools and instruments, the computer being only one example. Several possible kinds of everyday practices seem to include mathematics-based technology as well. We might claim that there is mathematics everywhere (Skovsmose, 2005).

This is at least one way of looking at things. One can also claim that the whole procedure of seeing mathematics everywhere does not say much about mathematics, nor about all these practices where mathematics is found. Instead it tells of the people who see mathematics everywhere and the interests they share (not the least of which is promoting mathematics education as a research field). Naturally, there is no privileged position from which one can argue or counter argue with respect to such controversies, but we can at least make the following observation: Whatever the case may be, mathematics is far from being a well-defined term. We cannot provide an unambiguous definition of mathematics that could settle controversies regarding to what degree a practice might include mathematics. Seeing or not seeing mathematics everywhere is an attitude established through discourses which include interpretations of mathematics. A restricted definition of mathematics ensures that mathematics can appear a rather pure and detached science, while a broad definition makes it possible to see mathematics as part of a variety of practices. Even mathematics is a run-away concept.

Mathematics is not a specific and well-defined parcel of knowledge, marked by a clear-cut conception of truth. But as any other form of knowledge, it is complex and confused. I will explore this point in the two following steps: First I will talk about *knowledge in action* and then *mathematics in action*.

2.1 Knowledge in action

Let me start with the classic definition of knowledge, which was indicated by Plato in the dialogue *Theaetetus*. According to this, knowledge is justified, true belief. The definition connects the notion of knowledge directly to the notion of truth. We can only know something that is true. This observation was also made by René Descartes, who applied a method of universal doubt, and in this way he eliminated from the stock of assumed knowledge whatever could be doubted, i.e. what might not be true. After applying this all-sweeping doubt, one single statement remained, impossible to doubt. And from this axiom, *cogito, ergo sum*, Descartes deduced what he considered to be genuine knowledge: a body of eternal truths.[6] In this way, throughout the Western tradition, the notion of knowledge has been shackled to the notion of truth.

Unfortunately, truth itself is not such a reliable concept, and has been seen to run away from even the most earnest pursuers. According to perspectivism, which can be traced through the work of Friedrich Nietzsche, the notion of truth must be handled with care.[7] This is not a concept that can be defined in any simple way. Any statement about truth says little regarding the truthfulness of something; rather it speaks of the person who makes the statement, or about the perspective from which the truth-claim is made. This is a radical shift in epistemology, because it helps us understand how statements of truth are more often about the subject position of the speaker than about the object to which one refers. One could say that there are no truths about, say, a particular house. The colours of the house could be seen as rather dull if in the fog, or rather radiant if seen at sunset. One could claim, however, that from whatever perspective we look at the house, the number of rooms in the house does not change. But a more radical form of perspectivism could claim that this number depends on what is considered to be a room. The discussion could go on, and one could reach absolute perspectivism and claim that there is nothing beyond perspectives. There is no reality on which one could have a perspective. There in no perspective *on* anything. There are just perspectives.

In a postmodern context, where perspectivism seems to infuse much of our understanding of truth, it seems appropriate to shift our attention to the processes by which knowledge gains truth in particular contexts. I suggest that we consider how knowledge can be acted out in different ways. I find it important to consider *knowledge in action*. This naturally also invites an analysis of perspectives in action. How does a certain perspective become acted out? How does it become 'real'? Actions are in need of reflections, and this brings us to consider in what sense *knowledge in action* in a given context could operate in a functional or in a critical way.

The connection between knowledge and action has been explored in relation to tacit knowledge, emphasising that tacit knowledge, although not explicit, can nonetheless emerge through our actions.[8] I would add that all forms of knowledge, both tacit and explicit, are enacted in complex implicit ways. It often appears as though knowledge is *presented* through our actions, but it is more often the case that knowledge is *constructed* through our actions. In the latter case, knowledge becomes part of the discursive terrain, a fluid concept that is negotiated in context. It is these knowledge constituting actions that also situate the actor in particular contexts in which particular power relations hold. Knowledge need not be personal, but it is always situated in systems, organisational structures and scientific theories. It can serve as a resource for technological innovations, constructions, and decision making. It can be acted out in many different ways.

These observations concerning knowledge in action have a particular significance in a knowledge society. Knowledge in such a society has gone on the market. In fact, *knowledge in action*, in various codified forms, has become a commodity. Here we can reconsider the functioning of the invisible hand as presented by Adam Smith. The assumption is that the invisible hand will regulate the market in a way that, according to basic liberal assumptions, is the best possible. The invisible hand makes sure that commodities are brought to the market in proper measures and that the prices will find an equilibrium. The labour market is a particular section of the free market but, according to the liberal assumption, the invisible hand will ensure the right balance between supply and demand in the case of labour as well. But how would this invisible hand manage the situation in which knowledge itself is put into an exchange market? How is the *knowledge market* managed by this invisible hand?[9] How does demand for knowledge determine supply?

2.2   Mathematics in action

Like other forms of knowledge, *mathematics* can be acted out in different ways, and each of these actions can be framed within the functional-critical distinction. This distinction pertains to the sorts of capacities or competencies that educators may build in successful learners. The functional and critical competencies are directly related to conceptions of mathematics in action because educators are reputedly preparing students to enter the workforce, and school mathematics seems to play a key role in this preparation. When mathematics is put in operation and new practices are established, one can also witness an *ethical filtration*. All actions require reflections, but somehow mathematics-based actions seem to escape this requirement, partly due to the assumed nature of mathematics. An ethical filtration can take place any time mathematics is brought into operation in order to provide reasons, arguments and decisions.

The action-dimension of mathematics has been neglected in classic philosophies of mathematics, in which action is reduced to mathematical modelling, an activity through which one is assumed to construct a more or less reliable picture of reality. This picture theory of mathematical modelling has been presented as part of the formalist philosophy of mathematics.[10] It has also been presented in many discussions about mathematical modelling in mathematics education. The picture theory preserves mathematics, and mathematical modelling, as an activity detached from any functional-critical controversy because it does not recognise the fluid definition of mathematical knowledge. The picture theory assumes a fixed definitive notion of mathematics, akin to earlier attempts to delineate a clear definition.

To facilitate the analysis of mathematics in action, I suggest that we move away from the traditional notion of mathematical modelling as a picture of reality, and instead consider mathematics as discourse. Mathematics is a way of acting in the world. It is a way of speech-acting in a discursively constructed world. Mathematics in action provides a principal value in the knowledge market of society, as mathematics in action is a constituting part of modern technology. By technology, I refer to any form of technological instrument, fabrication, construction, as well as to forms of production, automating, organising and managing. Next, I show how *mathematics in action* is actually constitutive of reality.

The mathematics-based conception of risks provides an example of mathematics in action. If we consider an event A, then the risk, $R(A)$, related to the event A taking place, is often described through the following equation $R(A) = P(A)C(A)$. Here $P(A)$ refers to the probability that A takes place, and $C(A)$ refers to the consequences of A taking place. From such an equation, some 'facts' can be formulated. For instance, with respect to the operating of an atomic power plant, one can claim that a certain procedure is not dangerous; that there are no risks for the environment, and that protection of the workers is adequate. But such 'facts' are fabricated through the modelling. Let me try to indicate this through some questions. What meaning are we to attribute to A? What kind of events are we dealing with? What meaning are we to attribute to $P(A)$? A very small number, one may suppose. What are we to think of $C(A)$? What unit should be used to measure consequences? Normally, the unit is money, but what if consequences were conceived of in terms of lost lives? What is the value of a person? In fact, there are many mathematical models for estimating the value of a person. One approach is to consider values from an insurance perspective.

My point is that a whole discourse of risks is established through mathematics, and that 'facts' about risks become manufactured through this discourse; that is, that certain risks become so small that they can be ignored. Mathematics-grounded discourses about risks are applied with respect to many aspects of life; for instance, with respect to new products put on the market: they are properly tested, we are told. Discourses could be established with respect to acceptable degrees of pollution, e.g. the pollution is so minimal that it does not cause any problems. However, the meaning 'properly tested' and 'acceptable degree' becomes fabricated from the grammar of mathematics. The discursive practices of mathematics might bring us sliding towards the most radical form of perspectivism, as mathematics in action becomes fact-producing. A mathematical discourse can be functional by establishing facts which demonstrate affinities with political, industrial or other interests.

In any process of technological construction, it is important to carry out hypothetical reasoning. In any new design of, say, an aircraft, its stability must be investigated. However, the stability is not explored through direct empirical investigations in the sense that aircrafts with different shapes are produced and launched, one after the other. The variation of the shape of the aircraft is tried out through experimentation with mathematical models. One experiments with designs that exist only in a mathematical form. The whole analysis is based on 'hypothetical reasoning' which has the form: if p then q, without p in fact being the case. Through hypothetical reasoning, one explores possible consequences of p, without trying out p. This form of reasoning is made possible as p is brought into existence through mathematics. Possible implications of a technological innovation are then identified though investigations of this 'existence'. Experimental reasoning takes place in all possible forms of technological design and decision making and, in many cases, this form of reasoning is the only way to investigate the possible implications of the designs and decisions. In particular hypothetical reasoning is basic to any mathematics-based formulation of risks.

In hypothetical reasoning, mathematics is an indispensable tool.[11] It is also a highly problematic tool. When one constructs a model on which one bases a hypothetical reasoning, one is also constructing a particular situation. The model need not, in any adequate way, represent any real design. Some important elements might be ignored due to the very nature of the mathematical model. In other words, the very form of mathematics might include a systematic misrepresentation. A mathematical model only includes what can be represented in a mathematical discourse. This is one of the principle features of risk constructions. Implications of what we design and decide can be systematically overlooked due to the mathematical nature of hypothetical reasoning. Nevertheless, constructions are brought in operation (being an atomic powered plane or an airplane) and decisions are made (about the acceptable degree of pollution, for instance). In this sense mathematics comes to make part of reality. It becomes, what I call, *realised*.[12]

Mathematics in action can be exemplified in many ways. In my book *Travelling Through Education* (Skovsmose, 2005), I comment on how mathematics can be used in designing strategies for overbooking flights. This is an example of a mathematics-based approach for maximising profit; such approaches are used in all possible forms of business. I also refer to how mathematics is used in economic policy making. In these descriptions, and also in my general description of mathematics and risk, I have emphasised the functionality that might accompany mathematics in action. However, it is also possible to accompany mathematics in action with reflections, thus opening the way for critical considerations of such forms of actions. I will now discuss an example of *mathematics in action* in an educational context. In particular, I am interested in exploring what it could mean to address actions, and also mathematics-based actions, as an ethical challenge: What does it mean in an educational context to establish an ethical perspective on mathematics in action? Let me try to indicate how it is possible to address some of the features of mathematics in action through project work in mathematics education.

The project 'Family support in a Micro Society' takes place in a secondary school.[13] The intention of the project was that the students would come to experience how mathematics can be brought into action—how it may become part of decision making processes and, in this way, become part of peoples' reality. The students were divided into groups, and each group had to think of themselves as directing a micro society of 24 families. The description of the families had been provided to the students in the form of longer essays describing: the members of the family; the number of children; the parents' situations; the children's interests; and whatever they might find relevant to describe. The description of the 24 families was the basis for the following part of the project.

Each group had to formulate principles according to how they wanted to distribute child benefits among the families. The amount of money available was given, but each group could formulate any criteria according to how they wanted to distribute it. Next, they had to provide an algorithm for distributing the money. What this could mean was clarified in the following way: You must identify an algorithm so you can hire a person to do the calculation of the distribution of the child benefit based on given information about the families without the person needing to request further details.

The groups tried to turn their original principles for the distribution of child benefits into algorithms. It soon became obvious that the functioning of an algorithm presupposes that some parameters are identified. When the values of the parameters are known, then the calculations can be completed – but not too many parameters! The final proposals for distributing benefits among the 24 families presented by each group of students were compared. In the process of turning the verbally-formulated principles for distribution into functional algorithms, the students experienced how the original principles needed to become simplified. At times the principles were almost ignored when mathematics was brought into operation to do the distribution. The students experienced the general phenomenon that when mathematics is brought in action, a new discourse takes over. The ethical principle, which might have guided the initial considerations, becomes substituted by the technical administration of the system. This is an ethical filtration, and it is a common consequence of bringing mathematics into action. A main idea of the project was to address this phenomenon, not only as a particular feature of the project, but as a general feature of bringing mathematics into action. In this sense, the project might indicate what 'being critical' could mean in educational practice. The mathematics-based design and decisions have to be accompanied by reflections.

3. MATHEMATICAL COMPETENCIES IN THE KNOWLEDGE MARKET

Mathematics in action has value in the knowledge market. There are value issues related to all the dimensions of mathematics in action. Mathematics brought into action is an indispensable resource for technological innovations. It can fabricate facts and administrative procedures. Administering family support is an illustration, but one can think of the operation of any economic system, with the tax system being only one example. Mathematical structures, algorithms and patterns become 'realised' through such systems. Finally, mathematics in action can include an 'ethical filtration', which can have an important functional value. In many cases, what is valued is the operational aspect of knowledge, not its reflective elements.

In the knowledge market, we find that considerable value is attributed to *competencies*. The elaborate international comparisons of mathematical abilities and the concern for specifying possible levels of performance in mathematics demonstrate a value-interest for competencies. Competencies gain their significance in relation to the ways mathematics operates in different practices. Competencies determine power relations across discourses and thus influence the ways in which learners are addressed within the given discourse.

A closer look at what is in fact taking place in mathematics classrooms partially reveals the sorts of competencies that are in fact valued in the knowledge market. School mathematics can be characterised as exemplifying the *exercise* paradigm: a large part of students' activities is concentrated on performing exercises. Mathematics lessons often follow the same pattern. First, the teacher presents a new topic, which may include a careful exposition of some details. This exposition may well be organised as a communication between the teacher and the whole class. Second, the students are asked to solve particular exercises. This can be done individually or in groups, and then some exercises can be assigned as home work. Third, a part of the lesson is reserved for the teacher to control the students' possible learning and understanding. Exercises are often then checked and worked out at the blackboard. Students can be questioned about results as well as about their interpretations of particular notions. It appears then that the school mathematics tradition is characterised through variations of three types of activities: teacher presentation; students solving exercises; and teacher control of students' work.

As numerous studies have indicated, such instructional models do not appear to be an efficient way of establishing mathematical understanding. Instead, it appears that this style of instruction maintains a learning environment where students cannot see much meaning in the suggested activities, where they need to be dragged through a lesson, and where they enter a state of apathy, if not anxiety. Research in mathematics education does not indicate that mathematical creativity can be established through a long row of exercises. The school mathematics tradition has not been identified as a promising or effective form of learning mathematics. In fact, there appears to be broad agreement among researchers in mathematics education regarding the inefficiency of the school mathematics tradition. It seems, therefore, that mathematics education, as a school practice, is in a condition of socioeconomic dysfunction. How could it be that such a dysfunctional practice continues to operate? From a market perspective, it seems as though the practice is a generally accepted world-wide waste of resources. One then wonders, suspiciously, how the school mathematics tradition functions as an integral aspect of our knowledge society.

Let us take a closer look at what is taking place as part of the school mathematics tradition. It includes a massive effort to distinguish between what is right and what is wrong. Quite obviously a solution to a well-defined exercise can be right or wrong. Exercises are always well-defined, as their formulation includes necessary (but not more than necessary) information for providing the one-and-only-one correct answer. However, the school mathematics tradition establishes many other things as being right or wrong. One can copy the given information from an exercise incorrectly, requiring the teacher to correct it: "You wrote 118 in stead of 198, so now your whole calculation is wrong." One can do the wrong exercise: "This exercise is not for today." One can use the wrong method for a particular task: "When solving quadratic equations, you have to use the formula on page 42." One can also answer a question without having raised one's finger. In Denmark, students can err by not putting double lines beneath the final result.[14]

Could it be that the students learn something significant through such corrections, although it may not be related to understanding mathematics? Could it be that students, through the school mathematics tradition, develop a readiness to follow orders and prescriptions? In fact, it seems that the whole school mathematics tradition establishes a *prescription readiness*. Could it be that the school mathematics tradition in this way ensures a disciplining, which meets a demand of the knowledge market – a demand that is met through mathematics education, although such a demand has little to do with the understanding of mathematics?[15]

One might assume that knowledge is valued in a knowledge market, and that the more knowledge one possesses the better. What could be better than having a plentiful and highly *qualified* work force saturating the labour market in a society that values knowledge? Unfortunately, the functioning of a knowledge society need not presuppose high qualifications of everyone, but instead could presuppose the careful distribution of knowledge profiles: some need to be highly qualified; others need competencies that enable them to complete particular job-functions; and some need to be ready to accept low-paid manual work. Maybe an important demand of the labour market of the knowledge society is to have people *meticulously labelled*, so that it is easy to pick out a person with exactly those competencies that are required. The increasing international interest for formulating, differentiating and evaluating different competencies might be an indication of this. It might be that the school mathematics tradition is efficient in providing this functional labelling.

This discussion provides a new perspective on what is taking place in mathematics education. The crucial task may not be to ensure that as many students as possible learn as much mathematics as possible, but rather that they be explicitly labelled according to a functionality grid. Maybe the knowledge society only needs a minority of students capable of managing the more advanced parts of mathematics. And, perhaps most importantly, in ensuring a vibrant knowledge market, these few students must be identified quickly and easily. Others have to function at other levels, such that they should be able to follow manuals (in a broad interpretation of manual). Some people need to be nothing more than consumers of knowledge-based products, and they need to be able to do all the transactions which are expected of a consumer. Being a consumer is one of the key functions of citizenship within the capitalist framework. Finally, many appear 'disposable' for the functioning of today's informational economy, as such an economy is defined in its liberal and capitalist form. And, in order for this economy to function, it is important that those labelled as 'disposable' acknowledge their disposability themselves and, as a consequence, become ready to take the poorest jobs.

4.   BEING FUNCTIONAL? BEING CRITICAL?

Many of the work practices (in shops, banks, insurance companies, hospitals), structured through *mathematics in action*, presuppose accuracy in dealing with prescriptions. Bringing school mathematics into action means a re-configuration of classroom routines into workforce compliance. Manual-guided work may be a particular outcome of structuring work routines through mathematics. Such job functions presuppose a readiness to follow prescriptions. It could be that, in fact, mathematics education helps to ensure functionality by preparing for a prescription readiness. As such, mathematics education helps to constitute these subject positions and to map the power relations between them.

As previously mentioned, functionality needs to be clarified in relation to particular practices. Thus, we can call a competence functional if the person with this competence can enter the practice in question without raising questions and concerns about the practice. A functional competence fits smoothly into a given context. Most often people in the labour market must demonstrate functional competencies in order to get a job. When we consider the innumerable forms of work routines that can be established when mathematics is brought into action, it is less difficult to imagine how school mathematics serves to generate prescriptive readiness, which is in such great demand in the knowledge market.

It might be that mathematics education, as it is widely practiced at the university level in the form of lectures, exercises, tests, etc., helps to prepare for such a functional expertise. A study by Herbert Mehrtens (1993) indicates that mathematics education, during the 1930's, demonstrated a surprisingly high degree of functionality by cultivating an expertise which easily fit into the overall industrial and military priorities of Nazi Germany. In such instances, it is evident that establishing functional expertise includes an ethical filtration. It could be that mathematics education prepares people to believe that value judgements are not relevant. Thus, at the university level, the exercises that form part of mathematical studies, including the mathematical courses in any form of engineering education, are detached from ethical considerations. They do not invite any reflection on mathematics in action. In this sense, mathematics education might help to instil a functional attitude by completing an ethical filtration. This is crucial when we consider that such an ethical filtration runs counter to the very premise of critical reflection.

These observations apply not only to those obtaining a mathematics-based expertise, but to all people who become involved in mathematics-based job routines as shop assistances, nurses, construction worker, etc. In all such work-situations one could follow the provided 'manuals' in a painstaking way. With respect to a wide range of job-functions, the school mathematics tradition might turn out to ensure a far reaching functionality. Indeed, this tradition might be at the heart of all functionality within the knowledge society.

But what could it mean to move beyond the idea of functionality? Let me consider the notions of literacy and mathemacy. First, the notion of literacy can refer to the capability to read and write. This is a narrow definition of the term. One can also associate literacy with a capacity to read and write a text, not only a text in a literal sense but text as situation and action. As mentioned previously, Paulo Freire's interpretation of literacy is broad in this sense, and he tried to establish literacy as a socio-political force, as a vehicle for 'conscientização'. The ability to read and write is basic for citizenship in any society today. When literacy is considered in a broader sense, it comes to include the capacity to 'talk back' to power, as well. This opens the way for understanding literacy as being not only functional but also critical. The second notion, mathemacy, can be discussed in parallel with literacy. One element of mathemacy is to read and write numbers and figures. But like literacy, mathemacy can also be interpreted more broadly, referring to a capacity to be involved in mathematics-based actions and to reflect on such actions. Mathemacy can include a critical dimension, in terms of a capacity for reading and writing the world as being open to change.[16]

When we consider mathematics in action, we consider *actions*. Actions can be hesitant, considerate, risky, audacious, careful, selfish, and many others things. They call for reflections. When one does not hear that call, then one acts in a functional way. Mathematics education is functional if it prepares people for operating in a non-reflective manner. A critical mathematics education tries, one way or another, to open the way for reflections on actions. These actions are always prescribed in some measure by the structure of school mathematics, and they call for reflection. I do not dare to claim any specific direction for such reflections.[17] They must be established in response to new actions in new contexts.[18] The project 'Family Support in a Micro Society' illustrates an attempt to make reflections on mathematics-based actions relevant for students in secondary school. When the students, at the end of the project, presented the way they had distributed the support among the 24 families and comparisons were made between the different proposals, they were able to reflect on the results of performing this action. How could it be that the distributions turned out to be so different? Had the groups not formulated relevant standards for being fair? In fact, the students came to realise that the mathematical way of handling the problem made them forget about the original principles. They came to operate as functional administrators. But they also came to reflect on this act of ethical filtration.

5.   BEING IN DOUBT

I have no doubt that I have now run into analytical difficulties. Somehow I have operated with a duality between being functional and being critical. But this duality is itself in play, as it is expressed through run-away concepts. The lived experience of school mathematics for certain groups may appear functional in one sense, and critical in a different sense. As an illustration, I can refer to the following example.[19] Barcelona has many immigrants living in deprived neighbourhoods. In these locations, however, there are educational initiatives taking place, also in the name of critical mathematics education. It is emphasised that mathematics education has to be contextualised within the students' world of experiences. The students should experience meaningful mathematics. Some are concerned, however, that through this critical programme, the students may miss opportunities to gain access to further education. The educational programme which in fact provides such access is not at all critical. Instead, it is the traditional programme where students learn to master prescribed mathematics curriculum. Thus, in this Barcelona case, critical mathematics education could result in maintaining social exclusion, while a traditional schooling in mathematics could appear empowering from the students' perspective.

Faced with this dilemma, one might realise that 'critical' and 'functional' are two of the most uncontrollable run-away concepts in circulation. It might be that they are, at best, analytically meaningless. We may have reached a discursive limit, bound by the binary itself, which makes it impossible to distinguish between 'being functional' and 'being critical'. It may also be that we must recognise the way such a binary shapes our discourse and determines our choices of action. Indeed, we need to recognise the run-away nature of this distinction. As a consequence, one might give up operating with the functional-critical distinction and accept absolute relativism, which the radical form of perspectivism invites. For me, however, absolute relativism all too often leads to a problematic nihilism. Therefore, I cannot escape the dilemma. I have to face it, but face it with doubt. Being critical and being doubtful become integrated.

ACKNOWLEDGEMENTS

I want to thank Anne Kepple for completing a careful language revision.

REFERENCES

Alrø, H. and Skovsmose, O. (2002). Dialogue and Learning in Mathematics Education: Intention, Reflection, Critique. Dordrecht: Kluwer Academic Publishers.

Borba, M. and Skovsmose, O. (1997). The Ideology of Certainty in Mathematics Education. *For the Learning of Mathematics, 17*(3), 17-23.

Bourbaki, N. (1950). The Architecture of Mathematics. The American Mathematical Monthly, 57, 221-232.

Clark, M. (1990). Nietzsche on Truth and Philosophy. Cambridge: Cambridge University Press.

Curry, H. B. (1951). Outlines of a Formalist Philosophy of Mathematics. Amsterdam: North-Holland Publishing Company.

D'Ambrosio, U. (2006). Ethnomathematics: Link between Tradition and Modernity. Rotterdam: Sense Publishers.

Dieudonné, J. A. (1970). The Work of Nicholas Bourbaki. The American Mathematical Monthly, 61, 134-145.

Gadotti, M. (Ed.) (1996). *Paulo Freire: Uma Biobibliografia*. Sao Paulo: Cortez Editora.

Gutstein, E. (2006). Reading and Writing the World with Mathematics: Toward a Pedagogy for Social Justice. New York and London: Routledge.

Freire, P. (1972). *Pedagogy of the Oppressed*. Harmondsworth: Penguin Books.

Hales, S. D. and Welshon, R. (2000). Nietzsche's Perspectivism. Urbana and Chicago: University of Illinois Press.

Mehrtens, H. (1993). The Social System of Mathematics and National Socialism: A Survey. In S. Restivo, J. P. van Bendegem and R. Fisher, R. (Eds.) (1993), Math Worlds: Philosophical and Social Studies of Mathematics and Mathematics Education (219-246). Albany: State University of New York Press.

Plato (1992). Theaetetus. Edited with an Introduction by Bernhard William. Indianapolis: Hacket Publishing Company.

Polanyi, M. (1966). The Tacit Dimension. New York: Doubleday.

Skovsmose, O. (1994). Towards a Philosophy of Critical Mathematics Education. Dordrecht: Kluwer Academic Publishers.

Skovsmose, O. (2005). Travelling through education: Uncertainty, mathematics, responsibility. Rotterdam: Sense Publishers.

Skovsmose, O. (2006). Reflections as a Challenge. Zentralblatt für Didaktik der Mathematik, 2006(4), 323-332.

Skovsmose, O. (forthcoming). Challenges for Mathematics Education Research. In J. Maass and W. Schlögelmann (Eds.), New Mathematics Education Research and Practice. Rotterdam: Sense Publishers.

Skovsmose, O. (forthcoming). Mathematical Literacy and Globalisation. In B. Atweh et al. (Eds.), Internationalisation and Globalisation in Mathematics and Science Education. New York: Springer.

Skovsmose, O and Yasukawa, K. (2004). Formatting Power of 'Mathematics in a Package': A Challenge for Social Theorising? Philosophy of Mathematics Education Journal. (http://www.ex.ac.uk/~PErnest/pome18/contents.htm)

Wright Mills, C. (1959). The Sociological Imagination. Oxford: Oxford University Press.

---

[1] Some concepts may appear to be possible to control: like 'force' within classical physics and 'function' within the established theoretical organisation of mathematics. But if one opens up a discussion of how the notion of force might include metaphysical elements,

and how the notion of set might include logical contradictions, then such concepts appear less well-defined.

[2] In Skovsmose (1994), I refer to such concepts as being 'explosive'.

[3] For a general presentation of Freire's educational approach see Gadotti (Ed.) (1996). See also Freire (1972).

[4] See Bourbaki (1950) and Dieudonné (1970).

[5] See, for instance D'Ambrosio (2006).

[6] The clarification of knowledge with reference to truth is an ever running concern in epistemology. Thus, the rationalist tradition followed Descartes, while the empirical tradition denied that we can be quite certain of any empirical fact. (Only in formal sciences, like mathematics, certainty can be obtained.) If we claim that knowledge presupposes truth, empirical knowledge is, strictly speaking, impossible. However, new epistemic routes open up if 'true' is substituted by 'a high degree of probability', and this is the approach of the empirical tradition.

[7] For a careful analyses of Nietzsche's perspectivism see Hales and Welshon (2000). For an analyses of the notion for truth in relation to perspectivism see, for instance, Clark (1990).

[8] For a discussion of tacit knowledge, see Polanyi (1966).

[9] There are very many notions that could be used instead: Mode -2 society, learning society, information society, informational society, network society.

[10] See, in particular, Curry (1951).

[11] In Skovsmose (2005) the use of mathematics-based hypothetical reasoning in economic policy making is described.

[12] See Skovsmose and Yasukawa (2004) for a discussion of mathematics-based cryptography and 'mathematics in a package'.

[13] The project is described in Skovsmose (1994, Chapter 7), where I discuss the formatting power of mathematics and not mathematics in action.

[14] This exaggerated use of the right-wrong distinction has been addressed in terms of an ideology of certainty. See Borba and Skovsmose (1997).

[15] In Alrø and Skovsmose (2002), the notion of bureaucratic absolutism is suggested in order to clarify these possible aspects of mathematics education.

[16] See Gutstein (2006). See also Skovsmose (1994) for a development of the notion of mathemacy.

[17] See, however, Skovsmose (2006).

[18] The project 'Terrible Small Numbers', described in Alrø and Skovsmose (2002), illustrates how the discussion of risks can be addressed though project work in mathematics in secondary school.

[19] This example was presented to me by Núria Gorgorió and Núria Planas during my visit to Barcelona in 2003.

MORE THAN MARK(ET) DRIVEN? SCENES FROM A CONTINUING CONVERSATION
A Response to Ole Skovsmose

Kathleen Nolan and Paul Muir
University of Regina; Saint Mary's University

KN[1]: On the issue of action and/or reflection, O.S. states: "All actions require reflections, but somehow mathematics-based actions seem to escape this requirement, partly due to the assumed nature of mathematics." (p. 163)

In our telephone conversation, you spoke about how you object to this sentence because it portrays applied mathematics—and, more specifically, mathematical modelling—as an unreflective process. From your perspective as a numerical analyst, you spoke about your experience of mathematical modelling as an iterative process—where a model is developed, a solution to the model is computed and then reflected on in terms of how well it agrees with known results, and then the model is modified in an attempt to find a better one for the situation being studied. Could you say more about this—your objection to the sentence and your experience that contradicts it?

PM[2]: It's important to emphasize that it comes from my own perspective which I think is somewhat outside the norm. Mathematical modelling-type people represent a small percentage of people. I would stand by my position that within *that* world, the models are understood to be just that—models, or, approximations to reality— and when first formulated, such models are expected to have to go through some modification to get them to an adequate level. This might only involve trying to select approximate values for some of the unknown parameters in the model or it might involve something more fundamental like introducing time-dependence into a steady state model, etc. Even at the end of the analysis, the models are understood to still only be approximations to reality and it would be of no surprise to the modeller if a better model were to be developed later. The point I am making is that within this world (of mathematical modellers) critical reflection upon the model is an essential part of the process. Looking at how the model agrees with whatever real data is available is how the model gets improved.

Having said that, if we broaden the discussion to the wider population, then I suspect there is less appreciation that the mathematical model is nothing more than an approximation to reality. I suspect that, within the general public, there is the mistaken belief that the mathematical model is (somehow) a "true" representation of whatever is being modelled and, therefore, that whatever comes out of the model is true; and thus not subject to critical reflection. The latter would be seen as of no use, I suppose. People might assume that if the equations work out to give a certain answer then that answer must be correct, assuming the equations are *solved* correctly.

So, many people might not be used to the idea of distinguishing between correctly solving a given mathematical equation and deciding if, in fact, the given equation is actually the correct one to solve in the first place. I should add that I am troubled by my use of "correctly" and "correct" in the previous sentence. "Appropriately" and "appropriate" might be better words. In the latter case, I think that there is no such thing as "the correct equation" since all equations must only be models of the real world - some might be better than others but none would be exact models. In the former case, the concept of correctly solving an equation is also not so appropriate, since most useful equations cannot actually be solved exactly and approximate solutions are therefore all that one can seek, as is done in numerical analysis. In this case, one would talk about computing an approximate solution for which the associated estimate of the error is within the tolerance prescribed by the person who is trying to solve the problem.

So, when the wider population is considered, I would agree with O.S.'s statement—or at least be more willing to agree that it is likely the case. It is just not true in general.

KN: Surrounding this same sentence on action and reflection from O.S.'s chapter were terms like "ethical filtration" and "mathematics in action" and you indicated to me that you preferred to think of these words or expressions in terms of ones more familiar to you. For example, you said that in your reading you would mentally replace "mathematics in action" with "applied mathematics" throughout the chapter. Did this somehow make your reading and reflection on the chapter more accessible? What does ethical filtration mean to you in the context of this chapter?

PM: I would agree that when I replace "mathematics in action" with "applied mathematics", in this sense, that I understand it—that is, using mathematics to help understand real world problems—then the chapter seemed to be more understandable to me.

Regarding "ethical filtration" ... I think it means taking something more general or complex and reducing it by removing some of the complexity according to a given set of rules (prescribed by a set of ethics—I think of ethics as a set of rules to follow). If so, I would agree that this is a necessary step in developing a model of a given reality. The model can only represent a few aspects of a given reality and the modeller must decide what aspects she or he might hope to approximate within the model. So what gets ignored represents the filtering and the decision process for ignoring things represents the set of rules or ethics.

It occurs to me that ethical *selection* might be a more appropriate term than ethical *filtering* as filtering seems to require describing what will not be included in the model and that might be a very long list of things, many of which the modeller is not actually aware of.

KN: The primary section of the chapter that we decided to focus on for this response conversation is that which looks at the mathematical competencies which, O.S. proposes, are valued in the knowledge market. O.S. introduces the idea that school mathematics is like an exercise paradigm, where the teacher presents a new topic through an exposition of details, then the students are asked to solve particular exercises related to the teacher's presentation, along with some assigned homework, and then finally the exercises are checked and worked out on the blackboard as a mechanism of teacher control over student learning and understanding (pp. 167-168).

PM: At one point, he makes a comment about this process being useful for society. He says that this is what the knowledge market wants. But it's not like the teachers are explicitly agents of the knowledge market. It's not as if they've been hired and trained by whatever the knowledge market might be. I agree with some of what he's saying though. It seems that mathematics is being taught in a skill-based way without much attention to what mathematics is really all about - the higher thinking and the relationships in mathematics. There's much more of an emphasis on skills. He has the theory that that's useful for society—that it's more useful to have people who will be able to handle routine mathematical tasks, rather than having people who can think about mathematics in a more general way.

KN: But I wonder... if you described this exercise paradigm to your typical teacher or professor, without reference to the rest of the chapter, would they not believe that this process is actually efficient in creating people who understand mathematics? I'm thinking that if they were to read the part of the chapter that I summarized above—and they were to think about their own education and this exercise paradigm with which they're so familiar—that they would actually equate it with being a *learning paradigm*, not just an exercise paradigm. For instance, many of the preservice teachers I work with would read about the exercise paradigm and they would likely think that this is how one *learns* mathematics. I don't think they would agree with O.S. (and the rest of his chapter) in saying that this particular exercise paradigm feeds into the menial tasks of following manuals or other 'lower-level' knowledge market competencies.

PM: As I said, I really don't think there's some kind of knowledge market agent who is out there explicitly affecting education, but there are other factors that, I think, are driving the process—like the experience of the teachers themselves and their vision of what mathematics is—making mathematics more of an exercise based/skill based thing.

There's a good chance that some of the people who are teaching math in the elementary or high schools think mathematics is about those skills, so they think that a mathematician is someone who's good at arithmetic, good at algebra, knows the values of the trig functions, etc. They might think that a good mathematician is someone who can do everything that you'd want to do in first year calculus. As well, I think the general public considers mathematics to be a skill-based activity. They don't know it as anything else. It seems to me that when people say "Do the math", they often mean "Do the arithmetic". ☺

KN: So, what role do you think mathematics skills, and a focus on them, should play in learning and doing mathematics? O.S. thinks the knowledge market depends on them, maybe too explicitly and at the expense of thinking.

PM: Well, I know for me—for example, if I'm with a group of non-mathematicians and somebody's trying to do some arithmetic, they all look at me, and I'll say, "Oh, I don't do arithmetic." Everybody thinks that's bizarre, but yet that makes perfect sense to me because I don't do arithmetic – and I don't do algebra anymore either. I have computer software I use that can do arithmetic and algebra far better than I ever could when I'm trying to figure something out. I don't consider arithmetic or algebra to be mathematics. There's a difference between the creative process of mathematical thinking and the skills that you need to solve a mathematical problem.

KN: I would agree with you—skills are *not* the be-all-and-end-all of mathematics. But then, how is this exercise paradigm approach continually (and so effectively, it seems) perpetuated? I believe the picture of mathematics classrooms as portrayed by O.S. is a reality and I agree with him in saying that "mathematics education, as a school practice, is in a condition of socioeconomic dysfunction" (p. 168). Yet I don't think teachers are aware of feeding into this market driven society.

PM: I agree. Unless there's a conspiracy of some kind, of which I'm un-aware, I don't think the entire education of math teachers is being driven by the knowledge market in any explicit way. But, in terms of your ques-tion about what drives the process, I do have some thoughts on that. One I have already discussed: it is the only mathematics that most people know. It seems to me, from the students I get in my classes, that (by and large) the experience they've had of mathematics is that it's a skill-based thing.

My second thought is that, even if we consider people who have taken some higher-level math courses where they experienced a sense that mathematics isn't about just skills – it's about thinking—that's a lot harder to teach. I know it's very challenging to teach school, and so, as a high school teacher for instance, I might feel that I've only got 2 or 3 people in my class who could possibly appreciate higher level mathematics. Every-body else is struggling just to get the skills, so I would end up resigning myself to providing a skill-based, exercise-based, mathematics experi-ence.

And then the third thought I have – and I see this myself with my own undergraduate mathematics majors—is that *students* are often much, much happier, or more comfortable, with something that's skill-based. And so they are customers of a different kind; students will voice their preference for basically a skill-based course. I don't think it's a conspiracy on their part, but they can get a better handle on something which boils down to a recipe. And so if I can say, "When you get this kind of problem, here are the steps you should take to solve it", they think that's perfect, and they think they're doing mathematics at that point.

KN: Right, but how do we stop feeding into that third observation of yours—giving into students' resistance to thinking? Do you attempt, in your courses, to introduce the idea of mathematical creativity and thinking as be-ing a part of learning math?

PM: I would say in my courses yes, because I insist upon it. I refuse to let the class have a sense of accomplishment based on mastering the skills alone. I say, "Yes, we're coming along with the skills, but to tell you the truth, I don't care if you make mistakes while you are trying to apply these skills. I want to see that you're trying to attack this particular ques-tion by thinking about what you already know, and then reaching the part where you've decided what skills are the right ones to use…"

My experience is that—the part where they're trying to figure out what combination of tools might be useful in trying to understand something—that is the part that my students sometimes consider to be the frustra-tion/waste-of-time part. They don't consider that to be mathematics. They'll say, "We don't know what to do here, you know. You've given us a question where we don't know what to do. We've read the book. We've looked at the notes you gave us. We still don't know what to do." And I say, "What's your point? I gave you a question and now you're going to have to go away and think about it. You've got all the pieces you need, but you need to think about how to put them together." They're often shaking their heads at that because it seems to them to be outside their experience of what mathematics is – of what being a math student is.

The prevalent experience, as far as I can tell from them, is that, for example, word problems are tossed in at the end of a treatment of something. A word problem is interesting... you have to extract from it what could be an expression of a mathematical problem that you could then attack with some of the tools you've learned. And really it's that part at the beginning, before you start to apply the skills, that I consider to be the mathematics; the actual application of the skill—be it long division, be it integrating a function, or something like that—I don't consider that to be mathematics anymore, assuming that standard techniques are applicable.

So within my classroom, there's an attempt, by me, to get us to move philosophically with respect to what we consider mathematics to be. My sense of what people have experienced coming out of high school is that it is much more exercise-based and skill-based.

KN: But, what keeps that exercise-based and skill-based school tradition going if, like you said, the teachers aren't consciously agents of this economic knowledge market?

PM: Those three prongs that I've mentioned—many don't really know what teaching math in a less skill-based way would be like, and, even if they do, it's more difficult to teach it that way; and, even if they're willing to take on the challenge of trying to teach math in a less skill-based way, the students don't want it, because learning is more difficult for them.

I do know that some people don't share my belief that the skills—and using them to get to the right answer—are less important. Many in the mathematics community would insist that students become strong at the skills before they try to tackle higher level thinking in mathematics, giving the teachers the message that emphasizing the skills is the correct thing to do. The issue comes down to whether or not you think it is OK for people to do math and not necessarily get the right answer.

I've heard people talk about poor algebra skills and how good algebra skills are critical to success in calculus. But it depends on what you mean by success in calculus since, in many cases, calculus is taught in a skill-based context. I'd like to teach a computer software-based calculus or linear algebra course some time and take the emphasis off the skills. I am much less interested in having people learn how to get the right answer than I am in having them learn how to take a good mathematical approach to figuring out a problem.

KN: Yes, we hear complaints about lack of skills at the middle years and high school levels too—that "they don't know fractions" or whatever the topic is. Well, that's true… each skill builds on others, so it is very noticeable if students lack a particular skill, especially if everything done in the mathematics classroom is skill-based. But I'm trying to have the students approach things from a problem-based perspective: start with a problem, identify what approaches and skills are needed in order to solve that problem, and then proceed to learn those skills, with the help of the teacher and other students, of course. But this approach is so unusual for my students that it is generally unwanted and rejected by them.

PM: I'm sure it's not a conspiracy among generations of students. They're obviously showing up in my classrooms with an honest expression of the experience they had in their mathematics education, and I assume from what I see that education has put a lot of emphasis on trying to get the skills right, and I think at a massive cost of having left out the part that really matters. I think there's a real insistence that the basics be in place before you can do something else.

What I'm saying is, the way I think math gets taught, the students spend the whole time learning low-level skills; they are only infrequently given the chance to experience math at a higher level. There's such an emphasis on skills that almost no one gets beyond them. And so two things happen. People end up thinking that mathematics equals skill acquisition. And, except for the occasional soul who can stick with it until they can get into some higher level mathematics courses—the soul who finds the learning of the skills to be enough of a reward in itself—the standard experience of learning math turns people off it. I can't tell you the number of bright, intelligent people I've met who have told me that they hate math and that they got turned off math in school because they could never see why it mattered and they did not have the motivation to blindly work on math skill acquisition without any bigger picture in sight. For them it was like spending years learning how to dribble, pass, and shoot without ever getting to even see, let alone *play*, a basketball game.

KN: If this particular school tradition, based just on exercises and skills, does, in the end, 'train' people for this market society—so that some people will be able to follow manuals—how is it that a few people *do* still go on, in spite of the system, to study mathematics and become higher-level thinkers and problem solvers? What, in that school tradition, works for them? Or are they achieving in spite of the school tradition?

PM: I think the last thing you said is the case. They actually are better at the skills than average, so they get an ego kick out of that. They get a sense of success coming from their better than average skills, and they can stay with it longer. I think we're cutting off a lot of people who might well be able to participate in society in a more quantitative way. I'm not even suggesting that the world needs more mathematicians. But a society that doesn't "hate math"— that is, a society more comfortable with quantitative thinking—would be a good thing.

So it seems that – in answer to your question—the people who do well eventually, probably had very little exposure to the higher end of things, but they were able to do better with the skills and that basically gave them a chance to get to the next level. My own experience was that I was good at the skills. Then, when I got into the higher-level math courses, having comfort with the skills didn't get in the way when I was trying to learn something else.

KN: But you're saying that [the higher-level math courses] were a very different kind of math for you? The skills were there but you were learning something completely different than what they called math in school?

PM: Yes, I mean, it's not black and white because a lot of what I learned as an undergraduate was still skill-based, and to some extent my perception of the big picture, while I was an undergraduate, was pretty limited. I got A's in a lot of courses, but it was a struggle for me at that point to appreciate the big picture. Now I can sit here—almost 30 years after my undergraduate degree, and in particular after I've taught many of these courses many times—and have these visions about what it is to talk about, for example, linear algebra. I have a whole landscape that I think of now when I say linear algebra. And little of it is skill-based. But I've acquired that perspective over years of teaching.

KN: So would you say that it's essentially fortunate—for lack of a better word—that we even manage to fill our knowledge market with the higher level thinkers that we need based on the school system we have?

PM: Yes, although it seems that O.S.'s thesis here is that the knowledge market doesn't really need a lot of higher-level math thinkers. It's difficult to tell though—if there were more people with that capability, maybe there would be more use for them. It could be quite a transformation. Obviously many people are doing whatever they do in the real world, and they're doing it with a fairly limited view of mathematics.

KN: That's interesting. Maybe it's like saying that right now what we have is a market driven school system but, in fact, if the school system changed we might end up having a school driven market system, where we *did* have a place for more of these higher level thinkers, these problem solvers.

---

[1] Kathleen Nolan, Mathematics Education Professor, University of Regina.
[2] Paul Muir, Mathematics and Computing Science Professor, Saint Mary's University.

LIVING MATHEMATICALLY: A POET'S RESPONSE
A Response to Ole Skovsmose

Carl Leggo
University of British Columbia

a+

Concepts run away in all possible directions. (Skovsmose, p. 159)

SOMEWHERE I HAVE NEVER TRAVELLED

I want to be a verb, since for too long I have
been written a noun only, but no longer satisfied
with being the name, the namer, the named,
I want to name endlessly, be the verb's verve

like Ole Skovsmose's concepts, poetry pushes at edges
into spaces where language refuses clarity,
coherence, composition, even comprehensibility,
amidst literally infinite alliterative possibilities

like holograms, the part in the whole,
rhizome connections in the earth,
the sheer certitude of everything spilling
and spelling out in fractal inevitability

as poems refuse to be consumed, preclude
easy access, even a ready location for readers
who are invited to find, if they can, their positions
for responding in a tantalizing textualizing

as poems invite the words to flow around
the reader, even in and through the reader
who must surrender the desire to hold the text
in place, must carry the memory of mystery

and sift the fragments like hypertextual links
to somewhere untracked to other places,
like e. e. cummings, somewhere i have never
travelled, gladly beyond

b+

Mathematics is not a specific and well-defined parcel of knowledge, marked by a clear-cut conception of truth. But as any other form of knowledge, it is complex and confused. (Skovsmose, p. 161)

GRADE NINE GEOMETRY

in grade nine geometry
I learned about points, lines,
rays, planes, and a parade
of polygons, spheres, pyramids,
and cones that always left me
hungry for ice cream

learned how to divide
the white page with angles,
precise and contained,
admired the saucy
isosceles angle, fell
in love with the acute angle,
was never sure about
the obtuse angle, always
wanted the right angle

learned axioms,
self-evident truths,
and theorems, less evident,
but available to proof (and
I loved the scent of approval
from all that proving)

learned the world is the word
of a cosmic comic mathematician
who set all relations spinning
like a tot with a Spirograph

learned to take the measure
of the world with my compact
smart K-Mart math set,
compass protractor ruler,
all the tools a geometer could
need to drum earth's rhythms

only now in middle age
have learned the world
is more than geometric,
now seek to embrace
the chaotic and scribbled lines
of light and love dazzled
within wild imagination

must not forget when
I have lined my world in
crayon congruent polygons
and rest with a satisfied grin
in the cube of my self-creation
to ask, at least occasionally,
about worlds outside
my box, other worlds
beyond the painted panels
of my geometric control:
no story is the whole story

c+

Mathematics is a way of acting in the world. It is a way of speech-acting in a discursively constructed world. (Skovsmose, p. 164)

A TANGLE OF LINES

we need a poetic line,

not a prosaic line,
          a line that plays   with possibilities of space,
     draws attention to itself,
                    contravenes convention,
                              will not parade from left to right margins,
               back and forth,   as if there is nowhere else
to explore,   knows instead lived experience
          knows little of linearity
               knows the only linearity
                    we know is the linearity
                         of the sentence
which waddles across the page like lines of penguins,
sentenced by the sentence   to the lie
                         of linearity,
     chimeric sense of order,   born of rhetoric,
     and so instead artists weave their ways in tangled lines,
     know wholeness
                    in holes and gaps,   in fragments
     that refract light   with fractal abandon,   and savour
     the possibilities of   prepositions   and   conjunctions

d+

What does it mean in an educational context to establish an ethical perspective on mathematics in action? (Skovsmose, p. 166)

LIGHT ECHOES

I jam with the wild lunacy
of the wind tangled in alders,
the day's light in the aspens

&
silence spilled in the forest's arteries
spells the heart's endless desire

&
located in the earth, I will learn
to keep the heart calling earth's rhythms
with roots seeking deep and deeper,
the whole earth sung in veins of long light

&

as the sun falls lower and lower,
the sun chants and I chant with the sun
in ancient blood rhythms

&

in the whirligig of wild imaginings
I breathe raucous ramblings with no anchor point
like a deflating balloon that never runs out of air

&

the lyrical light fall of rain remembers
the morning star in a heather-blue sky

&

these rhythms are the flow of blood,
breath, breathing, breath-giving,
the measure of the heart, knowing
the living word to inspirit hope, even
in the midst of each day's chaos

$$e \neq$$

Research in mathematics education does not indicate that mathematical creativity can be established through a long row of exercises. (Skovsmose, p. 168)

ALGEBRA

I loved grade ten algebra.
I've never been more sure
about the world and my place in the world
than I was in grade ten math class.
I teased out intricate equations
with unknowns of x and y,
and glowed with the confident knowledge
I could always find the correct answers
in the back of the book.

x+y

Being critical and being doubtful become integrated. (Skovsmose, p. 172)

PREPOSITIONS

I write my lines

across
        in
between
        through
over
     inside
on
   under

your lines in dozens
of prepositional possibilities,
a lineal writing, defying
linear measure or equation

Chapter 8

BUILDING POLITICAL RELATIONSHIPS WITH STUDENTS

An aspect of social justice pedagogy

Eric Gutstein
University of Illinois - Chicago

Abstract: Teaching is is a difficult, knowledge-intensive endeavour, requiring multiple knowledges, but rarely do we consider what, specifically, teachers need to know and do to teach for social justice. I argue here that building "political relationships" with students is key and illustrate these through examining aspects of several teachers' pedagogy. I also claim that what other subject-area teachers can do, mathematics teachers can also. Despite different contexts and specificities, there are common elements of critiquing knowledge, challenging oppression, and standing in solidarity with students, their families, and their communities. These elements support the development of students' sociopolitical consciousness and sense of social agency as they grow into becoming change agents in the struggles for their own liberation.

Key words: social justice; mathematics education; critical pedagogy; anti-racist pedagogy; education for liberation.

Rico,

> *Well this past week, as you know, you told me about what things we go under or what kind of "educational system" we're under. That made me think a lot. It now makes a lot of sense, like why you teach us math the way you do. Another thing that I realize now, that you said long time ago, was why they call the U.S. America, if there's North and South America. I guess what I'm trying to tell you is that there's a lot of (excuse me but) B.S. things that exist today that people know it's false, but they still teach it. Like why is there a national holiday for "Columbus Day" if they know that the Native Americans were there first. Why did the U.S. history start there and just forget*

about the Native Americans. Well, thanks for telling me that and I'm glad I asked you. Now I realize a lot of things.

(Angel's math journal, 12/13/98, eighth grade, in "Rivera," a Chicago public school.)

1.   INTRODUCTION

Most of us realize that teaching is a difficult, knowledge-intensive endeavor. The literature on teacher professional development suggests a number of areas about which teachers need to be knowledgeable. These include content knowledge which, in some subjects like mathematics, has been broken down into "common" knowledge (what most learned adults would know) and "specialized" knowledge of content (knowledge needed to teach the subject) (Hill, Ball, & Schilling, 2004). Shulman (1986) described two other forms of knowledge, *pedagogical content knowledge* (PCK) and *curriculum knowledge* (CK) . PCK is knowledge of how students learn a particular content area, as well as their potential conceptual difficulties, while CK is knowledge of how a particular subject matter is generally taught and presented in schools and texts. Although there are variations on these knowledge bases, and obvious intersections between them, various kinds of basic knowledge are usually considered to be necessary for student learning.

Beyond these basic knowledges, scholars of color and others have made the point (based on the wisdom of practice of successful teachers of students of color) that knowledge of students and their families, communities, contexts, experiences, cultures, and languages is also essential (e.g., Foster, 1997; Jordan Irvine, 1990; Ladson-Billings, 1994, 1995). Although such knowledge also has various descriptions, Ladson-Billings (1995) characterized it as *culturally relevant pedagogy*. Among progressive educators, this latter knowledge is recognized as equally essential as the knowledges I describe above, if not more so, especially when students are, to use Delpit's (1988) phrase, "other people's children"—that is, differences exist between teachers and students along the dimensions of "race," ethnicity, culture, social class, etc.

In this chapter, I examine what is necessary for "successful" teaching by building on Ladson-Billings' work. In *The Dreamkeepers: Successful Teachers of African American Children*, she reappropriated and redefined success:

Parents, teachers, and neighbors need to help arm African American [and other marginalized] children with the knowledge, skills, and attitude needed to struggle successfully against oppression. These, more than test scores, more than high grade-point averages, are the critical features of education for African Americans. If students are to be equipped to struggle against racism they need excellent skills from the basics of reading, writing, and math, to understanding history, thinking critically, solving problems, and making decisions; they must go beyond merely filling in test bubbles with Number 2 pencils. (1994, pp. 139-140)

Ladson-Billings (1995) clarified further that "success" has three components: academic success, cultural competence, and sociopolitical consciousness. Cultural competence means that students can "maintain their cultural integrity while succeeding academically" (p. 476) and do not need to be assimilationist. The development of sociopolitical consciousness refers to understanding the social, political, economical, and historical genesis, complexities, and dialectics of various phenomena in society (Freire, 1970/1998). Clearly, Shulman's (1986), and Hill, Ball, and Schilling's (2004) knowledges, with or without further specification, are involved in supporting the academic success of students, but how they relate to cultural competence and sociopolitical awareness is unclear.

The question I deal with here is: What (else) do teachers need to know and do to teach "successfully?" My evolving response is that they need to develop and enact social justice pedagogies that derive from Freire's praxis. The purpose of such an education should be to create conditions for learners to participate, as fully actualized people, in the struggles for humanization and liberation and for an end to oppression and exploitation. Education is always and inherently political, as Freire repeatedly pointed out, and serves to promote or impede peace and justice—and due to the complexities of life, sometimes simultaneously to promote *and* impede social movements and political struggle. Given the goals of stopping the domination of one people, country, or region by another, and of ending the forms of economic and political rule that produce and extend misery, poverty, inequality, and injustice in various forms—e.g., capitalism and neoliberalism—then the aims of social justice pedagogy are relatively straightforward. Students should develop whatever academic competencies are necessary to achieve this larger purpose and to (re)claim their own humanity as part of the process of their liberation (Freire, 1970/1998; Freire & Macedo, 1987).

Given these aims, the question of which sorts of teacher knowledge are necessary for student learning becomes even more complex. Part of my motivation in addressing this question is my research and collaborative work to understand social justice mathematics teaching and learning. I conducted an extended, multi-year practitioner-research study of teaching and learning mathematics for social justice in a Chicago middle school (Gutstein, 2006b), and for the last few years have been working in a new social justice high school in Chicago with a small team of mathematics teachers, a colleague with similar goals, and a growing core of student co-researchers (Gutstein, 2007a, 2007b; Gutstein, Blunt, Bobo, Jackson, Robinson, & Sia, 2006). I focus on the question of what teachers need to know so as to teach for social justice because of my reflections on my own teaching, my and others' political activism, and our work in the new school with teachers who are becoming mathematics teachers for social justice. I argue here that within the dialectic between social justice *curriculum* (in the narrow sense of text, materials, activities) and *pedagogy*, that the various basic knowledges by Hill, Ball, & Schilling (2004) and Shulman (1986) are not sufficient. Although this assertion may appear apparent, as the literature on teacher development is beginning to document, we need to more clearly specify what is important in both teachers' knowledge and dispositions to teach for social justice.

This chapter is not a research report per se, but rather an analysis of my own and others' work that is grounded in a political conceptualization of social change and the emergence of critical consciousness. Without belaboring the details, this chapter also grows out of my history as a white political activist in social movements in the U.S. from my youth through to the present. I was fortunate enough to come of age during the 1960s, growing up in inner-city New York, and strongly influenced by the Black Liberation Movement, the anti-Vietnam War movement, and other social movements at the time. I was a politically active high school student, graduating in 1970, and I have been involved in political struggles ever since. My path took me eventually to academia (late), and I have been a mathematics educator since 1993.

This chapter is about mathematics education, but it is also about teaching and learning in general. There are, of course, particularities about any subject matter, and mathematics has plenty. Nonetheless, there are strong commonalities about critical pedagogy that cross content lines, even if the research in critical mathematics education is relatively thin. My analysis here mainly examines non-mathematics teachers, but the lessons apply to all subject areas. A principal argument here is that what teachers do in other subject areas, mathematics teachers can too.

2.   BUILDING POLITICAL RELATIONSHIPS
WITH STUDENTS

In my report of my study on teaching and learning mathematics for social justice, I described how my students and I co-constructed a classroom oriented toward social justice (Gutstein, 2006b). I outlined three features that were necessary in my context (and by no means do I assume this is true for all situations). These were what I called "normalizing politically taboo topics" (e.g., making discussions about racism and injustice part of ongoing classroom discourse), creating a "pedagogy of questioning" (Gutstein, 2006c), and developing "political relationships" with students that

> ... subsume the personal, supportive relationships with students that some teachers see as essential to their pedagogy. Many teachers build quality relationships with students both in and out of class, and they spend time with students and families when appropriate; share stories from their own lives; and talk, listen, and respond to students about any concerns they have. However, political relationships go further. They include taking active political stands in solidarity with students and their communities about issues that matter. Political relationships also entail teachers sharing political analyses with students as much as possible. Finally, they include talking with students about social movements, involving students themselves in studying injustice, and providing opportunities for them to join in struggles to change the unjust conditions. (Gutstein, 2006b, pp. 132-133)

These political relationships can occur and develop in many different ways. In the following sections, I give examples of these relationships. Each story has a different theme and context, but commonalities exist. I conclude the chapter by briefly discussing how teachers who do not have such relationships might develop them.

2.1   The Politics of Language

In *The Silenced Dialogue: Power and Pedagogy in Educating Other People's Children*, Lisa Delpit (1988) recounted a discussion between a Black teacher and a Black high school student in the South. The teacher gave the student (himself a speaker of Black language) a children's book written in Black language.
Teacher: What do you think about that book?
Joey: I think it's nice.
Teacher: Why?
Joey: I don't know. It just told about a Black family, that's all.
Teacher: Was it difficult to read?
Joey: No.
Teacher: Was the text different from what you have seen in other books?
Joey: Yeah. The writing was.
Teacher: How?
Joey: It use more of a southern-like accent in this book.

Teacher: Uhm-hmm. Do you think that's good or bad?

Joey: Well, uh, I don't think it's good for people down this a way, cause that's the way they grow up talking anyway. They ought to get the right way to talk.

Teacher: Oh. So you think it's wrong to talk like that?

Joey: Well...[*laughs*]

Teacher: Hard question, huh?

Joey: Uhm-mmm, that's a hard question. But I think they shouldn't make books like that.

Teacher: Why?

Joey: Because they not using the right way to talk and in school they take off for that and li'l chirren grow up talking like that and reading like that so they might think li' that's right and all the time they getting bad grades in school, talking like that and writing like that.

Teacher: Do you think they should be getting bad grades for talking like that?

Joey: [*Pauses, answers very slowly*] No...no.

Teacher: So you don't think that it matters whether you talk one way or another?

Joey: No, not long as you understand.

Teacher: Uhm-hmm. Well, that's a hard question for me to answer too. It's, ah, that's a question that comes up a lot in schools now as to whether they should correct children who speak the way we speak all the time. Cause when we're talking to each other we talk like that even though we might not talk like that when we get into other situations, and who's to say whether it's—

Joey: [*Interrupting*] Right or wrong.

Teacher: Yeah.

Joey: Maybe they ought to come up with another kind of ... maybe Black English or something. A course in Black English. Maybe Black folks would be good in that cause people talk, I mean Black people talk like that, so...but I guess there's a right way and a wrong way to talk, you know, not regarding what race. I don't know.

Teacher: But who decided what's right or wrong?

Joey: Well that's true...I guess White people did.

[*Laughter. End of tape.*] (pp. 294-295)

In the discussion, the teacher positioned herself with the student and Black language when she said, "Cause when we're talking to each other like that..." She also challenged his assumption about what "right" language use is and contextualized it in terms of social power relations, thus creating the chance for him to reflect on his knowledge and experiences within a broader frame. She acknowledged her own ambivalence and struggle to make sense of the situation ("that's a hard question for me too"). But she ends the conversation by again challenging his ideas by asking "who decided what's right or wrong?" Hers is a problem-posing pedagogy (Freire, 1970/1998) that "makes oppression and its causes objects of reflection by the oppressed, and from that reflection will come their necessary engagement in the struggle for their liberation" (p. 30). Implicit in her words is the knowledge of how to provide contexts in which students can examine racism and the politics of language, and grow politically—and the process of developing critical consciousness is evidenced in the dialogue.

2.2   Confronting Racism

Ladson-Billings (1994, 1995) conducted an indepth study of eight teachers and, from her research, developed a theory of culturally relevant pedagogy. One of her vignettes demonstrates a teacher developing political relationships with students. The teacher, Julia Devereaux, was teaching reading using a Greek myth and asked her African American fourth graders to describe the princess in the story. A student described a princess with long blond hair (nowhere in the story). When others concurred and added that none of them could be princesses since they all lacked that hair, Ms. Devereaux read the students a story about an African princess. Afterwards, she

> leads a discussion … about how they had come to believe that only long haired, blond (White) women could be seen as princesses. They talk about ways in which everything around them devalues Blacks and elevates Whites. The students share examples of how news media portrayals construct Blacks as criminals, homeless, and/or on welfare. Ms. Devereaux reminds the students that they have many instances in their daily lives that contradict those images. She asks the students to begin enumerating them as she lists them on the board. The lesson that began as a reading lesson with a Greek myth as text has become one that explicitly challenges notions about racial superiority (Ladson-Billings, 1997, p. 135).

Notwithstanding the possible deconstruction around gender in which Ms. Devereaux could have engaged her students (which illustrates the complexities in teaching for social justice), this story shows her confronting cultural myths by drawing on students' knowledge and experience and by refusing to allow racist notions to go unchecked. Challenging racism, during reading class, by having students problematize media stereotypes and acknowledge positive counter examples represents a powerful way for students to read their world (develop political consciousness) as a precursor to reading the word (developing literacy)—which may then lead to students writing (changing) the world (Freire & Macedo, 1987):

> Reading the world always precedes reading the word, and reading the word implies continually reading the world....In a way, however, we can go further and say that reading the word is not preceded merely by reading the world, but by a certain form of writing it, or rewriting [emphases original] it, that is, of transforming it by means of conscious, practical work. (p. 35)

2.3 The Politics of Knowledge

"Only when lions have historians will hunters cease to be heroes." African proverb[1].

"Most of my students have trouble with the idea that a book—especially a textbook—can lie. That's why I start my U.S. history class by stealing a student's purse." (Bigelow, 1998, p. 17).

Bigelow's purpose in stealing the purse (with the cooperation of its owner) was to provoke a discussion with his students about discovery. He claimed to have discovered the purse to link it to Columbus' supposed discovery of the Americas. The ultimate goal, bolstered by having students read Columbus' own journals and other primary texts, was for students to begin to challenge the truthfulness of texts and examine the politics of knowledge.

Bigelow had students examine history from multiple perspectives to question and critique dominant interpretations and explore alternate positions. After reading extracts from Columbus' journal and letters, as well as other texts which examined events from the viewpoint of the indigenous Tainos, his students had to find and critique a traditional history text. His intent was to have students understand that a particular telling of history serves a particular segment of society. Evidence that some took him seriously about critiquing knowledge is found in the student response:

> I still wonder... If we can't believe what our first grade teachers told us, why should we believe you? If they lied to us, why wouldn't you? If one book is wrong, why isn't another? What is your purpose in telling us about how awful Chris [Columbus] was? What interest do you have in telling us the truth? What is it you want from us? (Bigelow, 1998, p. 21)

Bigelow added that these "were wonderful questions" and his answer to them is that students do indeed need to challenge the words of trusted teachers and question the validity of all texts. Ultimately, his goal was that students carefully critique and ask, "Why is it like this? Who benefits and who suffers? How can I make it better?" (p. 21)

A similar approach is taken by Bigelow's co-teacher, Linda Christensen (both are editors of *Rethinking Schools*). Christensen taught writing at Jefferson High School and her book, *Reading, Writing, and Rising Up* is rich in examples of her political knowledge and relationships with her students (2000). One example is how she and her students critiqued the SAT, examined its epistemological bases and racist beginnings, and developed their "own" SAT. Christensen did this to deal with how many students internalized feelings of "failure" from their test results. She also wanted them to understand that they had valid knowledge and that the test questions reflected particular class and race biases. Students deconstructed and demystified the tests and "when kids saw it [the SAT] as [merely] an obstacle, ETS no longer held the same kind of power over them" (p. 62). Students "became skeptical of tests, of any measure or device used to include some and exclude others. Beyond that, they sharpened their analysis of who would want devices that promoted and protected inequality" (p. 62). Both Bigelow and Christensen, through the nature of their political relationships with students, have created conditions for them to challenge and critique "official knowledge" (Apple, 2000); that is, to develop understanding of the political nature of knowledge in society.

2.4   Anti-Colonial, Liberatory Education

Patrick Camangian teaches English at Crenshaw High School, a large urban school of almost 3,000 students in South Central Los Angeles, with about 70% African American and the reminder Latina/o students. Below is a transcription from his classroom in which he pushed students to grapple with the purpose of their education in a no-holds-barred way. Admittedly few teachers can easily emulate this style, but he has life experiences similar to his students' which affords him certain connections. Camangian referred to challenging his students as "reframing the purpose of learning," and commented that "it's not always pretty." Students had been giving verbal presentations and Camangian interjected:

> It's not, this isn't for a grade, this is for our life! They're [student presenters] not talking about question number one, or question number two, or question number three. Or the SAT or the textbook. They're talking about your life. So if we don't take our lives serious, we will never live! And we will continue to be these slaves, we will continue to be these colonized people they want us to be! We will be our own enemy because

our enemy has created us in their own image. And if you're down with that, you're going to do your work the same way they did it, not necessarily them, but work like that. And what we want instead is for us to do work like we're trying to survive in the world. [*slowly*] Read, write, speak, think, like our lives depend on it. Cause your life depends on it. Your children's lives depend on it. And if you want to go out like a punk, then go out like a punk. I don't! Cause I hate losing. This isn't basketball or football that we're talking about, we're talking about bloodshed. We're talking about livelihood. Food, clothing, shelter. Peace of mind, self-esteem. [*pause*] And if you don't value those for you or people that you love, then you will continue to think that being knowledgeable is about getting a grade and not about saving our lives. I want you to go up there, speak to us, teach us like our lives depend on it. (Camangian, 2006).

Camangian's analysis of students' context is that South Central Los Angeles is an objectively occupied, colonized territory and that students need to prepare themselves for serious political struggle. His students study critical social theory from graduate university texts, and they go outside the classroom to investigate, analyze, and challenge the political realities of their neighborhoods. His orientation is to channel student resistance away from fighting him as a representative of the colonizers and, with him at their side, toward active engagement in the struggle to change oppressive systems. He has signs in his classrooms reflecting his views, such as, "If you feel like banging [participating in gangs], bang for freedom!"

The essence of Camangian's relationships with students is solidarity. He positions himself as part of students' community and struggles, and lives in the neighborhood. Freire (1970/1998) is clear on this essential requirement of the unity of students and teachers in the struggles against oppression: "...we cannot say that in the process of revolution someone liberates someone else, nor yet that someone liberates himself [sic], but rather that human beings in communion liberate each other" (p. 114). This concept is fundamental to Camangian's praxis.

2.5   Teaching Mathematics for Social Justice

Mathematics teachers can develop political relationships with students just like other subject teachers. The principal requirement is that students use mathematics in explicitly political ways. For example, I have done a complicated data analysis and probability project on racial profiling with several classes (Gutstein, 2002, 2006a, 2006b; Gutstein, González, & Masionette, 2007). We start by showing students a powerful clip about racial profiling from the movie "Hurricane," telling them that African Americans and Latinas/os claim racial profiling exists, and giving them space to relate their own experiences and understandings. Next, we pose the questions: But how do we know if there really is racial profiling? And how can mathematics help us? We tell students that a major goal of the project is to check up on the police because they generally deny racial profiling exists. We then simulate random traffic stops using real data, analyze our results, compare the actual numbers, and go from there. So we use mathematics to investigate reality, to see if racism exists and in what forms. We tell students that we are using mathematics to serve the people, and that orientation remains clear and explicit.

In the new social justice high school in Chicago, we have evidence that students readily identify mathematics with reading the world and identifying injustice. Recently (October 2006), we held in-depth focus groups with over half the sophomore class of about 100 students. Our purpose was to get student input on our plan to create and teach a multi-week unit about *displacement* in their communities (displacement means gentrification in the African American community and expulsion of undocumented immigrants in the Mexican community). Not a student blinked about the idea of using mathematics to investigate displacement, and almost every single student took the issue quite seriously, posing questions, providing feedback, and extending our thinking. Our analysis is that although the *Interactive Mathematics Program* (Fendel, Resek, Alper, & Fraser, 1998) is the school's main mathematics curriculum, we have normalized the political nature of mathematics in the school through doing mathematics projects (like the racial profiling project), spending time talking to students about political uses of mathematics, holding focus groups with students about teaching mathematics in these ways, and recruiting students to co-present at an education research conference—in other words, through the process of developing political relationships with students.

When I taught mathematics in middle school, my classes regularly used mathematics to study a whole host of justice issues, many of which directly related to students' lives, while several others were farther afield (Gutstein, 2006b). But the key ingredient in all the investigations was that students used mathematics to critique, question, and challenge relations of power, issues of racism, and other forms of discrimination. Furthermore, out-of-math-class conversations also played a central part. For example, when one class was in eighth grade and some students tested for a magnet high school, we discovered that they needed certain standardized test scores (from seventh grade) to even test for the school, including a vocabulary score in stanine six. Omar, a student, wrote the following journal entry:

...I really would like to go there and it's not fair. I'm a bilingual, and how many people with a stanine six [in vocabulary] can say that. People like Rosa [a classmate] miss a chance to go there when she really deserves to go. That can be one way of discrimination because those tests don't show the hard transition from coming from a Spanish talking home to learning a whole new language, yet we are not rewarded by getting a better education that we have earned and reached very hard for.

My response to Omar was:

I don't quite know what to say—yes, you are absolutely right. It is unfair, and it is racist and anti-immigrant. Rosa is not the only person who deserves to go there, there are a lot of you in this class who deserve to go there—and there are a whole lot of other students at Rivera [a pseudonym] who deserve to as well. Those tests do NOT show, as you put it, "the hard transition from coming from a Spanish talking home to learning a whole new language." And yes, you are right, you are not rewarded for all the hard work you have done. The people at Whitney Young [the high school] would say something like, "well there are lots of kids who've worked hard, and not everyone can get to go to WY." And you know what? There needs to be a whole lot more schools like WY so that youth have the opportunity to learn. Every high school needs to be a WY, and there's no real reason in this world why it's not like that. We already know how to build a WY—it's not that we don't know.

So we have to fight. That's what life is, a never-ending fight for freedom and justice, at least in this world where some control lots of "cookies" and others have crumbs[2]. And the purpose of education should be to prepare students to fight for justice, like we saw the HS students in the Chicano History Video [about the "East L.A. Blowouts"[3]]. Without their fight, many other students would not have learned as much as they did, because it's partially because they stood up that bilingual education ever happened at all. Do you know who Frederick Douglass was? He said, "Freedom is a constant struggle." And I'm sure he knew what he was talking about.

Take care and do not give up on this one!

Discussions that name racism, examine historical lessons of struggle, and politicize the overall context of mathematics can be important to developing political relationships with students, even/especially in mathematics classes.

3.   CONCLUSION

I have tried to show, briefly, what different teachers do to develop political relationships with students: examine the politics of language; confront
racism; critique the political nature of knowledge; engage in anti-colonial,
liberatory educational practices; and teach mathematics for social justice so
that students use mathematics to examine (and ultimately try to change) injustice, while explicitly naming racism and other forms of discrimination. To
reiterate, I am not suggesting a formula nor prescribing how these relationships occur. They are based in part on who teachers are, their own strengths,
weaknesses, experiences, knowledge, and orientations/dispositions toward
knowledge, social movements, and political struggle. Clearly, like any social
process, this is complicated. But people are doing this work, and we need to
learn the lessons.

The challenge is to support the development of others to use and further
develop social justice curriculum and pedagogy. Traditional teacher education programs are not oriented toward, nor, in my view, able to prepare social justice educators. Some have proposed ideas on social justice teacher
education (e.g., Darling-Hammond, French, & Garcia-López, 2002; Gau-
Bartell, 2005). While there is no room in this chapter to examine the question of initial teacher education, I offer some closing thoughts.

First, the life experiences that contributed to the sociopolitical knowledge
of the teachers presented in this chapter most likely occurred out of school
and in social interaction. If we subscribe to general notions of "learning by
doing," we would accept that one learns about social activism by being involved in the struggle. Freire (1998) called on teachers to do so:

> We are political militants because we are teachers. Our job is not ex-
> hausted in the teaching of math, geography, syntax, history. Our job im-
> plies that we teach these subjects with sobriety and competence, but it
> also requires our involvement in and dedication to overcoming social in-
> justice. (p. 58)

In short, if one wants to teach for social justice, then it is important to
concretely express solidarity with one's students and their communities, in
both words *and* deeds. The various teachers I mention in this chapter have an
ongoing commitment to participating in political and social movements.

Second, teachers whose lives have not yet taken them towards political
action need the opportunity to take such steps. The challenge for those who
have some of the knowledge required to teach for social justice—much of it
gained through participation in social struggles—is to then find ways to support others' development. Collective study of, for example, Freire's work
within teacher inquiry groups would certainly help, but it is not sufficient.

Another viable way, which we are attempting to do in the Chicago social justice high school, is to work together in collaboration, including with students, to design, teach, study, assess, and learn from and through social justice mathematics, while also concentrating on developing political relationships with students. Bringing students in as co-researchers, and working together to address how to improve our collective understanding of these issues is important to the process. And we have yet to begin working with parents and other community adults whom we are confident will share many of our goals (Gutstein, 2006d), but who will also challenge and expand our thinking and direction.

Finally, we need to document the process of developing and implementing social justice curriculum and pedagogy, as this chapter attempts to do. In the end, social justice education will be meaningful to the extent that students, teachers, and community members work together in and out of school settings to build a new society.

I end with a quote from Lupe, a student whom I taught in seventh and eighth grades. This is from a focus group interview with her and three classmates when they were ninth graders (the students were all working-class, bilingual Latinas/os from immigrant families). When students were in my class, many of us became involved, one way or another, in the community-led struggle against gentrification affecting the neighborhood. I took Lupe and others to city hearings involving the gentrification, which we studied mathematically (Gutstein, 2006b). I sat next to her at the hearing and had not planned to speak out, but she pushed and pushed, and finally, I testified. In the statement below, which took place during the group interview as we were discussing solidarity, Lupe directed her comments to me. Her words suggest how she, and probably other students, viewed the issue of teachers becoming involved in, and taking a stand with, their struggles—a key aspect of political relationships.

> Well, when we went to the TIF hearings—you don't live here. What the hell do you care about this neighborhood? You could care less as long as you just come [to teach]. But you were there with us. And it mattered a lot to us, definitely. And you went with us, and it was like you were standing with us for something that belonged to us. Something that made us who we were. And that just made everything stronger. (Lupe, April 17, 2000)

ACKNOWLEDGEMENTS

I would like to acknowledge Patricia Buenrostro, Phi Pham, and Joyce Sia, my math team colleagues in 2005-06 at the social justice high school in Chicago. The work I describe in this chapter regarding the school was entirely collaborative and distributed across the four of us.

REFERENCES

Apple, M. W. (2000). Official knowledge: Democratic education in a conservative age. New York: Routledge.

Bigelow, B. (1998). Introduction. In B. Bigelow & Peterson, B. (Eds.), Rethinking Columbus: The next 500 years (pp. xx-xx). Milwaukee, WI: Rethinking Schools, Ltd.

Camangian, P. (2006, March 30). Transformative teaching and youth resistance. Talk given at DePaul University, Chicago, IL.

Christensen, L. (2000). Reading, writing, and rising up: Teaching about social justice and the power of the written word. Milwaukee, WI: Rethinking Schools, Ltd.

Darling-Hammond, L. French, J., & Garcia-López, S. P. (Eds.). (2002). Learning to teach for social justice. New York: Teachers College Press.

Delpit, L. (1988). The silenced dialogue: Power and pedagogy in educating other people's children. Harvard Educational Review, 58, 280-298.

Fendel, D., Resek, D., Alper, L., & Fraser, S. (1998). Interactive mathematics program. Berkeley, CA: Key Curriculum Press.

Foster, M. (1997). Black teachers on teaching. New York: The New Press.

Freire, P. (1970/1998). Pedagogy of the oppressed. (M. B. Ramos, Trans.). New York: Continuum.

Freire, P. (1998). Teachers as cultural workers: Letters to those who dare teach. (D. Macedo, D. Koike, & A. Oliveira, Trans.). Boulder, CO: Westview Press.

Freire, P. & Macedo, D. (1987). Literacy: Reading the word and the world. Westport, CN: Bergin & Garvey.

Gau-Bartell, T. (2005). Learning to teach mathematics for social justice. Unpublished dissertation. University of Wisconsin, Madison, WI.

Gutstein, E. (2002). Math, SATs, and racial profiling. Rethinking Schools: An Urban Educational Journal, 16(4), 18-19.

Gutstein, E. (2006a). Driving while Black or Brown: The mathematics of racial profiling. In J. Masingila (Ed.), Teachers engaged in research: Inquiry into mathematics practice in grades 6-8 (pp. 99-118). Reston, VA: National Council of Teachers of Mathematics.

Gutstein, E. (2006b). Reading and writing the world with mathematics: Toward a pedagogy for social justice. New York: Routledge.

Gutstein, E. (2006c). "So one question leads to another": Using mathematics to develop a pedagogy of questioning. In N. S. Nasir & P. Cobb (Eds.) Diversity, equity, and access to mathematical ideas (pp. 51-68). New York: Teachers College Press.

Gutstein, E. (2006d). "The real world as we have seen it": Latino/a parents' voices on teaching mathematics for social justice. Mathematical Thinking and Learning, 8, 331-358.

Gutstein, E. (2007a). Connecting community, critical, and classical knowledge in teaching mathematics for social justice. The Montana Mathematics Enthusiast, Monograph 1 (pp. 84-93). Missoula, MT: Montana Council of Teachers of Mathematics.

Gutstein, E. (2007b). Developing social justice mathematics curriculum from students' realities: A case of a Chicago public school. Manuscript submitted for publication.

Gutstein, E., González, C., & Masionette, J. (2007). The Young People's Project and mathematics for social justice. Manuscript submitted for publication.

Gutstein, E., Sia, J., Blunt, A., Bobo, G., Jackson, A., & Robinson, C. (2006, September). Rethinking mathematics: Teaching mathematics for social justice. Paper presented at the regional meeting of the National Council of Teachers of Mathematics, Chicago.

Hill, H.C., Ball, D.L., & Schilling, S.G. (2004) Developing measures of teachers' mathematics knowledge for teaching. Elementary School Journal, 105, 11-30.

Jordan Irvine, J. (1990). Black students and school failure: Policies, practices, and prescriptions. Westport, CT: Praeger Publishers.

Ladson-Billings, G. (1994). The dreamkeepers: Successful teachers of African American children. San Francisco: Jossey Bass.

Ladson-Billings, G. (1995). Toward a theory of culturally relevant pedagogy. American Educational Research Journal, 32, 465-491.

Ladson-Billings, G. (1997). I know why this doesn't feel empowering: A critical race analysis of critical pedagogy. In P. Freire (Ed.), Mentoring the mentor: A critical dialogue with Paulo Freire (pp. 127-141). New York: Peter Lang Publishing.

Shulman, L. S. (1986). Those who understand: growth in teaching. *Educational Researcher, 15,* 4-14.

---

[1] Thanks to Mamokgethi Setati for sharing this proverb.

[2] The "cookies" refers to a project in which we simulated the relative wealth of continents using cookies as wealth and the people in the room as residents of the different continents.

[3] The East L.A. Blowouts were Chicana/o high school student walkouts in 1968. Up to 10,000 students protested what they saw to be racist school policies.

FEAR OF THE POLITICAL
A Response to Eric Gutstein

Elizabeth de Freitas
Adelphi University & University of Prince Edward Island

When responding to the question, "What (else) do teachers need to know and do to teach 'successfully'?" Gutstein suggests that even mathematics teachers have to enact social justice pedagogies if they are to teach successfully. He points out that providing social justice curriculum is not sufficient in this regard, and that teacher disposition remains crucial in developing a commitment to teach for social justice. But what sort of disposition?

When one of my pre-service teachers in a secondary mathematics methods course at a small regional university in Canada stated to the class, without hesitation, "I'm not one for social justice", and another, echoing her political neutrality, said, "I'm just one of those math for math sake people", and the rest, despite their mandatory courses in educational foundations, said nothing, I wondered why they felt entitled to abstain from a political vision of their teaching and to what extent they were drawn to mathematics precisely because they perceived it as apolitical. I wondered if there were tacit ideological assumptions shared by these soon-to-be mathematics teachers as they collectively resisted the critical pedagogy advocated in the course readings. Research in critical pedagogy suggests that students will not spontaneously critique the practices or institutions that have validated their own success unless they are triggered to do so (Wink, 1999; hooks, 2000). The challenge, therefore, is to generate particular strategies that function as triggers in this regard. Course readings, and discussions thereof, may work as a catalyst in the reorientation of pre-service teacher thinking, but often resistance emerges, as documented by the refrain, "I'm not one for social justice". Leonard and Jackson Dantley have recorded similar resistance from Philadelphia pre-service teachers, pointing to comments such as "Here we are playing the race card again. I have to seriously disagree with this article. Math is math period! How can a link be made between math and culture?"

(Leonard & Jackson Dantley, 2005, p. 98). Like Leonard and Jackson Dantley, I believe that such comments demand attention.

I do not mean to suggest that my pre-service teachers willfully or consciously choose to support a system that legitimates and defends their social status while further disenfranchising those who are different. Rather, I am suggesting that their actions and choices are implicitly informed on an ideological level, and that they perform their ideology when participating in the power economy, and that, most importantly, they can disrupt the system of cultural reproduction by developing a critical perspective on the ways mathematics education re-inscribes hegemony. Rodriguez and Kitchen (2005) suggest that reluctance to see success in school mathematics through a socio-cultural lens may be related to a sense of entitlement – granted and validated through previous school success – and may inhibit prospective mathematics teachers from embracing a social justice agenda. They state: "Teacher educators should consider the entitlement granted prospective secondary-level mathematics teachers as a potential reason why they may resist efforts to prepare them to teach for diversity." (Rodriguez & Kitchen, 2005, p. 35)

By addressing pre-service teacher resistance to social justice pedagogy, I hope to trigger a process of self-interrogation that may lead to an increased sense of responsibility. By questioning the naturalness of an apolitical position—indeed by creating some discomfort around that position—and demanding that pre-service teachers examine the ways in which their own status and privilege is sustained by the claim of political neutrality, I am borrowing the critical strategies of Boler & Zembylas (2003) who advocate for a "pedagogy of discomfort" in generating critical dialogue. They point to the significant emotional impact caused by our problematizing of "common sense" beliefs and assumptions, arguing that feelings of discomfort are crucial aspects of transformative learning about self and society. If teachers are able to be comfortable with discomfort, to move towards struggle instead of away from it, to enter the political arena of the communities where they teach, much like the "political solidarity" of Camangian who "positions himself as part of students' community and struggles," and who "lives in the neighborhood," then perhaps students will begin to see the power of mathematics as a political tool.

REFERENCES

Boler, M. & Zembylas, M.(2003). Discomforting truths: The emotional terrain of understanding difference. In P.P. Trifonas (Ed.), *Pedagogies of Difference: Rethinking Education for Social Change*. New York, NY: Routledge-Falmer. 110-136.

hooks, b. (2000). *Where we stand: Class matters*. New York, NY: Routledge.

Leonard, J & Jackson Dantley, S. (2005). Breaking through the ice: Dealing with issues of diversity in mathematics and science education courses. In Rodriguez & Kitchen (Eds.), *Preparing mathematics and science teachers for diverse classrooms: Promising strategies for transformative pedagogy*. Mahwah, NJ: Lawrence Erlbaum Associates, Publishers. 87-118.

Rodriguez, A.J. & Kitchen, R.S. (Eds.). (2005). *Preparing mathematics and science teachers for diverse classrooms: Promising strategies for transformative pedagogy*. Mahwah, NJ: Lawrence Erlbaum Associates, Publishers.

Wink, J. (2000). *Critical pedagogy: Notes from the real world* (2nd. Ed.). New York, NY: Allyn & Bacon.

CRITIQUING KNOWLEDGE, CHALLENGING OPPRESSION AND STANDING IN SOLIDARITY IN TEACHER EDUCATION
A Response to Eric Gutstein

Carol Fulton
University of Regina

The class period is about to end and I ask the pre-service teachers if they have any questions or concerns before we depart.

"I can see how to include topics related to social justice in social studies and language arts in our lesson and units plans, but it's a lot harder in mathematics and science," complains Steve. "I just don't see how it's relevant."

A few of his classmates speak up.

"What about having the class research statistics about child poverty in Canada?" offers Janet.

"Or maybe you could have students calculate their ecological footprint and compare a middle class Canadian's footprint to that of someone in Africa, for example," says Lori. "It really helps to show how industrialized countries are using most of the world's resources at the expense of others."

"In our practicum, Ethan and I had the students research the wages paid to immigrant Canadians who are doing the same jobs as people who were born here, and then create graphs to compare the differences. That really opened their eyes," Brady reports.

A few heads nod in agreement.

"But why can't we just stick to the curriculum? Social justice is about teaching kids how to do math and science so they can be productive members of society and compete for jobs, isn't it?" Steve demands.

"Yes, certainly," I say, "but in this program we are trying to do more than help students become productive members of society who compete for jobs. Do we not also want to help our students recognize and take action against inequalities and injustices? Besides, mathematics and science are often seen as objective, neutral subjects, but middle-class, Eurocentric values and assumptions underlay the development of curriculum and how students are taught and assessed. These values and assumptions are invisible or "normal" to us because we are part of the dominant group in society that has been raised on them. There are some minority groups, however, for whom mathematics and science have served as barriers to academic achievement because these subjects appear irrelevant to the students' lives. Instead, we need to help students see these subjects as tools for social change."

Steve leans back in his chair looking somewhat skeptical. I mentally search for some practical examples of what I am trying to explain, in a manner that he might understand.

"I have found *Rethinking Mathematics* (Gutstein & Peterson, 2005) really helpful," says Terry. "That might be a place to start, Steve."

Steve crosses his arms, nods and says, "Ok. Thanks. I'll check into it."

The preceding exchange represents typical conversations I have had with my students over the past two years in our new teacher education program oriented to teaching for social justice, or as we prefer to say, "teaching for a better world[1]." Like Gutstein, we are trying to develop (prospective) teachers' abilities to critique knowledge, challenge oppression, and stand in solidarity with students and their families and communities, although such an undertaking is not without its challenges. It is our hope that our motto, "Empathy, Critique, Hope and Action" will come alive for our prospective teachers as they try to put the theory into practice during their practicum experiences.

Although our context is different from Gutstein's—that is, the people most oppressed by the effects of colonization in this country are the First Nations, Métis and Inuit peoples of Canada—many of the issues Gutstein identifies are the same. As I read Gutstein's chapter, I was filled with a renewed sense of purpose and hope despite some challenges I see for initial teacher education.

The first challenge relates to facilitating the development of a critical consciousness in our prospective teachers, most of whom are white, middle class and female. Discussions around race, class, gender, and homosexuality are uncomfortable for some students and have been met with resistance on occasion, particularly when their religious and political beliefs differ from (and even clash with) the beliefs of others. Ironically, we, as professors also struggle with our own acceptance of other peoples' views, particularly those we see as intolerant.

Another challenge involves helping prospective teachers understand that teaching for social justice is best accomplished through meaningful action projects that arise from real problems in a community. Gutstein suggests that students become empowered by collecting local data and using mathematics to address and change the adverse conditions in their communities. In our teacher education program, we often send these soon-to-be teachers into their practicum experiences armed with well-prepared unit plans designed to raise students' awareness of larger global issues such as child labour, HIV/AIDs in Africa, world hunger, climate change and so on. Rarely, however, are they able to recognize or work with students on issues in their own communities.

Closely related to this challenge is the ability of our pre-service teachers to explain to cooperating teachers how action projects are related to the curriculum and how they contribute to in-depth, meaningful learning. Having our prospective teachers identify and carry out their own action projects (related to issues that had meaning for them in their own lives) helped to develop their understanding of the importance of the projects for learning, as well as how the projects can relate to curriculum. It also gave the pre-service teachers the confidence to justify action projects to their cooperating teachers or others who may question what they are doing in schools.

A final challenge relates to the structure of our program, which limits the amount of time prospective teachers actually have to work on meaningful social action projects within communities. Although it is much easier to carry out projects during their four-month internship in schools than in their other more brief (three-week) practicum experience, our pre-service teachers may never have a chance to experience what standing in solidarity with a community might mean. At the very least, however, they can (as Gutstein suggests) begin to normalize "politically taboo topics", create a "pedagogy of questioning" and develop "political relationships with students" (p. 193) within such a time frame.

Although Gutstein acknowledges that he does not address initial teacher education in this chapter, he provides a vision of the difference that prospective teachers can make when they teach for social justice. My dream as a teacher educator is to see these enthusiastic, idealistic, future educators strive to work in solidarity with their students and communities using subjects such as mathematics as powerful tools for change. Then I can rest.

REFERENCES

Gutstein, E. & Peterson, B. (Eds.) (2005). Rethinking mathematics: Teaching social justice by the *numbers*. Milwaukee, WI: Rethinking Schools.

---

[1] This is a four-year undergraduate teacher education program that prepares teachers for working with middle years (grades 6-8) students. It is part of a larger Elementary Teacher Education program. Applicants who have a first degree are accepted into the program with undergraduates who are in their third year.

A LIFE FOR APRILE: SOCIAL JUSTICE AS A SEARCH OF/FOR THE SOUL
A Response to Eric Gutstein

Dalene M. Swanson
University of British Columbia

> Dalene
> Thank you for your love and support over the last 2 years.
> I feel like I could shout from the roof tops.
> I did it.
> I have always wanted to be a teacher and now I have done what I had previously
> believed that
> I could not do.
> I feel empowered, honored and grateful.
> You were such a positive and caring role model and I know will continue to be.
> I promise to keep in touch.
> Truly
> Aprile

School mathematics is a discourse of power! The prevalent, but false, understanding of mathematics is one of an objective discourse that affords positions of political "neutrality" within its discursive parameters. This understanding is one which gives license to the use of mathematics as an instrument of capitalist relations of production and, in doing so, advances the cause of neo-liberalism globally. In other words, "neutrality" and "objectivity" serve as a cover for neoliberal and neocolonial discourses. It doesn't take much to notice that standard (Westernized) school mathematics curricula are underpinned by particular value systems (Bishop, 2000; 2001) that reify individualistic and civil libertarianism, and underscore the advancement of technocentric, progressivist, and capitalist tenets (see Bishop, 1990).

Common progressivist and utilitarian rhetoric on the 'importance' of mathematics learning in schools often make claims to 'good citizenship' and vocational advancement. A 'successful citizen', according to this tenet, is one that has access to the power of mathematics to 'know the world'. As an example, the chapter entitled 'Introduction to Mathematics" in the British Columbia Mathematics K-7 Integrated Resource Package (2007), which refers to the Prescribed Learning Outcomes for elementary school mathematics, a description of the nature of mathematics is given as "one way of trying to understand, interpret, and describe our world" (p. 13). Yet, the politics of such 'coming to know' is most commonly denied, such that school mathematics enables its knowing subjects to 'describe our world' in ways that are purportedly divorced from subjective influence and human interference. According to such readings, mathematics has great utilitarian worth, but is untainted by the messiness of politics and human vulnerability. 'Failure', in these terms, is therefore constructed, ironically, as a condition of being an unknowing mathematical subject.

Consequently, a citizen's purpose and worth is defined by their access to mathematical numeracy: "Numeracy ...(is)... required by all persons to function successfully within our technological world" (BC Mathematics K-7 IRP 2007's "Rationale"), suggesting that someone without access is a problem to the state and a 'failed' citizen. Yet, access to mathematics must nevertheless be differentiated to satisfy the socio-economic and political requirements of the nation state. Not all citizens are allowed to excel at mathematics! There is ideological investment in the fact that mathematics is most often the most divisive subject in the school curriculum (Dowling, 1998). In school mathematics, standardized testing, streaming/tracking systems and pronounced differentiated teaching practices in this subject, along with other gate-keeping controls, ensure that a differentiated hierarchy of access is produced. Such a hierarchy emulates, assists, (re)produces, and is (re)produced by itself within capitalist relations of production. The high status of mathematics in the "social division of labour of discourses" (Bernstein, 2000) within schools and society, makes it a high-stakes game to play, and its "strong grammar" (Bernstein, 2000) provides it with significant cultural caché for those with the good fortune and privilege to have access to it as knowing subjects and citizens.

"Successful citizenship", therefore, is constructed accordingly along the lines of privileged access to mathematical culture, but referenced in terms of 'innate capacities' and 'ability' to ensure that the privileged access is hidden, normalized, and often even justified under the auspices of being "democratic". It is generally considered "democratic" for students to have differentiated access to mathematics according to their "needs", "learning styles" (often euphemistic for legitimizing constructions of "ability"), "interests", and "aptitudes." Such a critique of what is deemed "democratic' is important to consider in coming to an understanding of what it might mean "to do" social justice mathematics education, while problematizing these terms for their oxymoronic tendencies.

It is with these issues in mind that I come to a remark made by Eric Gutstein in his chapter—a premise that underpins his chapter in reference to advocating for a social justice approach to mathematics (an approach that I greatly admire): "A principal argument here is that what teachers do in their other subject areas, mathematics teachers can do" (p. 192). This remark places mathematics evenly alongside other subjects in the school curriculum, denying the role it plays in the hierarchy of power within schools and the nature of its particular forms of oppression. Ironically, his remark also gives credence, rather than contestation, to the perception that mathematics has less to do with issues of power and social injustice than other subjects— subjects that are commonly considered to have a more 'natural' orientation to these issues. I would like to invite a restating of this position to the following: "Given (Western) mathematics' current role in schools as a powerful discourse in perpetuating and entrenching oppression and social and ecological injustice globally, it is even more important for teachers of mathematics, as compared to those of other subject areas, to approach the teaching of mathematics from a social justice perspective."

I believe that teaching mathematics for social justice needs to go further than just an extraneous use of mathematics to conscientize students to issues of injustice and problematic dominant truths. The approach should also trouble the way in which mathematics is intrinsically conceived as having a 'true nature', of how access to mathematics is afforded and denied, of *how* mathematics is taught along with *what* is taught and *why*, and how power and privilege play out to reproduce the status quo and entrench the forms of injustice being addressed extrinsically. I believe there is a call for a pedagogy that is more liberatory than those currently being espoused, by providing students with inside knowledge of how power operates to enable them to take action, rather than just using mathematics' descriptive powers to evidence it.

My discussion thus far contributes to Eric Gutstein's overarching question that he wishes to address in his chapter: "what (else) do teachers need to know and to do to teach 'successfully' [for social justice]?" (p. 191). I would argue that what is required is more than knowing how to manipulate mathematics towards its political utilitarianism, but requires a will and ability to critically analyze and critique the nature of power itself, and the way in which mathematics is complicit in the reproduction of injustice. Those labeled the "can dos" and the "can't dos" of mathematics need to see how power operates to have produced these categories, rather than accepting them as truths about themselves as the victims of the mathematical subjectivities of 'unknowing' and 'unable.'

Further to my discussion, Eric cites Gloria Ladson-Billings' work to affirm and recommend that teachers of social justice get to know their students, their backgrounds and their needs. Although this seems an obvious prerequisite for social justice education and advocacy work in education, it is not without its complications, and should, in itself, be troubled. Robyn Zevenbergen (2003) showed how teachers made judgments about students' mathematics "abilities" based on their perceptions of the students cultural and socio-economic backgrounds. In my own work (see Swanson, 1998; 2000; 2002; 2004; 2005), I have shown how teachers, even with the best of social justice intentions in mind, have participated in social difference discourses to position students in ways that perpetuate and advance what I refer to as "the construction of disadvantage" and the "pedagogizing of difference". In my research, disadvantage became a lived curriculum for those without access to school mathematics due to the differentiated practices that teachers participated in based on their perceptions/constructions of students. These perceptions, viewed through linguistic productions, were aligned with hierarchies of oppression related to race, gender, social class, language, culture, and ability.

Another missing element that troubles the notion that to do social justice work teachers need to know certain forms of knowledge is the element of 'context'. It is a victim-producing discourse to deny the elaboration of principles of power related to the context of production of social justice education. Context provides affordances and constraints. Certain repertoires of positions become possible in context while others are delimited (Bernstein, 2000). While it is very important for teacher candidates to 'know' key aspects of how 'to do' social justice education in mathematics, this 'knowing' becomes 'successful' in practice under different conditions, emphases, and forms of elaboration, based on the possibilities for successful engagement derived from the context. If institutional messages mitigate against a political approach to education, this "success" is recast as "failure" according to the prevailing rules of the institution in which the approach is undertaken. The pre-service teacher then becomes a victim of a particular advocacy that if enacted in a context outside of the legitimizing context of the teacher education classroom (such as a schooling (practicum) environment that does not support such advocacies) then the student (or new) teacher is made to be unsuccessful in that practice, even though it was deemed "successful" in the context of its advocacy in the teacher education program.[1] Consequently, there is no 'one knowing' of how to do social justice education in mathematics for all contexts—as if contexts are neutral and smooth—since the issues are beyond 'what you need to know and do' and more toward a consideration of adaptability, understanding what is possible, pushing boundaries as far as possible while still being "successful" in context, and being aware of how power operates to construct, delimit and enable.

Nevertheless, even after problematizing the element of context, understanding the constraints of context should never be a ready excuse for 'doing nothing'. Having grown up in apartheid South Africa and having participated in student advocacies within the anti-apartheid movement during my university years, I, like Eric, have life long commitments to social justice and the amelioration of suffering and oppression. These commitments are reflected in my teaching, research, mothering and the way I choose to lead my life. Limitations in one context provide, for me, avenues of opportunity in another, or afford opportunities to change approach and seek out ways of sparking hope and possibility where none appears to exist. I have learned some of these lessons through experiencing the humility and hope of the people in contexts of extreme constructed socio-economic poverty in informal (township/shanty town) communities in South Africa. I also learned, through the humbling spiritual power of the people living in "impoverishment" in those communities, that this humility and collective presence and solidarity with the people—often referred to as Ubuntu, an *isiXhosa* proverb[2], in the Southern African context—is perhaps the greatest opportunity for affording possibility and resistance to oppression through its promise of collective transcendence.

Sometimes though, this collective transcendence happens in the small successes of one life at a time. This is social justice in action, as a search of/for the soul. Aprile, a student teacher in my "Diversity Cohort"[3] mathematics methods course, transcended the victimizing institutional messages that constructed her as having a "learning difference" that would prevent her from becoming a successful teacher. She wanted to be a teacher more than anything else. She was one of the constructed "can't dos" of mathematics when she came into the program. She turned out to be an exceptional advocate of social justice mathematics education and excelled at teaching from and through these perspectives. She beat the system in more ways than one! As a witness to her development as a person and her social justice advocacy in mathematics education, as well as the way in which she was able to transcend institutionally-informed oppression herself, I recognize that Aprile is an exceptional teacher and human being of which I am most 'humbly' proud!

REFERENCES

Bernstein, B. (2000). Pedagogy, Symbolic Control and Identity: Theory, Research and Critique. NY: Rowman & Littlefield.

Bishop, A. J. (2001a). What values do you teach when you teach mathematics? In P. Gates (Ed.), Issues in Mathematics Teaching (pp. 93-104). London: Routledge Falmer.

Bishop, A.J. (2001b). Educating student teachers about values in mathematics education. In F.L. Lin and T. Cooney (Eds.), Making Sense of Mathematics Teacher Education (pp. 233-246), Holland: Kluwer,

Bishop, A. J., FitzSimons, G. E., Seah, W. T. & Clarkson, P. (2000). *AARE-NZARE 1999 Conference Papers*. AARE-NZARE 1999 Conference, Melbourne, 27 November - 2 December 1999, www.aare.edu.au/99pap/bis99188.htm, Available [online]: Values in mathematics education: making values teaching explicit in the mathematics classroom.

Bishop, A.J. (1990). Western mathematics: the secret weapon of cultural imperialism. Race and Class, 32 (2), 51 – 65.

British Columbia Mathematics K-7, Integrated Resource Package 2007, online [available]: http://www.bced.gov.bc.ca/irp/mathk72007.pdf

Dowling, P. (1998). The Sociology of Mathematics Education: Mathematical Myths / Pedagogic Texts. London: Falmer.

Swanson, D.M. (1998). Bridging the Boundaries?: A Study of Mainstream Mathematics, Academic Support and "Disadvantaged Learners" in an Independent, Secondary School in the Western Cape, (South Africa). Unpublished Master's dissertation, University of Cape Town, South Africa.

Swanson, D.M. (2000). Teaching Mathematics in Two Independent School Contexts: The Construction of "Good Practice". Educational Insights 6 (1) [on-line] available: http://www.csci.educ.ubc.ca/publication/insights/online/v06n01/swanson.html

Swanson, D.M. (2002). "Disadvantage" and School Mathematics: The Politics of Context. The International Journal of Learning, 9, 1471 – 1480.

Swanson, D.M. (2004). Voices in the Silence: Narratives of disadvantage, social context and school mathematics in post-apartheid South Africa. Unpublished PhD dissertation, The University of British Columbia, Vancouver, Canada.

Swanson, D.M. (2005). School Mathematics, Discourse and the Politics of Context. In A. Chronaki & I. Christiansen (Eds.), Challenging Perspectives on Mathematics Classroom Communication. Greenwich, CT: Information Age Publishing.

Zevenbergen, R. (2003). Teachers' beliefs about teaching mathematics to students from socially-disadvantaged backgrounds: Implications for social justice. In L. Burton (Ed.), Which Way Social Justice in Mathematics Education? (pp. 133-151). Westport, CONN/London: Praeger.

---

[1] A common example of this is when teacher candidates enter their long practicum in the field with a university faculty advisor that has a different philosophical and pedagogical orientation to the teacher candidate and faculty member responsible for the mathematics methods course in which a social justice approach has been advocated. Often an 'efficiencies model' of education is imposed on the teacher candidate that constructs 'good practice' in a particular way, reinforcing classroom control, unit plans, and other normative technologies in order to dismiss social justice advocacies in the classroom. In such a context, a social justice approach might be viewed as 'not sticking to mathematical content', and irrelevant to the discipline of mathematics being taught. Power relations come strongly into play as a result of the fact that the teacher candidate is being evaluated by the practicum faculty advisor and school representatives, and so there is a risk that she will be constructed in terms of 'failure' if she persists with a social justice approach.

---

[2] Here, in the interests of challenging our stated commitments to social justice as colleagues, and done in friendship and solidarity with his social justice approach to mathematics education, I invite Eric not to homogenize Africa as one reducible entity in his reference to an "African proverb" and I ask the question in support of this: is a Mohawk proverb an "American proverb"?

[3] The "Diversity Cohort" is a two-year elementary and middle school teacher education cohort with a social justice focus at The University of British Columbia. It began in 2004 as a joint venture between the Vancouver School Board and the David Lam Chair of Multiculturalism at UBC. I was invited to teach mathematics methods in this cohort by Professor Graeme Chalmers, the David Lam Chair at the time. I have taught the course in all of its subsequent offerings thus far.

Chapter 9

AFTERWORD

Bootleg Mathematics

Peter Appelbaum
Arcadia University, USA

I suspect that many children would learn arithmetic, and learn it better, if it were illegal. - John Holt (1989, p. 45)

Søren Kierkegaard once wrote of sitting in the Frederiksberg Garden on a Sunday afternoon, asking himself what he was going to do with his life. Wherever he looked, practical men were preoccupied with making life easier for people. Those considered the "benefactors of the age" knew how to make things better "by making life easier and easier, some by railways, others by omnibuses and steamboats, others by telegraph, others by easily apprehended compendiums and short recitals of everything worth knowing, and finally the true benefactors of the age ... (making) spiritual existence systematically easier and easier...". Kierkegaard decided, "with the same humanitarian enthusiasm as the others," to make things harder, "to create difficulties everywhere." (Kierkegaard, 1947, p. 194) I was reminded of this story re-reading Maxine Greene's (1978) essay "Toward Wide-Awakeness," in her compilation entitled *Landscapes of Learning*. Like Kierkegaard, and like the authors in this current volume, Greene is concerned with 'civilizational malaise', reflecting the inability of a civilization directed toward material triumphs and improvements – higher incomes, better diets, miracles of medicine, ... - to satisfy the human spirit. In education, as in social life in general, we seek out simple slogans, 'best practices', 'test score increases', and other forms of simplicity that make everything 'easier'. Kierkegaard noted that, with so many people trying to make things easier, the only thing left would be to make things harder; he imagined people would soon be seeking out the difficulties of life, and he would be there ready. The authors in this volume, too, worry that, at least within the field of mathematics education, we find ourselves embracing the "easier" without addressing the difficulties, and, like Kierkegaard, these thinkers are here, ready for us, now that we have had enough with "the easier" and its dissatisfactions. Maxine Greene writes that making things harder for people means "awakening them to their freedom"; it means "communicating to them in such a way that they … become aware of their 'personal mode of existence,' their responsibility as individuals in a changing and problematic world." (Greene, 1978, p. 162) Reading the contributions to this volume communicates our collective and individual responsibilities as mathematics educators in a changing and problematic world.

Static Electricity

The poet and slam champ Matt Cook (2005) captures this same feeling of dissatisfaction in the context of education. "Remember static electricity?" he asks. "That sure seemed to come up a lot when we were younger." People would rub balloons against their heads and then stick the balloons to the walls. "People would make examples out of the balloons they stuck to walls. The suggestion was that they were illustrating a principle…" But, as Cook notes, "there *were* no applications – it was just people rubbing balloons against their heads and sticking balloons to walls, and saying *static electricity*." In my own experience, much of school activity unfolds in exactly this way. People 'illustrate principles', but all they are doing is simply showing something and naming it. They are making things easier and, in the process, removing what matters, the difficulties. We do the same thing in pedagogy: Readers of this volume do not need a recitation of the numerous weaknesses of the 'methods fetish' in teacher education that reduces all of the art and science of teaching to slogans and recipes, only to lead to teachers who feel and act like cogs in a machine, and students who see the equivalent of balloons stuck to walls, hearing the mantra 'static electricity' over and over again. The difficulties evoke the crisis of meaning in teaching and learning, a disconnection of education from the triumphs and devastations of contemporary social life, and a lack of wide-awakeness to the catastrophes of human suffering and inequality, both locally and globally.

In another poem, Matt Cook writes, "having your back against the wall … is actually more comfortable than facing the wall" (Cook, 2005, p. 32). He calls forth Greene's notion that wide-awakeness – *less* comfortable than *avoiding* awakeness, in Cook's words - has a concreteness: it is related to being in the world. In the immediate concreteness, short term comfort precludes long-term satisfaction. This goes beyond ordinary notions of "relevance" where education is concerned, toward the kind of heightened consciousness and reflectiveness that are associated with human projects. Such consciousness demands human undertakings, and careful efforts to avoid withdrawal from the intersubjective world. For mathematics education, this means the design of experiences "that enable people to pay, from their own distinctive vantage points, 'full attention to life'" (Greene, 1978, p. 163).

Power

Christensen, Stentoft and Valero use perspectives of *power* to "face the wall." An intrinsic perspective on power distribution calls our attention to the ways that mathematical skills are related to individuals as 'things' that might or might not be acquired. A technical perspective takes such 'things' to be acquired and situates them in a social context, so that skills and concepts may be viewed as residing independent of particular individuals, and asks us to consider the role of such 'things' socially and culturally. The structural inequality perspective moves further toward the social and cultural towards the political, focusing on the ways that mathematics education promotes equality and/or mariginalization and inequity. As Nolan notes in her thrice-told tale, there is a way in which educational events and social analysis could incorporate all three perspectives, shifting from a macro to a micro level of analysis and interpretation that would inform practice in multiple ways. The authors' response to their own chapter is especially interesting in its search for the construction of standpoints on power distribution itself. I prefer the notion of power made fashionable following Michel Foucault, understanding power as an attribute of relationships. This is similar to gravity in physics, rather than a hypostasized 'thing' that can be distributed, owned, and wielded, as in an economy of power (Appelbaum, 1995; see also Russell, 1938). The shift from distribution to attribute helps us appreciate power's role as an indicator of relation, leaving behind perspectives on power, and in the process making them studyable as theories themselves.

> Power in this sense does not simply prohibit or repress. It is a force that is dispersed. It circulates. It is not outside our relations. It produces relations. It is not simply a question of who or what exercises power, but rather how power is exercised in the concrete. (McCarthy and Dimitriadis, 2000, p. 189)

Foucault's maneuver was to collapse the distinction between power and knowledge, that is, to begin with a single category of power/knowledge. Within this scheme, all practices, including mathematics education practices, are understood as 'discursive', i.e., as readable and potentially critiqued in terms of providing clues to the meanings upon which they are based. Practices themselves become 'technologies of the social', sites through which power/knowledge relations are produced. In this sense, mathematics education practices are part of the apparati of government and are means of regulating the population; they are also historically constituted rather than being the product of universal and trans-historical structures (Appelbaum, 1995, p. 37). The implication of this approach for mathematics education is that it is imperative to trace the history of particular forms of discursive practices so that we can examine how the present 'truths' are constructed, and the effectivity of those truths in the government and regulation of the population.

Discourse

Skovsmose, Batarce and Lerman, and Ernest each contribute chapters to this book that address the discursive character of mathematics education practices. Applying the work of Derrida to the 'Math Wars' discourse, Batarce and Lerman interrogate the debate between mathematicians and mathematics educators, which they describe through a tale of attempts for members of the two 'camps' to "work together". In the Brazilian context, they note how new generations of mathematics educators have "moved away from mathematics" and in the process set up a "new era" with new communities of practice. They note as well that any attempt to understand debates among perspectives on mathematics education already presupposes prior notions of mathematics and mathematics education, and the commonalities and differences between these two nodes in a discourse. The set-up of a 'debate' or social-historical analysis of these terms is already implicated in a 'position on' a pre-established debate. In doing so, they further reify the categories of 'mathematician' and 'mathematics educator' as well, in ways that presuppose differences and positions attached to these terms. I personally work with mathematicians in the U.S. and globally who share more beliefs about mathematics education with me than with many mathematicians, and I know many mathematics educators in Brazil, the U.S. and elsewhere who share more beliefs and practices with many mathematicians than they do with me. I see myself as both a mathematician and a mathematics educator. I imagine I have different definitions of these terms than these authors, so I am not clear on the meaning of this constructed dichotomy. I assume that this analysis makes sense for the specific narrative of mathematicians (who apparently did not identify as mathematics educators) and mathematics educators (who apparently did not identify as mathematicians) in Brazil. My own perspective is that everyone is a mathematician, in the sense of the popular that I discuss later in this Afterword; I would also embrace the notion that everyone - including students and community members – can and often does act as a mathematics educator for others.

When we move from the social text of working together on policy and practice, toward the writing of mathematical text, as in the contribution by Paul Ernest, we see that the meaning of mathematical signs and texts are given by their social uses and functions rather than by their reference to some extra-textual domain of signification. In the context of school mathematics, the asymmetric relationship between teacher and student is enacted through the writing of mathematics primarily by the teacher and the reading of the mathematical text primarily by the student. We might change the power relationships if we work to change the nature of reading and writing mathematics in school. For example, if classroom work more closely resembled the kinds of reading that are done by research mathematicians, then, Ernest indicates, the reader is expected to assume the roles of reader and writer simultaneously, and to adopt as well the meta-role of critic of mathematics texts. In current classrooms, however, the majority of successful behaviors include rule-following and rule-challenging rather than reading and writing. In this respect, significant social and semiotic transformation is in order. The myth of neutrality and objectivity associated with mathematics serves to preserve at once both the asymmetric power relations and the textual interactions which carry their meaning. Taken as common sense, this neutrality and objectivity proscribe the universal nature of mathematics while 'teaching' students that mathematics is a boring collection of activities to be met with indifference:

> Common sense is both an individual possession and a social construction. It helps us learn, do, and teach mathematics and it also can hinder all those processes. ... School mathematics has historically attempted to mirror what has been sees as the abstract, context-free, universal nature of academic mathematics. Consequently, mathematics teaching has tended to concentrate on the promotion of skill in handling routine numerical, algebraic, and geometric operations divorced from meaningful contexts or realistic applications. Far from drawing on, let alone developing, learners' commonsense notions of quantity and space, instruction seeks out the rarified realm of abstraction, formalism, and generality. With few exceptions, learners respond to such instruction with boredom and indifference. (Kilpatrick, 2007, p. 161)

Ole Skovsmose, too, describes mathematics as discourse. He writes of mathematics as a way of acting in the world. This moves our conception of mathematics away from "a picture of reality" toward a way of "speech-acting in a discursively constructed world". Mathematics *in action* builds on the Wittgensteinian notion that meaning is found in use, so that the meaning of mathematical knowledge would only be evident in its construction through action. It is in the action that the functional and/or critical become part of the discursive terrain. Like Ernest, Skovsmose discusses the ways that an illusion of neutrality and objectivity can mediate this terrain, constraining the possibilities for action via an associated fixed notion of mathematics. This may be observed as an *ethical filtration* if mathematical action circumvents reflection-*in*-action and reflection-*on*-action. Skovsmose places knowledge in action in the contemporary context of a knowledge market. In this conception, knowledge is commoditized, and people seem to act as disciples of the economist Adam Smith, expecting the invisible hand of the knowledge market to regulate the knowledge economy. Skovsmose questions the assumption of the invisible hand, and analyzes why certain types of mathematical knowledge seem to be valued over others – value is based on functionality. What this conception does not explain, though, is agency. When, how and why does knowledge in action take on a critical capacity? In my own work, I read the text of mathematical practices in consumer culture as opposed to the knowledge market; in consumer culture, mathematical practices are at once commodities and cultural resources (Appelbaum, 1995). As commodities, they may be taken in the ways described by Skovsmose; as cultural resources, they are the discursive materials through which people construct and deconstruct identities and relationships. Because commodities can always be taken and enacted as cultural resources, and because cultural resources can always be taken and enacted as commodities, we can understand the constraining and enabling character of social structures at the same time as the reproductive and transformative nature of action. I think this is what Ernest is referring to when he writes that "mathematics refers to a semiotic space, a socially constructed realm of signs and meanings." It is also what I believe Skovsmose is seeking in promoting the critical in a world where the functional predominates. The critical does not always exist in action, just as the cultural resource is not always present in practice as anything but a commodity.

Waking Up

When the critical *does* exist in action, we get something other than "static electricity" repeated warmly and reassuringly; we get what Carl Leggo describes as a "... poetic line,/ .. a line that plays ... with possibilities of space,/ draws attention to itself,/contravenes convention ... knows instead lived experience...". Educational practices that promote such experiences shift our attention from education imposed on students from external sources to "the ways in which teachers and pupils make sense of their everyday classroom experiences, and how educational 'reality' is continuously reconstructed in the interaction of individuals" (Whitty and Young, 1976, p. 1). Linked to this change of emphasis has been a refusal to regard definitions of what counts as 'education' as somehow neutral and irrelevant to the way in which inequality is produced in school and society. From such a perspective, the practices of individual teachers and pupils, and the assumptions about knowledge, ability, teaching and learning, which are embedded in these practices, 'secretly' keep society going (Appelbaum, 1995). The authors here have reminded us of Whitty and Young's concern from the 1970s that "both the values embodied in current conceptions of curricular knowledge and the styles of pedagogy and assessment adopted by teachers, which help to sustain existing social hierarchies" (p. 1).

Eric Gutstein and Margaret Walshaw point in directions for practice that speak to the difficulties, and that illustrate potential practices that can support Maxine Greene's notion of wide-awakeness, in terms of pedagogy and professional research in our field. Gutstein writes of forging political relationships with students. "The purpose of such an education," he writes, "should be to create conditions for learners to participate, as fully actualized people, in the struggles for humanization and liberation and for an end to oppression and exploitation." Political relationships are created when students use mathematics in explicitly political ways, using mathematics to critique, question, and challenge relations of power, issues of racism, and other forms of discrimination. This is similar to the kinds of relationships that are developed in the stories shared by Skovsmose. However, in Skovsmose's knowledge-in-action he weaves a critical perspective on mathematics itself as part of the critical social practice. Students who interrogate the complicity of mathematics as a way of thinking and being (e.g., in the story of students' questioning the role of mathematical algorithms in the equitable and democratic distribution of government funds) do not accept mathematics merely as a critical tool. They also see that mathematics as a collection of social practices formats our very way of perceiving reality and "the way the world is."

Stories of meaningful mathematics in action, such as those offered here by Gutstein, Skovsmose, and Walshaw, which I discuss below, are often read by emerging teachers as something that is not consistent with common practice. We hear this in Carol Fulton's contribution, where even the well-meaning teacher educator laments the various institutional structures that apparently prevent such meaningful educational encounters and the development of political relationships. My only thought is to imagine a critical interrogation of both approaches. The teacher educator needs to find ways to redefine the program within which she works. Similarly, the emerging teacher needs to redefine the opportunities. My own recent approach to this is to work with 'replacement units' designed to meet both my own goals and those of others. For example, my undergraduate students are expected to plan lessons and implement assessment tools that are consistent with the school district curriculum framework; we do so by taking children out of their classrooms and leading them through 6-week social justice mathematics investigations, documenting through extensive assessment how the children are meeting the district objectives. When we are questioned about why certain things are transpiring, we simply present the documentation to demonstrate that we are meeting the goals that others have for us. In a high school context, teachers develop 'replacement units' for Algebra II, Geometry, or Calculus, planning social justice experiences and projects that will simultaneously accomplish the week or month of their traditional curriculum; they proactively explain to gatekeepers how their replacement unit will do a better job at attaining the traditional objectives. In both cases, we are developing political relationships through mathematics in action and, in the process, developing a critical perspective on pedagogy and mathematics.

The critical interrogation of the formatting function of mathematized systems of thinking, planning and decision-making is further evident in Margaret Walshaw's description of the New Zealand response to best evidence syntheses regarding diverse students in pāngarau/mathematics. Accepting the potential for collaborative, democratic, and systematic structures for reviewing research evidence already available in research practices, the New Zealand response recognized the central role that infrastructure, context, settings, and accountabilities play within the educational system. Applying postmodern notions of complexity, process, emerging relationships, and interconnections enabled a view of mathematics teaching as a collection of practices nested within systems that "function like an ecology," in which "the activities of the students and the teacher, as well as the school community, the home, the processes involving the mandated curriculum and education-at-large, are constituted mutually through their interactions with each other." Within the nested system, teaching is influenced by adaptive and interactive variables, rather than additive and isolated variables. Student outcomes, in turn, are shaped by teachers' active engagement with processes and people within the classroom and beyond.

As Tony Brown notes in his response to Walshaw, the complexity of the mathematics classroom extends well beyond the conscious processes of teaching and learning, of curriculum delivery and assessment practices. It includes the unconscious desires of those within the psychic space of the classroom, as well as the natural applicability of mathematics to representations of phantasy and of the desired worlds of those who live and work and learn in those classrooms. This echoes some of my own work in psychoanalysis and mathematics teaching and learning with my colleague Rochelle Kaplan (Appelbaum and Kaplan, 1998). What we noted in our study of teacher-student encounters was that students' mathematical conceptions are really a function of the negotiation between the participants' personal relationships with mathematics. Framed in this way as a truly psychoanalytical encounter, mathematical knowledge includes a meta-knowledge of how one 'does' mathematics as well as how one establishes relationships with various objects of mathematics. These relationships to mathematics, and to one's understanding of how they influence the mathematical conclusions that are drawn, become important considerations in and out of school. Many educational encounters serve the teacher as much as, or more than, the student in working through these relations, so that classroom experiences are often more about the teacher's construction of mathematical self than about student learning:

> The educational encounter is not the satisfaction of personal drives deriving from particular selves, but an ongoing establishment of relations with objects, within a particular social practice; an educational encounter is an evocation of selves. This is where critics of recent reform efforts in mathematics education may be wrong: by taking a tough-love stance they misinterpret reform-based mathematics as abandoning skill drill whereas reform-based curriculum merely intends to place its meaning in a new context. On the other hand, where the dream-of-love, child-centered assessment interpretation of reform-based mathematics goes wrong is in its fear of challenging the mathematics itself, and thus failing to enable more substantive changes. It avoids confrontation of the self and its relationship with the mathematics in its desire not to disrupt the dream. In our imagined curriculum, an experientially and reflectively aware aspect of the person is called into existence as the object of his/her own unconscious ego processes; that is, students and teachers become "subjects." Paramount are the perpetually changing object relations that make up a self, and how a teacher's relationship with this theory would change as her or his own object relations alter and coalesce in new ways through work with children. (Appelbaum and Kaplan, 1998, p. 42)

"So," in Brent Davis' words, "how do we get to the pretexts and the subtexts that are concealed in the presented-as-pristine text of *school mathematics* – especially when part of the power of mathematics resides in the concealment of pretexts and subtexts?" He, too, brings us back to the ways that the writers of the school mathematics text – those who literally write text materials, as well as the teachers whom Ernest describes as the writers of the 'texts' read by students – are using the educational encounters as tools for their own object relations. In his contribution, Davis emphasizes the shame in our vanity if we are eager to display the artfulness of our finished weaves/texts.

Stop Making Sense

Davis writes as well about Kierkegaard's fallacy of making things easy. "In the desire to pull learners along a smooth path of concept development, we've planed off the bumpy parts that were once the precise locations of meaning and elaboration." We have, he writes, "created obstacles in the effort to avoid them." In my own work on what Davis calls the "huh" moments – when mathematics stops making sense to us, and we grope for models apparently not available (Appelbaum, 1998) – I, too, have noted the potential for the non-sense-making characteristics of mathematics to generate different kinds of teacher-student relationships, and most significantly, different kinds of relations with mathematics within associated critical mathematical action (Appelbaum, 2003). The text to which Ernest refers hides the messiness, but more importantly constructs a false fantasy of coherence and consistency. As most professional mathematicians understand, mathematics at its core is grounded in indefinable terms (set? point?), inconsistencies (Gödel's proof? Cantor's continuum hypothesis?) and incoherence (the limit paradox in calculus?). At a more basic level, multiplying fractions ends up making things smaller even though multiplying means increasing to so many people; two cylinders made out of the same piece of paper (one rolled length-wise, on width-wise) have the same surface area but hold different volumes; we're taught to add multiple columns of numbers from right to left with re-grouping, when it is so much easier to think left to right starting with the bigger numbers. In some cases, it is impossible, speaking epistemologically, for mathematics as a discipline to 'make sense'; in others, it might be more valuable pedagogically to treat mathematics as if it does not make sense. Yet, so much of contemporary mathematics education practice is devoted to helping students make sense of mathematics! What if, instead, we stopped trying to make sense, and instead worked together with students to study the ways in which mathematics does and does not make sense?

Elizabeth de Freitas describes this as mathematical agency interfering with an abstract realm. Her tale of Agnes troubling the authority of the discipline, in order to belie the 'reasonableness' of mathematics, helps us understand how trickster proofs and carefully constructed forms of undermining mathematics' apparent claim to authority can, as Stephen Brown once wrote, help us to "balance a commitment to truth as expressed within a body of knowledge or emerging knowledge, with an attitude of concern for how that knowledge sheds light in an idiosyncratic way on the emergence of a self" (Brown, 1973, p. 214) The new teachers in Tony Brown's stories also grapple with autonomy and the authority of mathematics as well as with the authority of mathematics curriculum materials. "Obviously somebody somewhere with a lot of authority has actually sat down and written this Numeracy Strategy," says one teacher, "it's not like they don't know what they are talking about." Tony Brown blames the administrative performances that have shaped mathematics for masking what Brent Davis calls huh moments, and what Agnes in Elizabeth de Freitas' fable describes as the self-denial that accompanies "rule and rhythm." Teaching in this "senseless world of mathematical practice" need not abandon science and the rational. It merely shifts teaching away from method and technique toward what Nathalie Sinclair calls the "craft" of the practitioner, as she evokes the metaphor of teaching as midwifery from Plato's *Theaetetus* (see also Appelbaum, 2000). As midwives, teachers assist in the birth of knowledge; students experience not only the pain and unpredictability of the creative process, but also the responsibility for the life of this knowledge once it leaves 'the womb'. One must care for and nurture one's knowledge, whether it acts rationally or not. Can we be confident that the ways we have raised our knowledge will prepare it for when it is let loose upon the world? Will our knowledge be embodied with its own self-awareness and ethical stance?

A Global Imaginary

The contributions by Brent Eidsness, Shana Graham, Kathy Lawless, Devona Putland and Tara Stuckless, invite us to imagine new forms of mathematics education theorizing. "Imagination, according to Arjun Appadurai (1996),

> is the attempt to provide coherence between ideas and action, to provide a basis for the content of social relationships, and the creation of categories with which to understand the world around us. What is imagined defines what we regard as normal. Thus viewed, imagination is not an attribute possessed by a few endowed individuals but, instead, denotes a collective sense of a group of people, a community that begins to imagine and feel things together. (p. 5)

"There has been a shift in recent decades," he wrote, "building upon technological changes over the past century or so, in which imagination has become a collective social fact. This development, in turn, is the basis of the plurality of imagined worlds." (p. 5) We persist, as if it is our job as contributors to this book, in imagining new worlds. This is what defines our collective sense of the field of mathematics education. Foucault (1980) might have said that this was how we kept our profession afloat – by constantly defining problems to solve through our expertise. To Appadurai, this imagination, this collective sense of ourselves, characterizes contemporary diasporic spaces, resulting from the increased flows of ideas, people and cultures. In the past, much of the work of imagination was mediated through the nation-state. But now, imagination transcends national boundaries and emerges in a variety of ways. Indeed, the contributors to this volume hail from Canada, New Zealand, England, Denmark, Brazil and the USA. The product of our efforts is a diasporic space, resulting from increased flows of ideas, people and cultures of mathematics education.

My suggestions for further work center on taking advantage of, and critically analyzing, our own responsibilities within this 'Global imagination' – in which the notions of mobility, trans-culturalism, and diaspora would be especially significant. At one level, the terrain under globalization is a space of flows, an electronic space, a de-centered space, a space in which frontiers and boundaries have become permeable. But at another level, this space seems highly fixed: the center (i.e., the most powerful industrial nations) holds five monopolies: technology, worldwide financial markets, global natural resources (in terms of access), media and communications, and weapons of mass destruction (Stromquist and Monkman, 2000).

I encourage us to awaken through the "transnational imaginary" – the *as-yet-unfigured* horizon of contemporary cultural production by which national spaces/identities of political allegiance and economic regulation are being undone and imagined communities of modernity are being reshaped at the macro political (global) and micro political (cultural) levels of everyday existence. In what ways are mathematics education practices local expressions of the transnational imaginary of globalization, not restricted to the economic arenas of social life? Such practices are concerned with things other than the production, exchange, and consumption of goods and services, and related issues of industry and employment. In what ways are mathematics education practices expressed in and through mass media, converging information technologies, and the social institutions and movements through which we monitor and regulate our concerns about many quality-of-life issues, such as health and the environment? Globalization is expressed in our apprehension of new and increasingly complex patterns of interconnections – cultural processes that destabilize relationships between social organization and the spaces and places in which technologies, materials, media, and meanings are produced, exchanged, and consumed. (Gough, 2000)

As we work with, through and around this global, transnational imaginary, I raise several caveats. First, power is above all discursive; it is evidenced as technologies and practices of 'truth' that deeply inform how social individuals conduct themselves in relation to each other. Taken this way, mathematics education practices are the sites at which state, industry/ economy, and education meet the massive technologies of textual production and meaning construction. The focus of power struggles in the modern global/transnational society is not found in the classic sites of state politics, labor-capital arm wrestling, or the bulldozing actions of civil rights and union-based political actors and their detractors. Modern power struggles are quintessentially located in the deeply contested arenas of the popular, the domain of struggles over social conduct, popular commitments, anxieties and desire, and, ultimately, the disciplining of populations. (McCarthy and Dimitriadis, 2000, p. 189)

Second, students 'know' more about other social, racial, economic and cultural groups through electronic mediation, particularly film and television, than through personal or classroom interaction, or even through textbooks. Yet, these process are co-constitutive, since school textbooks, like academic books generally, have become part of a prurient culture industry with their high density illustrations, their eclectic treatment of subject matter, and their touristy, normalizing discourses of surveillance of marginalized groups. Individuals everywhere 'improvise' local performances from (re)collected pasts, drawing on foreign media, symbols, and languages, in a creolized interculture that destabilizes notions of 'intention' in power relationships, because any commodity can become a cultural resource for political action (Appelbaum, 1995, p. 188) In this sense, mathematics education is articulated to popular culture in ways that implicate broader cultural imperatives.

Third, practices of ethnocentric consolidation and cultural exceptionalism evident on a global scale now characterize much of the tug-of-war over educational reform and diversity, and the stakes could not be any higher, for all parties involved. Specific practices of identity displacement, in which the social actor consolidates his/her identity by a complete disavowal of the merits and existence of his/her social other, generate a sense of self only possible through annihilation or emptying out of the other, whether discursively or materially. At the same time, globalization has brought forth new opportunities for people to define themselves locally as a member of a group or diasporic category, counteracting the global sameness. These forces together construct openings for the creation of prejudice, misunderstanding, and inequitable action, and, as Una Hanley requests, "where the porosity of boundaries is deliberately made clear".

This is not intended to imply that mathematics has any sort of international or global position from which is warranted any particular transnational of global universality or privilege. Indeed, if anything, mathematics is the discipline most readily associated with colonialism and imperialism, given the particular history and recent cultural ascension of specifically European mathematics. That mathematics which developed in Europe in the 13th through 19th centuries has seemingly been accepted by professional 'mathematicians' internationally as defining their field of study, despite the wealth of ethnomathematical studies and regional mathematical practices that suggest the potential for alternative forms of mathematical practice. As Swanson writes in her response, "Given (Western) mathematics' current role in schools as a powerful discourse in perpetuating and entrenching oppression and social and ecological injustice globally, it is even more important for teachers of mathematics, as compared to those of other subject areas, to approach the teaching of mathematics from a social justice perspective." While professional (elite) mathematics is dominated by a received 'canon' of content and practices, local mathematical practices are rhizomatically spreading across diasporic flows. With Swanson, I suggest we craft "a pedagogy that is more liberatory than those currently being espoused, by providing students with inside knowledge of how power operates to enable them to take action, rather than just using mathematics' descriptive powers to evidence it." The subtle modification I would like to make in this Afterword is that we can not simply "provide" students with inside knowledge; a gift we give is not always received as a gift. We might instead work with students on using those funds of knowledge they bring with them, and to enrich their understanding of the ways that they can work with, as well as critique, mathematics in action.

My recommendation for mathematics education is to 'write' a transnational, global imaginary in which students and teachers are working together as mathematicians, critically appraising their mathematical work. Such work would be embedded in social action projects (Appelbaum, 2007), both using mathematics as a tool of social justice and developing a critical competence regarding the mathematical concepts and techniques themselves. I imagine with Una Hanley that this will look like the multiple offspring of an ill-sorted parentage. For me, though, the parentage is not mathematics and education, which would only perpetuate what I have already described as a false dichotomy; I offer instead the parentage of global and transnational practices - two terms that overlap but carry with them significantly different political sentiments, which will generate, I imagine, different forms of political relationships between teachers and students, and between teachers, students, and members of their diasporic communities. Critique implies the evaluation of one's own practices in relation to the differentiations (and hence inequalities or hierarchies) that they create (Brown and Dowling, 1989; Appelbaum, 1995).

Action in Concert: An ethnographic approach

For mathematics education, the development of political relationships in action, and the evaluation of one's own practices in relation to the differentiations that they create, demand that we design experiences "that enable people to pay, from their own distinctive vantage points, 'full attention to life'" (Greene, 1978, p. 163). Such experiences grow, writes Maxine Greene, where "people create themselves by acting in concert" (Greene, 1988, p. 134). She is speaking here of power as associated with consent. This is in the tradition of power as creating possibility, rather than the oppressive, negative notion of power that sometimes gets our attention. Evidence of this sort of power appears in actions that structure other actions, and in this sense, power is productive.

I suggest youth cultural practices can usefully inform and influence the ways we work and learn in the classroom. Understanding the ways that youth accomplish creative work in their everyday lives outside of school, we can organize school mathematics experiences so that youth can use the same ways of working in school mathematics. Ethnography is a form of qualitative research: the researcher works to understand lived practices, by 'looking, listening, collecting, questioning, and interpreting' (Sunstein and Chiseri-Strater, 2000, p.1). Ethnographers come to understand how the people they are studying make meaning in the world, realizing that they know little and the people who are part of the phenomena - the "natives"- know a lot (Gallas, 1994). When we make this analogous to teaching, it is our job as teachers to figure out how our students are mathematicians, instead of assuming that they are not or that they need to be taught how to be: the students become the teachers about what they know and do.

A teacher influenced by ethnographic practices recognizes that the student is involved in a practice, a craft, a habit of mind and body that enables the student to do the work of the popular culture form. The teacher must work to understand the how and why of the youth's popular culture practice, both because of centrality of the popular as deeply contested arenas of modern power struggles over social conduct, popular commitments, anxieties and desire, and, ultimately, the disciplining of populations, because creative practice within the popular – appropriation of commodities as cultural resources - is one way in which students make meaning in the world. Here's how you know when you are achieving this: You have a student and she's a poet. She is not just reading Vaclav Havel and Tupac Shakur; she's reading all over the place; watching and thinking in so many seemingly disparate ways that contribute to and make it possible for her to make meaning in this popular culture form. Or, you've got a student, and she is a mathematician. She is not just doing math homework or number crunching all day; she's thinking in creative, disparate and diverse ways that inform what she does as a mathematician.

Understanding youth cultural practices requires that we look at youth as inherently creative problem solvers, posers, solution-finders, etc. The teacher enters her/his room assuming that her/his students are already some form of mathematician, scientist, poet, architect, etc. Karen Gallas (1994), a grade 1-2 teacher, "suspend[s] [her] disbelief as a teacher and [leaves her] judgment in abeyance in service of a child's development" (p. 96). She references her experience with John (age 7) who, in science class, says that rap is science because 'rap is so exciting when you, when you never went to a rap concert, it's so exciting, like micro- and they're electric too…'. Gallas writes, "Rather than my 'teaching' John what science was, we struggled together to understand his changing picture of science" (p. 96). Edward Said (1994) would describe Gallas as a 'professional amateur', someone who doesn't limit themselves through their special knowledge of a discipline. Experts, Said contrasts, only feel comfortable approaching problems, issues, and ideas through their rarified knowledge. When someone presents an expert with a problem that grows out of their craft of popular culture, an expert often feels that s/he can't even discuss it because it is beyond the purview of her/his expertise. What they know has nothing to do with the problem. Teachers, too, often think of themselves or approach their subject as experts. A math teacher may see her/his job as teaching how to factor polynomials, and therefore cannot afford the time to link mathematics with national elections, or even be able to entertain a provocative tangent related to everyday life. Teachers as professional amateurs, on the other hand, voraciously pounce on these opportunities to think about things differently and learn from others. They relish the chance to get involved in conversations where they can take what they know and grow new understandings. They see their students as allies in a common project, expecting to learn from their students not just how to be a better teacher or how to understand fractions in a new way but also about the world in general. Students' experiences in popular cultural practices are resources for the 'professional-amateur' teacher's own understandings of academic subject knowledge in particular and the world more broadly.

Youth involved in popular cultural practices are professional amateurs as well. Consider Karl, a zine writer, whose cultural practice is to write handmade publications that he distributes to friends and through independent bookstores and CD stores. What makes Karl a professional amateur is the range and variety of things that he does that somehow influence how he writes his zines. For example, he reads widely and disparately (including *The Economist*, comic books, and *On the Road* by Jack Kerouac); he sculpts, makes films, attends rallies, views films, writes music, listens to music, plays pool with friends, and volunteers at a soup kitchen. He doesn't pursue these experiences because of his interest in zine writing; nevertheless, they inform and influence what and how he decides to write. Like Gallas, teachers who understand popular culture as a craft provide a space where students can see for themselves that the skills and concepts that they are developing within their popular cultural practices are assets in the classroom. All of Karl's varied experiences can be used in the classroom to do the work of the class. Thus, we are avoiding a deficit model of teaching: the student is not an empty vessel. Students as professional amateurs see their craft as informing and influencing the way they engage in the work of the class. They see academic disciplines and their popular cultural practices as equal resources for their work. Karl might do similar work in math class: reading widely from different sources including other students' summaries of what they have discovered or invented around non-continuous functions; organizing meetings to plan a class newsletter; forming an editorial board; recording images from films, sculpture, and comic books that can be used in his mathematics investigation; organizing a web blog of challenge problems for students around the world. The point is not to use the ways of working literally, but as a metaphor for the kinds of thinking and doing that happen in the classroom.

Action in Concert: Avoiding the false problem of mathematics education

As teachers, we are always trying to find something to do with our students. The problem is that our search for the best activities is never over; we're always hunting for more ideas. Jean Lave (1997) captures this perpetual crisis of teaching, comparing a curriculum that supports the cultural practices of youth with a curriculum that delineates what practice must be:

> The problem is that any curriculum intended to be a specification of practice, rather than an arrangement of opportunities for practice (for fashioning and resolving ownable dilemmas) is bound to result in the teaching of a misanalysis of practice ... and the learning of still another. At best it can only induce a new and exotic kind of practice ... In the settings for which it is intended (in everyday transactions), it will appear out of order and will not in fact reproduce "good" practice. (p. 32)

The global transnational imaginary I propose is more sustainable than the kind of curriculum that is built from daily lessons and one-off activities. It is *a way of being in the classroom*, not a collection of methods of teaching. Implementing this sort of curriculum gives teachers a 'solution' to the problem of constantly trying to find one day, one month or one hour of something to do in the classroom. Lemke (1997) reminds us that "practices are not just performances, not just behaviors, not just material processes or operations, but meaningful actions, actions that have relations of meaning to one another in terms of some cultural system" (p. 43). Thus, building a 'common culture' of 'professional amateurs' in our classrooms enables our students to "learn not just what and how to perform, but also what the performance means" (Lemke, 1997, p. 43). We build with our students a 'community of classroom practice' through a conception of popular culture as craft: One must know the meaning in order to appropriately deploy the practice, to know when and in what context to perform.

Maxine Greene (1986) offers the following invitation:

To engage with our students as persons is to affirm our own incompleteness, our consciousness of spaces still to be explored, desires still to be
tapped, possibilities still to be opened and pursued...We have to find out
how to open such spheres, such spaces, where a better state of things can
be imagined...I would like to think that this can happen in classrooms, in
corridors, in schoolyards, in the streets around. (p. 29)

   Modeling our pedagogy on popular culture 'craft' begins to affirm our
own incompleteness as well as our consciousness of spaces still to be explored - incomplete in that we do not know everything about our students;
realms of popular cultural practices are still to be explored with our students.
To support the crafts of youth culture in our classroom is to open and pursue
new possibilities. Perhaps a better state of things can be imagined when we
move away from the hierarchy of high culture vs. low culture to a more
common culture, where students as professional amateurs seize upon both
academic disciplines and popular cultural practices as resources for their
work. New things might happen in classrooms, corridors, schoolyards, and
the streets if the culture of the streets informs the way we work in classrooms. Youth cultural practices enacted as ways of being in the classroom
make each student "present" as who they really are, not just in the role of a
student but as someone who knows 'what they want to do today'.

Action in Concert: Projections

   One might imagine school mathematics finding such craft-based meaning
and social purpose through integration with other school subject areas. I
agree that this could be the case. However, I disagree that "subjects like music, computing and even some aspects of humanities are easier to discuss
with schoolmates, and thus become preferred subjects" (CIEAEM, 2006).
Instead, let's have students discuss mathematics with classmates in the same
ways that they talk about music, computing and humanities. I also disagree,
as has been suggested, that "mathematics ... needs a strong, long-term
commitment from the individual (based on deep mental concentration and
cumulative, systematic appropriation of knowledge), within an appropriate
environment (...silence)." (CIEAEM, 2006) I argue instead that the commitment will grow through personal connections to a self-designed investigation
or experiment. Such mathematics fosters social connection rather than 'social isolation', and routes to consumption rather than distraction.

   - **Can mathematics be taught in such a way as to become a subject
     that can be shared with schoolmates, a 'social medium'?**

Yes: Learning from youth cultural practices and taking a stance as ethnographer of everyday life, teachers make the ways of working in the classroom more closely approximate the ways of working that youth exhibit when they are productive, creative scholars and craftspeople outside of school. Schooling can be a vibrant context for youth to demonstrate the *funds of knowledge* that they bring with them to school, rather than a place of disconnect and the delay of future gratification.

- **Can the cultural values inherent in some aspects of mathematics be linked to other more 'popular' subjects?**

Yes: However, this occurs most effectively *not* through looking for clever connections to other subjects, *nor* by using other subjects as the motivating 'hook' that 'tricks kids into learning math', but instead by allowing those modes of thinking and working that students find personally meaningful to inform the ways that they work within school mathematics.

Observing and interviewing youth, we notice that they accomplish creative work by finding their own ways to meet criteria for the work that is valued; making their own decisions about how to use their time. Multi-tasking is at the heart of their productivity. Most importantly, they take what they have learned and find on their own some way to put their work back out into the world, so that their connections with people outside of their immediate (school) work have an impact, either on these other people or on themselves.

- **Some basic elements of the pedagogy I recommend:**

Start a unit with a common exploration of the global issues of a main theme; 2) Provide time for students to explore their own interests related to the theme; 3) Organize class time so that students can help each other identify personal or small group investigations; 4) Introduce mini-lessons on skills and concepts as related to the investigations that students have designed themselves; 5) Provide a deadline for putting one's work back out into the world; 6) Organize an archaeology of the work accomplished that facilitates students' awareness of the skills and concepts they have learned through their work, and of their ability to apply what they have been learning in new contexts.

Professional amateurs - students who work as mathematicians using the skills and concepts that they bring with them from youth cultural practices into the classroom - examine this very set of questions themselves as part of their work. In the process, they come to appreciate the ways that scientific, aesthetic, and other types of inquiry can inform their work in important ways.

- **Can the creative side of mathematical activity be incorporated into classroom tasks?** Using popular culture in school is not a new idea, and we can learn from other teachers' work. Here are some common ways that popular culture is used in the classroom: as entertainment and motivating force; as a connection to the 'real world'; as a unit of study; as social critique. While I have had success with each approach, I have come to realize that they don't take advantage of what popular cultural practices have to offer: the ways in which youth engage in the practices - how they do what they do.

Missing from much of current school practice – which explains the prevalence of 'static electricity' across the curriculum - is Aristotle's idea of *tekhne*: "the art in mundane skill and, more significantly, in day-to-day life...an intrinsic aesthetic or crafting that underlies the practices of everyday life... 'a reasoned habit of mind in making something'" (Cintron, 1997, p. xii). To explain this, I have developed a continuum of popular culture curriculum:

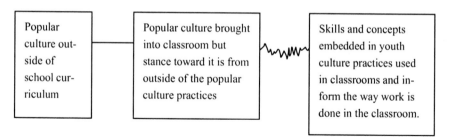

On one end of this continuum, the popular culture artifact or practice is outside the National Syllabi, State and Provincial Standards, and local school curriculum frameworks. To the right of this approach, students take on the roles of someone in popular culture. Students in English might publish their own Zines. Students may be filmmakers in history and graffiti artists in math. While there's a fine line that may be hard to see at first, I place myself to the right of this stance. I concern myself with the artificiality of playing a role, a subtle yet significant issue: Normally students play the role of 'student' in a classroom; if we ask them to play the role of graffiti artist, fashion critic, or film director, how is the experience of learning all that different from the same old classroom that doesn't concern itself with popular culture (Appelbaum, 2000)? In the classrooms on the left or middle of the continuum, the teacher has chosen one popular culture experience, artifact, or set of practices; s/he still must extrinsically motivate students. In my conception (to the right), I build instead on the skills and practices that students use in their engagement with and participation in popular culture, transporting these habits of mind and body into the classroom work at hand. I *design an infrastructure* for how we will work together in the classroom, *rather than an overt structure*, to support and capitalize on the wealth of skills and concepts that youth bring with them into the learning environment from all of the cultural work they are doing on the 'outside'.

Action in Concert: Curriculum for millennial students.

The current generation of *millennial children*, especially in the US, are shaped by cultural messages, including 'be smart – you are special' (children's TV, special stores for youth products, special magazines and other media, recreational programs); 'leave no one behind' (be inclusive of other ethnicities, races, religions and sexual orientations); 'connect 24/7' (it is good to be interdependent on/with family, friends, teachers); 'achieve now' (go to the right school, university, etc.); and 'serve your community' (think of the greater good). Mathematics experiences should be designed so that they can enact the values of these messages; they feel special and unique, sheltered (others often take the risks for them), confident (they have been told they are great since birth), team-oriented (from group pedagogies in school to participation in team sports to play-dates), achievement-focused (need to accomplish something they can point to), pressured (want the experience to contribute to recognition), and conventional (unlike baby-boomers who criticized adults, they share many values with the adults in their lives).

Part 1	Part 2 through Part 4	*Part 5*
Opening **Creating the Issue** Finding the Question *Generating the Interest*	**Doing the Investigation** *Three weeks devoted to active engagement in student designed investigation around curricular themes, issues, conflicts, problems*	*Archaeology* *Making explicit the knowledge gained*
Open-ended activities to elicit student-generated questions about issues or problems related to discipline concepts, curricular topic, or theme **Materials needed:** Mathematicians' Notebooks, Criteria,	Three parts devoted to mathematical investigations. Class time devoted to discussing work done, strategizing next steps, organizing mini-lessons and workshops on ideas generated by students, and putting the work back out into the world. **Materials needed:** Mathematician's Notebooks; Criteria specifications; conference forms; peer feedback; teacher feedback; center materials; new tools and materials as needed for investigations; assessment vehicles.	Time devoted in class to look back at the work done, to name what has been learned, and to extend it into new areas and directions. **Materials needed:** Mathematician's Notebooks; tests & other evaluation instruments;

books, Center materials, films, speakers, field trips, to help stimulate interest **Envisioned activities:** Quickies; Center work modeling Polya Phases, Specializing and Generalizing, and Problem Posing; Improv warm-ups; Discussions; lists of questions; experiments, background information **Culmination:** Each student identifies mathematically interesting and potentially significant ideas that they have been working with at a center (on posters, in discussions, in their notebooks, etc.); Students identify the center they will return to for their own investigation.	**Envisioned activities:** Interviews, experiments, debates, in-class writing and work time, peer-review of work in progress, reading discussions, mini-lessons and workshops developed by teacher, initiated by students, guest speakers, planning sessions, etc.	manipulatives; new problems **Activities:** Quickies, Improv; Core curriculum and Standards based conversations where investigations are linked to school, city and state expectations; challenges presented by teacher to show students they can utilize skills and concepts developed in their investigations; activities that encourage students to transport the skills and knowledge they learned to other areas. **Culmination:** Class addresses these questions: What should we do next? Starting a new project Leave taking, goodbyes, and plans for a reunion.

Developing the Investigation	**Doing the Investigation** *Can start this part sooner if students identify their investigation.*	**Putting the Work Back Out Into the World**
Activities: Quickies, Center Work, Polya Phases, Problem-Posing; Improv; Reflecting on their work; Discussions **Assessment:** Student work sample analyses; Center observation notes; Targeted interviews **Culmination:** Peer strategy session	**Activities:** Quickies, Center Work, Polya Phases, Problem-Posing; Improv; Reflecting on their work; Discussions of student work on large posters; mini-lessons and workshops as needed **Assessment:** Student work sample analyses; Center observation notes; Targeted interviews **Culmination:** Students identify a mathematically significant idea coming out of their investigation.	**Activities:** Quickies; Improv; Writing about the idea; brainstorming in groups; getting ideas up on big sheets of paper; practice meeting with potential audiences; actually doing the work of putting the work back out into the world. Questions guiding the critical activities: What do you want to do with what you've learned? What *should* you do? Do something that impacts on you, or that impacts on other people. **Assessment:** Student work sample analyses; Center observation notes; Targeted interviews **Culmination:** Taking the action of work back out into the world. Debriefing of the experience.

The five-part structure centers the above feelings by leading students through investigations of their own design, identifying findings and results by members of the community of mathematicians, relying on the class as a support team that helps individuals think through their ideas and/or leads to small group collaborations, and facilitates students' making an impact on the larger community based on what they have accomplished; the end of the experience enables them to recognize what they have learned and achieved, and to see that they have met goals that adults have set for them. The teacher introduces critical skill and concept goals and ways of working as a mathematician (e.g., Polya, 1945; Mason et al., 1982/85; Brown and Walter, 1983) through mini-lessons or 'clinics', understood by the students as helping them to accomplish their own investigations.

The specialness of each student is established in tandem with a 'team' through the *opening* and *developing the investigation*; initial experiences also satisfy conventionality (the topic is chosen by adults) and shelter (impossible to fail at identifying what one wants to accomplish, what one already knows about a topic). We introduce Polya, Mason, and Brown/Walter first by identifying how students already use these strategies on their own, and then as tools for helping them get unstuck when they do not know what to do next. Classroom conversations elicit ideas from other students as part of the supportive team, and highlight everyone as doing something special contributing to others' learning. Students use Polya's 'looking back' to repeatedly identify what they have achieved so far. Treating students as mathematicians refining their techniques to further achieve, we are taking advantage of students' confidence in themselves while also helping them meet pressures for success from family and society. At the same time, taking the accent off mastering prescribed mathematics material, and shifting the emphasis to using such material to see what they might be able to do with it, we make risk-taking easier, accommodating the need for shelter. Putting the work out into the world helps students use what has been done so far to connect with others outside of the class, working for the good of the larger community. The archaeology phase helps students see that they have indeed achieved, and to apply skills and concepts learned to other contexts beyond the specific investigation carried out.

My Brain is Open

To wake up, is, in Paul Erdös' terms, to greet everyone with the phrase, "My brain is open" (Schechter 2000). (In opening the research text, the editors and contributors to this volume maintain this spirit. The text is still open. We are awakened, to both new possibilities and the responsibilities they evoke. The difficulties have troubled our practice, and in so doing have made it possible for readers of this work to "affirm [their] own incompleteness, [their] consciousness of spaces still to be explored, desires still to be tapped, possibilities still to be opened and pursued." We can no longer open this text without taking seriously the notion that mathematics education research is about constructing standpoints or perspectives on power distribution and the physics of power relations (Christensen, Stentoft, and Valero); nor without an awareness of the troubling notion that critical mathematics education could result, to our disappointment, in maintaining social exclusion in contrast with the potential empowering social function of more traditional schooling practices (Skovsmose); nor without the consumer cultural perspective on mathematics as collections of commodities/cultural resources in a market-driven society. Concepts run away in all possible directions (Skovsmose), yet the run-away difficulties of the concepts we employ in making our professional decisions are the very things that keep our research text open, generate actions that structure other actions, and in this sense, foster possibility and hope. It is imperative that policy be informed by research that admits counter-scientific strategies in order to address both the needs of diverse learners and the patterns of systematic underachievement; in this way, we keep the negotiation and decisions processes vivid, in the moment, dynamic and complex (Walshaw). We have the opportunity to consider those realms of professional practice that involve unconscious desires, and to interpret our actions in terms of fantasy and dreams as much as target setting and 'solutions'; to recognize the ways that global disturbance and anxieties about 'big transnational crises' interact with micro-level actions where adults who harbor ambivalent attitudes towards adolescents might not be willing or able to engage with the very issues that are making the strongest impact on their practice (Brown); to coopt mathematics' rhetorical possibilities even as we remain aware of and challenge its role in imperialism and social reproduction (Swanson).

Discourses and talking past one another are part of the very fabric of this open text. Many of us feel that there are different 'camps' in the global mathematics education diaspora, manifesting themselves as localized instances of conflict and miscommunication. In this sense, we must be cognizant of those ways that the appearance of an open text is always leaving its trace in terms of hierarchies and privilege, sometimes in terms of who is the definitive voice on 'mathematics education', at other times in terms of who is even at the table, to 'play' *with* the mathematics education discourse (Batarce and Lerman). Some of us turn for solace to the work of Deleuze and Guattari, because their notion of a plane of immanence seems to represent so much of how we experience our own practice as researchers, teachers, students, policy-makers, and community participants. Jacques Derrida, too, made a repeated appearance; his work on grammatology and discourse has become fundamental to current efforts to open the text of our work. Still others turn to psychoanalysis or socio-linguistics. These are all tools from the last century that a mathematics educator today should not be without.

The same goes for concepts of globalization, a transnational imaginary, and consumer culture. Each of these tools may be used to write as an intrusive 'third space' (de Freitas); to embrace the semiotic recognition that action involves fitting new suggestions with a mostly non-conscious weave/web/ network/text of bodily base, culturally situated, and linguistically effected associations (Davis). There are complex layers of the social encoded in this 'opened' text, contrary to the myth of objectivity and impersonality; indeed, the texts of mathematics and of mathematics education research are fundamentally and idiosyncratically interwoven *as* the ongoing construction and reconstruction of self (Ernest, Stuckless, Brown). We are called to forge political relationships with our students using mathematics as a resource, indeed to recognize the increasing body of research that points to such relationships as critical to the most effective forms of culturally relevant pedagogy (Gutstein); to work with our students in developing new program structures, using the work of our colleagues who have already done so as models and provocations to take the next step (Fulton); to confront narratives of compliance as we refuse to make things easier for others (Nolan, Eidsness, Graham, Lawless, Putland, Stuckless).

The 'easy' is static electricity; the difficult is what keeps us open.

REFERENCES

Appadurai, Arjun. (1996). *Modernity at large.* Minneapolis: University of Minnesota Press.
Appelbaum, Peter, and Kaplan, Rochelle. (1998). An Other Mathematics: Object Relations and the Clinical Interview. *Journal of Curriculum Theorizing, 14*(2), 35-42.
Appelbaum, Peter. (1995). *Popular culture, educational discourse, and* mathematics. Albany, NY: SUNY Press.
Appelbaum, Peter. (1998). And We Built a Crooked Place: Beyond the Commodity/Cultural Resource Dualism Through Curriculum as Klein Bottle. JCT Conference on Curriculum Theory and Classroom Practice. Indianapolis, IN, Oct. 21-25.
Appelbaum, Peter. (2000). Performed by the Space: The Spatial Turn. *Journal of Curriculum Theorizing, 16*(3), 35-53.
Appelbaum, Peter. (2003). Critical considerations on the didactic materials of critical thinking in mathematics, and critical mathematics education. (Quasi-plenary lecture). In *Proceedings of the International Commission for the Study and Improvement of Mathematics Teaching*, Maciej Klakla (ed.). Płock, Poland. July 22-28.
Appelbaum, Peter. (2007). *Embracing mathematics: On becoming a teacher and changing with mathematics.* NY: Routledge.
Brown, Andrew, and Dowling, Paul. (1989). *Towards a critical alternative to internationalism and monoculturalism in mathematics* education. London: Centre for Multicultural Education, Institute of Education, Working paper No. 10.
Brown, Stephen I. (1973). Mathematics and Humanistic Themes: Sum considerations. *Educational Theory, 23*(3), 191-214.

Brown, Stephen, and Walter, Marion. (1983). *The art of problem posing.* Philadelphia: The Franklin Institute Press.

CIEAEM – International Commission for the Study and Improvement of Mathematics Education. (2006). *Changes in society: A challenge for mathematics education. Changements dans la societe: Un defi pour l'enseignement des mathematiques: Le commun et les differences.* Proceedings of CIEAEM 58, Srni (pp. 108-113). Plzeň, Czech Republic: University of West Bohemia.

Cintron, Ralph. (1997). *Angels' Town: Cheroways gang life and rhetorics of the everyday.* Boston: Beacon Press.

Cook, Matt. (2005). Static electricity. In *Eavesdrop Soup*: 33. San Francisco: Manic D Press.

Foucault, Michel. (1980). *Power/knowledge: Selected interviews and other writings.* Brighton, England: Harvester Press..

Gallas, Karen. (1994). *The languages of learning: How children talk, write, dance, draw, and sing their understanding of the world.* NY: Teachers College Press.

Gough, Noel. (2000). Globalization and curriculum inquiry: locating, representing, and performing a transnational imaginary. In Stromquist, Nelly and Monkman, Karen (eds.) *Globalization and education: Integration and contestation across cultures*: 77-98. Lanham MD: Rowman & Littlefield.

Greene, Maxine. (1978). Towards wide awakeness: An argument for the arts and humanities in education. In *Landscapes of learning*: 161-167. NY: Teachers College Press.

Greene, Maxine. (1986). In search of a critical pedagogy. *Harvard Educational Review.* 56 (4): 427-441.

Greene, Maxine. (1988). *The Dialectic of Freedom.* NY: Teachers College Press.

Holt, John. (1989). *Learning all the time: How small children begin to read, write, count, and investigate the world, without being taught.* NY: Addison-Wesley.

Kierkegaard, Søren. (1947). Concluding unscientific postscript to the 'Philosophical Fragments'. In *A Keirkegaard Anthology,* Robert Bretall (ed.). Princeton, NJ: Princeton University Press.

Kilpatrick, Jeremy. (2007). Developing common sense in teaching mathematics. In Uwe Gellert and Eva Jablonka (eds.), *Mathematisation and demathematisation: Social, philosophical and educational ramifications*: 161-169. Rotterdam: Sense Publishers.

Lave, Jean. (1997). The culture of acquisition and the practice of understanding. In David Kirshner and James Whitson, eds., *Situated cognition: Social, semiotic and psychological perspectives*, 17-36. Mahwah, NJ: Lawrence Erlbaum.

Lemke, Jay. (1997). Cognition, context, and learning: A social semiotic perspective. In David Kirshner and James Whitson, eds., *Situated cognition: Social, semiotic and psychological perspectives*: 37-55. Mahwah, NJ: Lawrence Erlbaum.

Mason, John, et al. (1982/85). *Thinking mathematically.* NY/Wokingham: Addison-Wesley.

McCarthy, Cameron, and Dimitriadis, Greg. (2000). Globalizing pedagogies: Power, resentment, and the re-narration of difference. In *Globalization and education: Critical perspectives*: 187-204. NY: Routledge.

Polya, Georg. (1945). *How to solve it.* Princeton, NJ: Princeton University press.

Russell, Bertrand. (1938). *Power: A new social analysis.* NY: Norton.

Said, Edward. (1994). *Representations of the intellectual.* NY: Pantheon Books.

Schechter, Bruce. (2000). *My brain is open: The mathematical journeys of Paul Erdös.* NY: Simon and Schuster.

Stromquist, Nelly, and Monkman, Karen. (2000). Defining globalization and assessing its implication on knowledge and education. In Stromquist, Nelly and Monkman, Karen (eds.). *Globalization and education: Integration and contestation across cultures*: 3-26. Lanham, MD: Rowman and Littlefield.

Sunstein, Bonnie and Chiseri-Strater, Elizabeth. (2000). *Fieldworking: Reading and writing research*. NY: Bedford/St. Martins.

Whitty, Geoff, and Young, Michael (eds.). (1976). *Explorations in the politics of school knowledge*. Nafferton, England: Nafferton Books.

SUBJECT INDEX

Mathematics Education Library

Managing Editor: A.J. Bishop, Melbourne, Australia

H. Freudenthal: *Didactical Phenomenology of Mathematical Structures*. 1983. ISBN 90-277-1535-1 HB; 90-277-2261-7 PB

B. Christiansen, A. G. Howson and M. Otte (eds.): Perspectives on Mathematics Education. Papers submitted by Members of the Bacomet Group. 1986 90-277-1929-2 HB; 90-277-2118-1 PB

A. Treffers: Three Dimensions. A Model of Goal and Theory Description in Mathematics Instruction. TheWiskobas Project. 1987. ISBN 90-277-2165-3

S. Mellin-Olsen: The Politics of Mathematics Education. 1987. ISBN 90-277-2350-8

E. Fischbein: Intuition in Science and Mathematics. An Educational Approach. 1987. ISBN 90-277-2506-3

A.J. Bishop: Mathematical Enculturation. A Cultural Perspective on Mathematics Education.1988 ISBN 90-277-2646-9 HB; 0-7923-1270-8 PB

E. von Glasersfeld (ed.): Radical Constructivism in Mathematics Education. 1991. ISBN 0-7923-1257-0

L. Streefland: Fractions in Realistic Mathematics Education. A Paradigm of Developmental Research. 1991. ISBN 0-7923-1282-1

H. Freudenthal: Revisiting Mathematics Education. China Lectures. 1991. ISBN 0-7923-1299-6

A.J. Bishop, S. Mellin-Olsen and J. van Dormolen (eds.): Mathematical Knowledge: Its Growth Through Teaching. 1991. ISBN 0-7923-1344-5

D. Tall (ed.): Advanced Mathematical Thinking. 1991. ISBN 0-7923-1456-5

R. Kapadia and M. Borovcnik (eds.): Chance Encounters: Probability in Education. 1991. ISBN 0-7923-1474-3

R. Biehler, R.W. Scholz, R. Sträßer and B. Winkelmann (eds.): Didactics of Mathematics as a Scientific Discipline. 1994. ISBN 0-7923-2613-X

S. Lerman (ed.): Cultural Perspectives on the Mathematics Classroom. 1994. ISBN 0-7923-2931-7

O. Skovsmose: Towards a Philosophy of Critical Mathematics Education. 1994. ISBN 0-7923-2932-5

H. Mansfield, N.A. Pateman and N. Bednarz (eds.): Mathematics for Tomorrow's Young Children. International Perspectives on Curriculum.1996. ISBN 0-7923-3998-3

R. Noss and C. Hoyles: Windows on Mathematical Meanings. Learning Cultures and Computers.1996. ISBN 0-7923-4073-6 HB; 0-7923-4074-4 PB

N. Bednarz, C. Kieran and L. Lee (eds.): Approaches to Algebra. Perspectives for Research and Teaching.1996. ISBN 0-7923-4145-7 HB; 0-7923-4168-6, PB

G. Brousseau: Theory of Didactical Situations in Mathematics. Didactique des Mathématiques 1970-1990. **Edited and translated by N. Balacheff, M. Cooper, R. Sutherland and V. Warfield.** 1997. ISBN 0-7923-4526-6

T. Brown: Mathematics Education and Language. Interpreting Hermeneutics and Post-Structuralism. 1997 ISBN 0-7923-4554-1 HB. Second Revised Edition. 2001. ISBN 0-7923-6969-6 PB

D. Coben, J. O'Donoghue and G.E. FitzSimons (eds.): Perspectives on Adults Learning Mathematics. Research and Practice. 2000. ISBN 0-7923-6415-5

R. Sutherland, T. Rojano, A. Bell and R. Lins (eds.): Perspectives on School Algebra. 2000. ISBN 0-7923-6462-7

J.-L. Dorier (ed.): On the Teaching of Linear Algebra. 2000. ISBN 0-7923-6539-9

A. Bessot and J. Ridgway (eds.): Education for Mathematics in the Workplace. 2000. ISBN 0-7923-6663-8

D. Clarke (ed.): Perspectives on Practice and Meaning in Mathematics and Science Classrooms. 2001. ISBN 0-7923-6938-6 HB; 0-7923-6939-4 PB

J. Adler: Teaching Mathematics in Multilingual Classrooms. 2001. ISBN 0-7923-7079-1 HB; 0-7923-7080-5 PB

G. de Abreu, A.J. Bishop and N.C. Presmeg (eds.): Transitions Between Contexts of Mathematical Practices. 2001. ISBN 0-7923-7185-2

G.E. FitzSimons: What Counts as Mathematics? Technologies of Power in Adult and Vocational Education. 2002. ISBN 1-4020-0668-3

H.Alrø andO. Skovsmose: Dialogue and Learning in Mathematics Education. Intention, Reflection,Critique.2002. ISBN 1-4020-0998-4 HB;1-4020-1927-0 PB

K. Gravemeijer, R. Lehrer, B. van Oers and L. Verschaffel (eds.): Symbolizing, Modeling and Tool Use in Mathematics Education. 2002. ISBN 1-4020-1032-X

G.C. Leder, E. Pehkonen and G. T rner (eds.): Beliefs: A Hidden Variable in Mathematics Education? 2002. ISBN 1-4020-1057-5 HB; 1-4020-1058-3 PB

R. Vithal: In Search of a Pedagogy of Conflict and Dialogue for Mathematics Education. 2003. ISBN 1-4020-1504-6

H.W. Heymann: Why Teach Mathematics? A Focus on General Education. 2003. **Translated by T. LaPresti** ISBN 1-4020-1786-3

L. Burton: Mathematicians as Enquirers: Learning about Learning Mathematics. 2004. ISBN 1-4020-7853-6 HB; 1-4020-7859-5 PB

P. Valero, R. Zevenbergen (eds.): Researching the Socio-Political Dimensions of Mathematics Education: Issues of Power in Theory and Methodology. 2004. ISBN 1-4020-7906-0

D. Guin, K. Ruthven, L. Trouche (eds.): The Didactical Challenge of Symbolic Calculators: Turning a Computational Device into a Mathematical Instrument. 2005. ISBN 0-387-23158-7

J. Kilpatrick, C. Hoyles, O. Skovsmose (eds. in collaboration with Paola Valero): Meaning in Mathematics Education. 2005. ISBN 0-387-24039-X

H. Steinbring: The Construction of New Mathematical Knowledge in Classroom Interaction: An Epistemological Perspective. 2005. ISBN 0-387-24251-1

M.Borba, M. Villarreal: Humans-with-Media and the Reorganization of Mathematical Thinking: Information and Communication Technologies, Modeling, Visualization and Experimentation. 2005. ISBN 0-387-24263-5 HB; ISBN 0-387-32821-1 PB

G. Jones (ed): Exploring Probability in School: Challenges for Teaching and Learning. 2005. ISBN 0-387-24529-4

D. DeBock, W. Van Dooren, D. Janssens, and L. Verschaffel: The Illusion of Linearity: From Analysis to Improvement. 2007. ISBN 978-0-387-71082-2

K. Francois and J. P. Van Bendegem: Philosophical Dimensions in Mathematics Education.2007. ISBN 978-0-387-71571-1

E. Filloy, L. Puig, and T. Rojano: Educational Algebra: A Theoretical and Empirical Approach. 2007. ISBN 978-0-387-71253-6

B. Barton: The Language of Mathematics. 2007. ISBN 978-0-387-72858-2

P. Winbourne, A. Watson: New Directions for Situated Cognition in Mathematics Education.2007. ISBN 978-0-387-71577-3

E. DeFreitas, K. Nolan: Opening the Research Text. 2007. ISBN 978-0-387-75463-5

Printed in the United States
118469LV00003B/125/A